Ladies of
Magna Carta

Dedicated to the memory of my Nan and Grandad, with all my love.

Ladies of
Magna Carta

Women of Influence in
Thirteenth Century England

Sharon Bennett Connolly

PEN & SWORD
HISTORY

First published in Great Britain in 2020 by
Pen & Sword History
An imprint of
Pen & Sword Books Ltd
Yorkshire – Philadelphia

Copyright © Sharon Bennett Connolly 2020

ISBN 978 1 52674 525 5

The right of Sharon Bennett Connolly to be identified as Author of
this work has been asserted by her in accordance with the Copyright,
Designs and Patents Act 1988.

A CIP catalogue record for this book is
available from the British Library.

Printed and bound in the UK by TJ International Ltd,
Padstow, Cornwall.

Pen & Sword Books Limited incorporates the imprints of Atlas,
Archaeology, Aviation, Discovery, Family History, Fiction, History,
Maritime, Military, Military Classics, Politics, Select, Transport,
True Crime, Air World, Frontline Publishing, Leo Cooper, Remember
When, Seaforth Publishing, The Praetorian Press, Wharncliffe
Local History, Wharncliffe Transport, Wharncliffe True Crime
and White Owl.

For a complete list of Pen & Sword titles please contact

PEN & SWORD BOOKS LIMITED
47 Church Street, Barnsley, South Yorkshire, S70 2AS, England
E-mail: enquiries@pen-and-sword.co.uk
Website: www.pen-and-sword.co.uk

Or

PEN AND SWORD BOOKS
1950 Lawrence Rd, Havertown, PA 19083, USA
E-mail: Uspen-and-sword@casematepublishers.com
Website: www.penandswordbooks.com

Contents

Acknowledgements

Writing my third book, the first for Pen & Sword, has been an incredible experience and I would like to thank everyone who has helped and encouraged me throughout the process. I would like to thank the staff at Pen & Sword, especially my editors Claire Hopkins and Danna Messer for giving me the opportunity to write this book and for their continuous support.

I would particularly like to thank Amy Licence, whose help, advice and friendship has been invaluable to me in my journey to become an author. I am also grateful to my fellow authors, Kristie Dean, Annie Whitehead and Susan Higginbotham, who have offered advice and encouragement throughout. Thanks to the wonderful Anna Belfrage and Elizabeth Chadwick, for all the little messages of support and discussions about our favourite women throughout history. And thank you to Darren Baker for allowing me a sneak peek at his latest book, The Two Eleanors, and for clearing up a couple of queries for me.

I owe a great debt to Rich Price, owner of the Facebook group King John's Letters, who continues to do an incredible job of following John's itinerary and transcribing his Patent and Close Rolls – and with whom I have had various discussions about John and his life, and his barons. Thank you, Rich, for all your help and for being a wonderful sounding board and fount of information on John's reign. I would also like to thank Rachael Rogers of Abergavenny Museum for all the chats we've had over the years about Matilda de Braose, chats that helped this book become a reality. Thank you, Rachael, for all the wonderful support you have always shown me, and to artist Frances Baines and Abergavenny Museum for allowing me to use the drawing of the Christmas Dinner at Abergavenny Castle. I am also grateful to Dean Irwin, whose knowledge and insights of the period and frequent suggestions of further reading have been invaluable to me.

Writing can be a lonely experience, you spend your time reading books for research, or sitting, staring at the computer screen, trying to think of something to write. But social media has changed all that, there are always friends just a 'click' away to give you a diversion or encouragement. I would therefore like to thank the readers of my blog, *History … the Interesting Bits* for their wonderful support and feedback. A special thank you goes, too, to my friends in the online community, whose amusing anecdotes and memes have given me that boost when I needed it, particularly Karrie Stone, Tim Byard-Jones, Karen Clark, Geanine Teramani-Cruz, Anne Marie Bouchard, Harry Basnett, Derek Birks and every one of my Facebook friends and Twitter followers. Also, the online author community has proved invaluable to me. So, I would like to extend a special 'thank you' to Mike Jones, Julian Humphreys, Nathen Amin, S.J.A. Turney, Tony Riches, Sarah Bryson, Matthew Harffy, Dr Janina Ramirez, Giles Kristian, Justin Hill, Mary Anne Yard, Paula Lofting, Samantha Wilcoxson, Bev Newman, Stephanie Churchill and Prue Batten for all your support and encouragement with this book and the previous ones.

And thank you to the various historical sites I have visited, including the British Library, Doncaster Museum, Conisbrough Castle, Lewes and Pevensey Castles, Lincoln Castle and Cathedral, and all the wonderful staff who have been happy to talk about all things Magna Carta. I would like to include some 'thank yous' to those who supported the release of my first two books, *Heroines of the Medieval World* and *Silk and the Sword: The Women of the Norman Conquest*. Particular thanks have to go to Sasha and Gill at Lindum Books for hosting my author talks and being so supportive of this local author and to Victoria, Nicola (no 'h') and everyone at Gainsborough Old Hall, for hosting my book signings and being my place of refuge when I need to get away from the computer.

Thanks go to Kristie Dean, Anne Marie Bouchard and Jayne Smith for their kind permission to use their wonderful photos, and to Daniel Gleave for taking a special trip to Westminster Abbey, just to get a photo for my book! A thank you must also go to my friends closer to home, particularly Sharon Gleave, Jill Gaskell, Di Richardson, and all my local friends, for their wonderful support and for dragging me out for a coffee every once in a while. I reserve a special thanks to my family, especially my sister, Suzanne, whose support has been incredible and very much appreciated, and my brother Stephen. And to my mum and dad for all their love and encouragement, and for their own passion for history. A huge thank you also goes to my research assistant and son, Lewis Connolly, who has travelled to various wonderful places with me in the process of making this book a reality and has turned into a fabulous sounding-board for my ideas and arguments. And to my husband, James, thank you for putting up with all the history talks. I could not have done it without all of you.

I also owe a debt of gratitude to the great historians who have gone before me, who gallantly edited and translated the great chronicles of the twelfth and thirteenth centuries, so that they are accessible and readable for all of us who have an interest in the period.

Every effort has been made to ensure the accuracy of this book. However, any errors that may occur are entirely my own.

Introduction

Here is a law which is above the King and which even he must not break.
This reaffirmation of a supreme law and its expression in a general
charter is the great work of Magna Carta; and this alone justifies the
respect in which men have held it.

Winston Churchill.[1]

Magna Carta is probably the most significant charter in English history and, today, its importance extends beyond England's shores, holding a special place in the constitutions of many countries around the world. Despite its age, Magna Carta's iconic status is a more modern phenomena, seen in the influence it has had on nations and organisations throughout the globe, such as the United States of America and the United Nations, who have used it as the basis for their own 1791 Bill of Rights and the 1948 Universal Declaration of Human Rights, respectively.

After more than 800 years, there are only four original copies of the 1215 charter which remain in existence. The best preserved of these four is thought to have arrived at Salisbury Cathedral within days of it being issued on 15 June 1215 and is housed in an interactive exhibition in the cathedral's Chapter House. A second is owned by Lincoln Cathedral, and is now housed in a new, purpose built, state-of-the-art underground vault in the heart of Lincoln Castle. The remaining two are owned by the British Library in London, one of which was badly damaged by fire in 1731 and has deteriorated over the years; however, the other is on display in the Treasures exhibition, a magnet to visitors from all over the world, who wish to see the iconic Magna Carta (for a full transcript, see Appendix A).[2]

Originally called the Charter of Liberties, it was renamed Magna Carta, or Great Charter, in 1217, when the Charter of the Forest (see Appendix C) was issued. Sealed (not signed) in the meadow at Runnymede in June 1215, the legacy of Magna Carta, down through the centuries, has enjoyed a much greater impact on history and the people of the world than it did at the time of its creation. As a peace treaty between rebellious barons and the infamous King John, it was an utter failure, thrown out almost before the wax seals had hardened, not worth the parchment it was written on. The subsequent armed rebellion saw a French prince invited to claim the English throne – if he could wrest it from John's hands – and John spent the last year of his life clinging desperately to his crown and lands. Just fifteen months after Magna Carta was sealed, King John was on his deathbed; he died in his forty-ninth year, at Newark Castle on the night of 18/19 October 1216. His 9-year-old son, Henry III, inherited a country mired in civil war, with half of it occupied by a French army.

The one good thing going for Henry III was that he was so young; his youth protected him from any association with his father's actions and allowed many rebel barons to see a way back into the king's peace. They could submit to Henry, where they would never have sought peace with John. The second advantage that Henry had was in the regent appointed to take charge of the country, while Henry was still too young to take on the personal rule of England: William Marshal. The first Earl of Pembroke was a man of reputed integrity, earning him the moniker of 'the greatest knight' from historians and novelists alike. One of Marshal's first acts as regent was to reissue Magna Carta and it would be issued again several times in the thirteenth century and beyond. It was revived again in the seventeenth century when the king was in conflict with the senior men of the land, who invoked Magna Carta in both the 1628 Petition of Right and the 1641 Grand Remonstrance. The English Civil War and Charles I's execution followed.

Of the sixty-three clauses, two stand out as the guarantors of liberty and the law, not only in England, but around the world. Clause 39 ensures that 'no man shall be taken or imprisoned or deprived or outlawed or exiled or in any way ruined, nor will we go or send against him, except by the lawful judgement of his peers or by the law of the land.'[3] This guarantee of justice for all may well have been inspired by John's treatment of Matilda de Braose, wife of William de Braose, Lord of Bamber, who was one of John's foremost supporters in the early years of his reign, but later fell afoul of the king and saw his family hunted and hounded, almost to destruction. This clause is supported by the one following, clause 49, which states categorically; 'To no one will we sell, to no one will we deny or delay right or justice.'[4]

The Magna Carta of 1215 reflects the needs and events of the time in which it was issued; an England on the brink of civil war, disaffected barons demanding redress, the church and cities such as London looking for protection. It was drawn up by barons looking for reparation and legal protection from a king whose word could no longer be trusted, who meted out arbitrary punishments and heavy taxes. It was not a charter that was intended to form the protection and legal rights of every man, woman and child in the land; though it has come to be seen as just that in subsequent centuries. Indeed, the common man does not get a mention, and of the sixty-three clauses, only eight of them mention women as a gender.

Only one clause uses the word *femina* – woman – and that is a clause which restricts the rights and powers of a woman, rather than upholding them. Clause 54 states: 'No one shall be taken or imprisoned upon the appeal of a woman for the death of anyone except her husband.'[5] At first glance, this has to be the most anti-feminist statement ever made, a woman was not allowed to give evidence of a murder unless it was her own husband who was killed. However, the barons believed they had justification for inserting this clause. In a time when a man had the right to face his accuser in trial by combat to prove his innocence, this right would be automatically removed if his accuser was a woman; women were not allowed to use force of arms. A female accuser was seen as being able to circumvent the law, and therefore the law was open to abuse. It was not just that a woman may bear false witness and the accused would have no right of redress in battle; it was also that a woman may be manipulated by her menfolk to make an accusation, knowing that she would not be required to back it up by feat of arms. Whereas her husband, father or brother may have been challenged to do just that.

However, while it is possible to see why this clause was written, it does not deny the fact that women were treated so differently and denied the fundamental right to justice simply because of their gender. This clause was used on 5 July 1215, when King John ordered the release of Everard de Mildeston, an alleged murderer. Everard had been accused of the murder of her son, Richard, by Seina Chevel. The charge was therefore forbidden under the terms of Magna Carta, and the accused released.[6]

It is, of course, true that many of the clauses of Magna Carta refer to people in general, rather than just men, and that women are included in such clauses, as well as in the eight which refer to them specifically. However, the significance of women in the Magna Carta story is not just their limited inclusion in the charter itself, but also in their experiences of the unsettled times in which they lived, in their influence on the charter and in their use of its clauses to exact recompence for injustices they have experienced. The political crisis which saw the issuing of Magna Carta, and the civil war which followed, was not just significant to the barons involved, but to their wives and families, tenants and retainers. The conflict tore families apart as they took sides in the struggle and saw more than one baron change sides mid-crisis. Wives and daughters were caught in the middle, often torn by divided loyalties; between their birth family and the family into which they had married; between their fathers and their husbands. For instance, Matilda Marshal was the eldest daughter of William Marshal, a man known for his staunch loyalty to the crown, but she was married to Hugh Bigod, son of Roger, second Earl of Norfolk, one of the leaders of baronial opposition; Roger and Hugh were both named among the twenty-five barons (see Appendix B) appointed to ensure that John adhered to the terms of Magna Carta. Some of the clauses are specific to the people on the political stage in 1215. Clause 59 of Magna Carta, for instance, refers to two particular women, two of the sisters of Alexander II, King of Scots, who had been held hostage by King John since 1209. John had promised to find husbands for the two princesses, preferably within the royal family. However, the marriages had never materialised and, six years on, the young women were now in their twenties, and still unmarried.

It behoves us to remember that John was not unique; in many ways he was a typical medieval king. John's story and, indeed, his very character, has been shaped and reshaped through the distance of time. Eight hundred years of re-examining King John has left few with the impression that he was a man of impeccable character. However, was he really as bad as he has been portrayed? Kings before and after could be just as ruthless, if not more so. And yet, John is vilified and labelled 'Bad King John', probably for eternity. Nevertheless, he did manage to hold onto his throne to the very end; and despite his travails, he did retain the loyalty of a number of high-profile barons, including William Marshal and Nicholaa de la Haye.

Matilda Marshal, Nicholaa de la Haye and Matilda de Braose are three of the best known, non-royal women of the era, but they were by no means alone. *Ladies of Magna Carta* serves to demonstrate how women influenced – and were influenced by – Magna Carta, and how they were a central part of the struggle to bring about the Great Charter, and to ensure its clauses were adhered to by the king. On the whole, it is within the family environments of these women, that we can see the effects of Magna Carta, and the crisis of which it was a part; in the marriage alliances and family loyalties. As a consequence, I have chosen to present the ladies within the context of their families; the English royal family, the Scottish royals, the Marshals, Warennes, Braoses, etc. Although some women have a chapter to themselves, it is hoped that placing them within their families will help to demonstrate the extent of the influence of Magna Carta and its effect on the family. (I apologise in advance for the number of Isabels and Isabellas in the book and hope to avoid confusion by clearly identifying their family origins and using different forms of the name where I can).

For ease of reference, you will find the full wording of the 1215 Magna Carta, the 1217 Charter of the Forest, and a list of the Twenty-Five Enforcers of Magna Carta in the Appendices at the end of the book. I have chosen to include the original wording of each charter, rather than subsequent versions, but will mention, where necessary, if events and actions have been influenced by the later versions, rather than the original.

The women associated with Magna Carta did not live in a feminist bubble, and so the men in their lives formed a large part of their own stories and I have endeavoured to give you as much of their stories, their lives, their loves and their struggles, as I can, based on what is known and can be inferred from the greater story that is the history of England and the birth of Magna Carta.

To discuss the impact of Magna Carta, however, in relation to these women and their families, we must first examine the life and reign of King John and the events that led to the creation of this Great Charter ...

Chapter 1

John: The Path to the Throne

The names of King John and Magna Carta are inextricably linked in history and the story of the thirteenth century. Magna Carta was a product not only of John's reign, but of John's actions and personality from his early years onwards. Medieval government in England was led by the king, its style determined by the character of the individual monarch. This is markedly true in the reign of King John. John's own distrustful nature and paranoia led to a domineering government and John himself coming down through history to be judged as a tyrant. He is still, and has always been seen as, 'Bad King John'. However, the story of a man – or king – is never so cut-and-dried that we can give him one label which explains the entirety of his life, career, and personality. John was just as complex an individual as any of us are. His nature was not just determined by his birth and family, but also by his life experiences; from being the youngest son of a reigning monarch, Henry II, to seeing his mother, Eleanor of Aquitaine, imprisoned, and the rebellions and deaths of his three surviving older brothers, John's experiences helped create the king he would become.

John, as the youngest son, was never expected to inherit the crown. He was probably born on Christmas Eve 1166, or maybe 1167, at Beaumont Palace in Oxfordshire – the confusion appears to be due to the slack recording of the chroniclers, who had little interest in noting the birth of this younger son. His mother was now in her early forties and he was the last of his parents' eight children, seven of whom survived into adulthood. The eldest son of Henry and Eleanor, William, had died in his third year. Of the three other boys, Henry, the Young King, was born in 1155, Richard, later King Richard I and known by the soubriquet 'the Lionheart', was born in 1157 and Geoffrey, later Duke of Brittany, was born in 1158. John's oldest sister, Matilda, born in 1156, had already left England before her little brother was born, in preparation for her marriage to Henry V, known as 'the Lion', Duke of Saxony and Bavaria, which took place in Minden Cathedral, Germany on 1 February 1168. Another sister, Eleanor (Leonor in her adoptive country of Castile) was born in October 1162 and married Alfonso VIII of Castile in September 1176. Of all his siblings, John was closest in age to Joanna, born in 1165. Given that there were nine years between John and the youngest of his older brothers, he probably had little to do with them growing up, nor they with him.[1]

John's lack of importance as a younger son was ably demonstrated by a peace treaty with King Louis VII of France, just a year after John's birth. In it, Henry II set out the division of his lands, should he die. His eldest surviving son Henry, the Young King, would get Henry's principal domains of England, Normandy and Anjou; Richard would get his mother's duchy of Aquitaine and Geoffrey would receive Brittany, which Henry had taken by force in 1166. There was nothing for John, earning him the nickname – which contemporaries believed had been given by his father – of Lackland, a name that has followed him doggedly down through the centuries. It is possible that John had been initially intended for the church; as a child he and Joanna were educated, for a time, at the great abbey of Fontevrault in France. As a consequence, John was literate and developed a love of books, his library included works in both French and Latin. However, little else is known of John's early childhood and education. His sister, Joanna, spent some time with their mother in Poitou, but John appears to have remained at Fontevrault until brought back to England by his father in 1174. The world surrounding John was far from stable, however; in 1173, when John was 6 years old, a family rift arose that would see the young prince's parents pitted against each other.

Henry II's desire to provide for his youngest son by marrying him to the daughter of the duke of Savoy, and giving him the castles of Chinon, Loudun and Mirebeau, spurred his oldest brother Henry, who held those castles, into rebellion. The Young King was encouraged by his father-in-law Louis VII, King of France, who was always happy to foment trouble in the family of his biggest rival for control of France and the current husband of his former wife; the marriage of Eleanor and Louis, had been annulled in 1152 after fifteen years and only two daughters, no son. Louis welcomed the disaffected Angevin prince to his court. Eleanor of Aquitaine, whose relationship with Henry II was strained by this time, to say the least, sided with her sons against her husband and sent 15-year-old Richard and 14-year-old Geoffrey to join their older brother at the French court, while she rallied her barons in Poitou. When the rebellion failed, Henry accepted the submission of his sons, but Eleanor, who was captured as she rode towards safety in France, was not so fortunate. While it was not encouraged for sons to rebel against their father, it was seen primarily as boys flexing their muscles. For a wife to rebel against her husband was practically unheard of, and went against the natural order of society, and therefore deserved harsher punishment. Unforgiven and defeated, she was sent to imprisonment in various castles throughout southern England. Although the terms of her imprisonment would be relaxed in later years, her freedom would only come with Henry II's death and Richard's accession in 1189.

With the revolt suppressed, John was granted the castles that had been the cause of the insurrection, plus substantial revenues. In September 1174 John was given £1,000 in annual revenues from England, plus the castle and county of Nottingham, and the castle and lordship of Marlborough.[2] He was also given 1,000 livres in revenues from Normandy and Anjou, and two Norman castles.[3] In addition, the death of William, Earl of Gloucester, in 1176, gave Henry II the perfect opportunity to provide for his youngest son, by betrothing him to the late earl's daughter and co-heiress, Isabella of Gloucester. While an earldom would ordinarily pass intact to the eldest son, when the earl left only daughters the inheritance was usually shared equally among all the surviving sisters. With Gloucester, this did not happen. Henry effectively disinherited Isabella's older sisters and their husbands, in order that the earldom should pass, intact, through Isabella, to John. Although the wedding did not take place immediately – in fact, it did not happen in Henry's lifetime – John was allowed to enjoy the use of his betrothed's lands and money, in anticipation of the marriage.

In May 1177 Henry had John named King of Ireland, and even asked the pope, Alexander III, to provide a crown for the occasion. It was, by all accounts, an empty gesture; John was still very much subject to his father's authority, being styled in charters as *filius regis* – 'the king's son'.[4] King Henry seems to have made a habit of promising lands and titles to his sons, without relinquishing to them any actual authority. Henry also had a habit of changing and rearranging the domains he allowed his sons to possess. The death of the Young King, John's oldest brother, in 1183, prompted one such change-around and launched John, now about 15, on his first political mission: to wrest Aquitaine from his brother, Richard. Richard had been groomed to be duke of Aquitaine from a young age, but Henry wanted it transferred to John, now that Richard was heir to Henry's entire empire. With the help of his only other surviving brother, Geoffrey, John launched an attack on Aquitaine, which failed; unsurprising, given that Richard was already an accomplished warrior, while John was an untested youth. Richard kept his mother's beloved Aquitaine and John remained landless for the moment.

In order to rectify this, John was sent to claim his kingdom of Ireland. The Anlgo-Norman lord, Hugh de Lacy, Lord of Meath, Henry's representative in Ireland, was enjoying a greater degree of independence than Henry wished, and it was decided that John would mount an expedition to curb Lacy's ambitions. The young prince was knighted in March 1185, before embarking for the crossing to Ireland. He was accompanied by Ranulf de Glanville, who was appointed as John's *magister* in 1183 and may have encouraged and developed John's later interest in the law. John's well-equipped and substantial force arrived in Waterford on 25 April.[5] The prince was also accompanied by the chronicler Gerald of Wales, who recorded that the 'undertaking ... auspiciously commenced' when the princes of Ireland made 'voluntary submission without delay, did homage to the king, and indisputably confirmed his right.'[6] However, it was not to last. According to Gerald:

the Irish people, who were so astounded and thrown into such consternation at the arrival of the first adventurers, by the novelty of the thing, and so terrified by flights of arrows shot by the English archers, and the might of the men-at-arms, soon took heart, through delays, which are always dangerous, the slow and feeble progress at the work of conquest and the ignorance and cowardice of the governors and others in command.[7]

According to Gerald, the Irish became experts with bow and arrow and 'practised in stratagems and ambuscades by their frequent conflicts with our troops,' which enabled them to mount a 'stout resistance'.[8] On arrival in Ireland, John built and garrisoned three castles, at Tibrach, Archfinan and Lismore. Unfortunately for John, this did nothing to alleviate the unrest and a series of ambushes followed. The garrison of Archfinan were set upon when out raiding, with nineteen of their number killed, while the men of Meath 'put one hundred of the invaders to the sword.'[9] John de Courcy lost thirteen men-at-arms as they returned to Connacht. Moreover, the Irish kings of Limerick, Connacht and Cork, apparently encouraged by Hugh de Lacy, soon took up arms again, as John started rewarding land grants to his own followers, with complete disregard for existing Irish rights.

This catalogue of disasters is explained by Gerald of Wales, who blames Henry II's failure to answer the pleas of Heraclius, Patriarch of Jerusalem, who sought Henry's assistance for the beleaguered Holy Land. Instead of launching a crusade the king sent John to Ireland 'with a retinue and outfit more sumptuous than profitable ... for his own aggrandisement, not for the cause of Christ'.[10] Further blame is attached to John who, when Irishmen loyal to England came to congratulate him, treated them not only with 'contempt and derision, but even rudely pulled them by their beards.'[11] The Irish judgement of John was not very flattering, Gerald of Wales reports that they 'found him to be a mere boy, surrounded by others almost as young as himself; and that the young prince abandoned himself to juvenile pursuits.'[12] Although Holingshed, in his *Chronicles of Ireland*, claims John was only 12 years old, he was, in fact, approaching his nineteenth birthday. Still young and experiencing his first real chance to exercise his authority, it seems he was not as mature or sensible as the Irish lords would have liked. Roger of Howden adds that John's own greed, and failure to pay his troops their due, led to their deserting to the Irish.[13]

In the end Henry II 'discarding the new-comers as totally incapable, if not cowardly and resolving to employ men who from the first had acquired experience in the conquest of the island,' sent John de Courcy to take overall command of the Irish expedition as John returned home.[14] A year later the death of Hugh de Lacy, who was 'treacherously slain and decapitated by the axes of the Irish under his dominion,' and the arrival of a crown, sent by pope Urban III, saw Henry planning a new expedition to Ireland.[15] However, the death of John's brother Geoffrey, Duke of Brittany, in August 1186, meant the new Irish enterprise was postponed indefinitely and the crown left unused, as Henry saw the opportunity for a far-reaching redistribution of the family domains. John remained 'lord of Ireland', a title held by all subsequent monarchs until Henry VIII, but the focus of all interest now rested on the inheritance of King Henry's vast empire. Henry II had only two living sons remaining: Richard and John. The fact John was widely perceived as the king's favourite son led to rumours, fuelled by Philip II Augustus, King of France, that Henry planned to disinherit Richard, his oldest surviving son, in favour of John. The fact that Henry refused to allow John to take the cross, when he, Richard and Philip Augustus did so in 1187, and Henry's own refusal to name Richard as his heir, further added to the speculation that John would supplant his older brother in the succession.

The refusal to name Richard finally pushed the warrior prince into the welcoming arms of Philip Augustus and open revolt against his father in 1188. Henry II's position rapidly became desperate, and with the fall of Le Mans, on 12 June 1189, John deserted his father to join the winning side. Many contemporaries believed that the news of John's betrayal was the final straw for Henry II, who died, defeated and all-but deserted, at Chinon Castle on 6 July 1189, apparently crying 'Shame, shame on a conquered king' before breathing his last. He was buried at the great abbey of Fontevrault in his native Anjou.[16] Richard was now king of England and ruler of the vast Angevin Empire that had been built by his father, with lands stretching 1,000 miles, from the Scottish border in the north to the Pyrenees in southern France. He had also, already, acquired a formidable reputation as a soldier, with one contemporary saying he cared 'for no success that was not reached by a path cut by his own sword and stained with the blood of his adversaries'.[17] Richard was crowned in Westminster Abbey on 3 September 1189, and immediately set about planning his crusade to the Holy Land in earnest.

Richard's accession saw John given possession of those lands and castles long promised to him by their father; the county of Mortain in Normandy and the honours and castles of Peverel, Lancaster, Marlborough and Ludgershall in England. He was also given the English honours of Tickhill and Wallingford and the counties of Derby and Nottingham, though without their castles. Even before Richard's coronation, John's long-proposed marriage to Isabella of Gloucester was finally solemnised, the wedding taking place on 29 August 1189. It was not without controversy, however, as the archbishop of Canterbury categorically opposed the match on the grounds of consanguinity; John and Isabella were both descended from King Henry I of England. A papal legate recognised the marriage as lawful, pending John's appeal to Rome against the Archbishop's prohibition; however, the fact that John never actively pursued the appeal meant the legality of the marriage remained conveniently ambiguous, therefore both lawful and voidable at any time.

The Gloucester estates included Bristol and the marcher lordships of Glamorgan and Newport. As a result, Richard provided John with an army and sent him to relieve the Welsh castle of Carmarthen, besieged by the Welsh prince Rhys ap Gruffudd, known as the Lord Rhys. Although John came to terms with Rhys and brought him to Oxford in October, Richard refused to meet him, suggesting he found the outcome of John's campaign unsatisfactory. However, Richard's generosity continued and in December 1189, John was given the counties of Cornwall, Devon, Somerset and Dorset, bringing his English revenues to somewhere within the region of £4,000 a year. John now had considerable landholdings, both in Normandy and England, and managed them efficiently from Marlborough.[18] The chronicler William of Newburgh suggests that Richard's love for his brother had led to such generosity, though Richard obviously did not trust his brother completely. In March 1190 he extracted an oath from not only John, but also his illegitimate half-brother, Geoffrey, making them both swear to stay out of England for three years, while the king was on crusade. It is possible Richard also recognised John as heir to the duchy of Normandy at the same time, though not England; and he did later lighten the restriction by allowing that his justiciar, William de Longchamp, could choose to release John from the oath if he saw fit to do so.

Although it seems highly unlikely that Longchamp released John from his oath, the prince was back in England by 1191; possibly on the insistence of his mother, Eleanor of Aquitaine. Now freed from captivity, the queen mother was once again in a position of trust and power, watching over her favourite son's domains while he was away on crusade. However, events took a turn when Richard himself recognised Arthur, still only a child of 5 years, as his heir, in peace negotiations with Tancred of Lecce in Sicily in 1190, in which he also agreed that Arthur would marry one of Tancred's three daughters. Richard was eager to continue on crusade and wanted a speedy resolution to the diversion that saw him rescuing his sister, Joanna, and settling the Sicilian succession crisis which had arisen on the death of Joanna's husband, William, King of Sicily. He may have only wanted to make Arthur a more attractive marriage prospect, dangling the possibility of his daughter becoming queen of England before Tancred. Richard's recognition of Arthur as his heir was a closely guarded secret; the only person in England who was meant to know was William Longchamp. However, it seems that Longchamp may have sounded out others to measure the level of support for Arthur. According to the chronicler William of Newburgh he passed on the information to the king of Scots, at least, and possibly some of the Welsh princes.[19] In early 1191 the news was widely leaked, and John came to hear of it.

According to William of Newburgh, John had 'expected to become the successor to the kingdom, should the king, perchance, not survive his laborious and perilous undertaking.'[20] Indeed, Richard's advancement of his brother since his accession, in giving John lands in England and arranging his marriage to an English bride, all seemed to support this expectation. Richard's actions in naming Arthur his heir, and Longchamp's support for this, threatened to undermine John's own claims and rights. In the late twelfth century, primogeniture was far from established in the rules of inheritance, and the son of a king (John) was often seen as having a greater right to a throne than the grandson (Arthur) of the same king, even if he was the son of the king's elder son. It did not hurt, either, that John was a grown man and would be able to take personal control, while Arthur was still a very young child and would be in need of regents.

A meeting between John and Longchamp, in March 1191, failed to resolve the issue and John set about building up his own support. According to Richard of Devizes 'certain nobles became busy'. The chronicler reported that 'castles were strengthened, towns were fortified, ditches were dug.'[21] In June of 1191 Longchamp demanded that Gerard de Canville, sheriff of Lincolnshire, relinquish his custody of Lincoln

Castle and swear allegiance to the justiciar. Canville refused and instead paid homage to John, recognising him as heir presumptive. John moved north to support Canville, quickly taking the ill-prepared royal castles of Tickhill (in Yorkshire) and Nottingham and demanding that Canville be reinstated. As Canville joined John at Nottingham, Longchamp laid siege to Lincoln Castle, which was under the command of Canville's wife, Nicholaa de la Haye, during his absence. In the meantime, having heard of the growing unpopularity of Longchamp, King Richard had despatched Walter de Coutances, Archbishop of Rouen, who was with the king in Sicily, back to England to restore peace. Coutances brought the two sides together at a conference in Winchester in July, though both John and Longchamp each brought a large number of troops with them, just in case.

Settlement was reached whereby John would return the castles he had taken, Gerard de Canville was reinstated, and Longchamp would withdraw his support of Arthur as Richard's heir and recognise John as heir presumptive. Longchamp would, however, remain in power; moreover, according to Richard of Devizes, King Richard had sent orders that his brother must obey Longchamp.[22] This uneasy peace was not to last the year, and when Geoffrey, the newly consecrated archbishop of York, was arrested for entering England on 18 September 1191, John exploited public opinion. Presenting himself as the champion of English liberties and raising a coalition against the foreign justiciar, he wrote to the bishop of London, who was acting as go-between for John and Longchamp:

> John count of Mortain to Richard bishop of London, greetings. As you love the honour of God and the Church and the king and kingdom and me, be present at the bridge over the Loddon on 5 October, between Reading and Windsor, because, God willing, I will meet you there to confer about certain important and serious matters concerning the king and kingdom.[23]

The mutual distrust on both sides saw skirmishes between retainers, on the road to Windsor, and one of John's knights was killed. Longchamp refused to meet John, claiming the prince was intending to usurp the throne. Within days John was being welcomed into London, recognised as heir presumptive and 'declared supreme governor of the realm, and ordered that all castles should be turned over to whomever he wanted.'[24] A conference was held in the Tower of London on 10 October, during which Longchamp resigned as justiciar and was replaced by Walter de Coutances. Coutances was no pushover, however, and John was denied full authority, having to work alongside the new justiciar.

In the meantime, Richard had reached the Holy Land in the summer of 1191 and enjoyed some notable victories; he had captured Acre in July and defeated Saladin at the battle of Arsuf in September, writing home that he hoped 'to recover the city of Jerusalem and the Holy Sepulchre within twenty days after Christmas, and then return to our own dominions.'[25] However, Richard had also begun to alienate his allies, especially Philip II Augustus of France. Richard's marriage to Berengaria of Navarre, while *en route* to the Holy Land, had finally ended his long-standing betrothal to Philip Augustus' sister, Alix. Claiming that Alix had had an affair with his father, Richard paid Philip Augustus 10,000 marks in compensation; but the humiliation caused a rift that was not so easily repaired. The two kings continued to quarrel as they arrived in the Holy Land, taking opposing positions in political disputes and unable to agree on how to divide the spoils of war. Claiming he was too ill to continue the war, Philip Augustus left the crusade in August 1191 and was home in France by Christmas. With his rival still in the Holy Land, Philip saw an opportunity to cause trouble for Richard; by nurturing a friendship with John, who he promised to recognise as ruler of the Angevin lands in France, in return for John marrying Alix, Richard's discarded fiancée. The fact John was already married to Isabella of Gloucester was seen as no hindrance, given the ambiguity of the marriage and the archbishop of Canterbury's declaration of its invalidity shortly after the nuptials. Ever one to grasp an opportunity, John was preparing to leave for France when his mother arrived in England. It took several meetings between Eleanor of Aquitaine, John and the king's ministers to persuade the prince that his interests lay in England; the threat of losing all his English lands and castles finally persuading John that it was in his best interests to remain there.

Meanwhile, Richard's crusade had stalled. At Christmas 1191, he was camped within twenty miles of Jerusalem, but did not have the men or machines to take the Holy City and so withdrew to Ascalon. A second attempt to take Jerusalem, in the summer of 1192, was again called off due to lack of resources and renewed negotiations with Saladin resulted in a four-year truce, which meant Richard could return home to deal with his recalcitrant brother. However, Richard had made many enemies in the Holy Land and his route home was problematic. He needed to avoid territories over which Philip Augustus had influence; his ships were driven ashore by storms on the north-east coast of Italy and he was arrested as he headed north, having strayed into Austrian territory.[26] Captured by his erstwhile ally, Duke Leopold of Austria, who was another powerful supporter he had offended in the Holy Land, Richard was handed over to Leopold's overlord, Henry VI, the Holy Roman Emperor.

News of Richard's capture and imprisonment in Germany saw the tables turned again. Philip Augustus renewed his overtures to John, who grasped the opportunity with both hands and met with Philip in Paris; in January 1193 he sealed a treaty by which he relinquished the Norman Vexin to Philip and agreed to marry Alix. While Philip took Gisors, the capital of the Norman Vexin, and gathered an invasion fleet together, John returned to England to gather support for his enterprise. However, the king of Scots was not receptive to his overtures, unwilling to join a rebellion against a crusader king. Despite his predicament, Richard was dismissive of the threat John posed, saying, 'My brother John is not the man to seize any land by force, if anyone meets his attack with even the slightest resistance.'[27]

In the end, John could do little but hire some Welsh mercenaries, with whom he garrisoned the castles at Windsor and Wallingford. John tried to persuade the king's ministers that Richard was dead, but they were not deceived by the ruse. They besieged John's castles and prepared to defend England against Philip Augustus' impending invasion. Seeing England prepared, the French king abandoned his plans. Loyalties were still conflicted, however, and in the north some magnates refused to join the siege against John's castle at Tickhill, Yorkshire, claiming to be his liegemen. It was a delicate balancing act for Richard's ministers. They had to keep John in check in order to protect King Richard's throne, but always had to keep in mind that, should anything happen to Richard, John was likely to be their next king. John was keenly aware of the quandary which faced the king's ministers and appears to have taken advantage of the situation whenever and wherever he could.

In April 1193 Hubert Walter returned from Germany, with the terms for Richards release; the huge sum of 100,000 marks was demanded in ransom.[28] Military action against John was draining the treasury and in order to facilitate the collection of the vast ransom, peace needed to be established as John and Philip Augustus were still conspiring against Richard. Together Philip and John offered a bribe to Henry VI, Richard's captor, to keep the English king in prison, or hand him over to them; John's contribution was to be 5,000 marks.[29] However, Richard himself deflected this counter-offer by offering a further 50,000 marks for his release. As news of this latest twist reached Philip Augustus, he sent a message to John, saying 'Look to yourself, the Devil is loosed!'[30]

Despite Philip Augustus' dramatic exclamation, Richard was not yet free as the ransom was still to be raised and paid. Frustrated at being forced to relinquish a number of his castles, John turned once again to Philiip Augustus who gave him the castles of Arques, Drincourt and Evreux. Despite the two offering Emperor Henry further payments to keep Richard imprisoned, the king of England was freed on 4 February 1194. When Richard arrived back in England in March, John was given forty days to present himself before the king, or he would forfeit any future claim to the kingdom. Richard then rode south, he was crowned for a second time, at Winchester Cathedral, on 17 April, and crossed to Normandy four weeks later, where John and Philip Augustus had captured more castles and were in the process of besieging Verneuil.

As Richard's army camped overnight at Lisieux, John came to meet his brother face-to-face. John fell at the king's feet in supplication. Raising him up, Richard gave his younger brother the kiss of peace, and despite John being 27 years old, he told his brother 'have no fear, John, you are a child and were left with bad guardians.'[32] Although Richard dismissed John's actions as those of a misguided youth, his reputation was badly scarred by his attempts to usurp his brother's throne; that he was trying to steal the lands of an imprisoned crusader king was unforgivable. In the call to crusade, the pope specifically promised that the property of crusaders would be preserved and protected while they responded to the church's call. John had broken this guarantee in a dramatic way; and had failed spectacularly. Where his failures in Ireland could be seen as youthful folly, and he was even praised for acting against the excesses of the unpopular justiciar William Longchamp, his betrayal of his crusading sibling exposed him as a disloyal, faithless brother. As William of Newburgh put it, John was 'heaping up endless curses on his own perfidious head.'[33]

Although Richard publicly forgave his brother, John's lands and castles were not returned to him, and his supporters lost their positions; Gerard de Canville was replaced as sheriff of Lincolnshire and castellan of Lincoln Castle. John's position as heir to the throne remained ambiguous. In 1190 Richard had named Arthur, but in 1191 the English council had recognised John. Nothing more was said on the matter, leaving John in a state of limbo. Perhaps, now reunited with his wife, Berengaria of Navarre, Richard hoped to produce a son and heir of his own?

Richard's immediate concern, however, was the recovery of the lands in Normandy, lost to Philip Augustus – with the collaboration of John – during his imprisonment. John was sent to retake Evreux, a task apparently made easier by the fact the defenders did not know John had changed sides, and the garrison were slaughtered. Although he enjoyed limited military success in the reconquest of Normandy, Richard recognised his brother's assistance and in 1195 'forgave his brother all the wrath and displeasure he felt towards him,' and restored some of his lands and titles.[34] John was once again Earl of Gloucester and Count of Mortain and was promised an income of £2,000 annually. John's ambiguous position as Richard's possible heir was given a boost in 1196 when Richard failed to gain custody of the alternative claimant, Arthur Duke of Brittany. Despite an invasion of Brittany, Arthur slipped through Richard's grasp and was spirited away to the French court by the Breton nobles. Richard could hardly promise his throne to Arthur now that he was in the hands of his greatest rival, Philip II Augustus.

By 1197 it was becoming obvious that the king was not going to father a son of his own, and so John's standing, though never officially recognised as heir, was once again in the ascendancy. However, relations between Richard and John again cooled in 1198 when the king received a missive from Philip Augustus, claiming that John was once more plotting with him. Chroniclers are divided on whether Philip Augustus was telling the truth, or merely attempting to sow discord. Richard, at least, found the claims credible and John was again deprived of his lands and titles. The brothers were still not reconciled when Richard began the siege of Chalus in 1199. On 26 March, while inspecting the progress made by his troops, protected only by helmet and shield, Richard was hit in the shoulder by a crossbow bolt fired from the ramparts. The wound turned gangrenous and he died on 6 April 1199; his mother, Eleanor of Aquitaine, was at his bedside. Richard I was buried at Fontevrault Abbey, beside his father, Henry II. Roger of Howden claimed that, on his deathbed, Richard named John as his heir.[35]

On hearing the news, John acted quickly and raced to Chinon to secure the Treasury. Although Arthur had substantial support in Anjou, England, Normandy and Poitou immediately recognised John as king – as did his mother and her duchy of Aquitaine. John's succession was not without concerns, however, and the *Histoire de Guillaume le Maréchale* tells us of a keen debate between William Marshal, Earl of Pembroke, and Hubert Walter, Archbishop of Canterbury, when the news of Richard's death reached them in Rouen four days later. According to the *Histoire*, while the archbishop backed Arthur as having the greater right, William gave his full support to John, arguing against Arthur due to his close links with the king of France.[36] More with a nod to hindsight (the *Histoire* was written in the 1220s), than the skill of prophecy, the archbishop cautioned: 'This much I can tell you, you will never come to regret anything you did as much as what you're doing now.'[37]

John was invested as Duke of Normandy in Rouen before departing for England and his coronation; he was crowned in Westminster Abbey on 27 May 1199. The fifth and youngest son of Henry II and Eleanor of Aquitaine, John was never expected to become king. The early deaths of three older brothers, and Richard's own inability to produce a son and heir had dangled the possibility tantalisingly in front of him. His own betrayals of his brother counted for nothing in the grand scheme of things and, in the end, John acceded to the throne with the support of his mother and the great magnates of Normandy and England. John's perfidy and self-interest, however, during the reign of his brother, had not gone unnoticed; his reputation as a 'mad-headed youth' who had become 'nature's enemy' not forgotten. Many must have looked forward to the new reign with mounting trepidation.

Chapter 2

The Road to Magna Carta

John was in Normandy when he heard of his brother's death – or perhaps in Brittany. According to *the Life of St Hugh*, which tells the story of Hugh of Avalon, the saintly bishop of Lincoln, John was in Brittany with his nephew, Arthur. Bishop Hugh was travelling to meet with King Richard at the time, and so may be well-placed to know John's whereabouts. If true, this would add credence to the accusations that John was yet again plotting against his brother, with Arthur and the king of France.[1] Having received a messenger with the news of Richard's death, John headed for Chinon in Anjou to secure the Treasury; it was at Chinon that he was reunited with his mother, who had ridden there from Richard's deathbed. Philip Augustus and Arthur were not idle and, having heard of Richard's death, moved to advance Arthur's own claims to the Angevin lands. Philip took Evreux as Arthur progressed towards Le Mans, John escaping the city just before his nephew's arrival. Arthur paid homage to Philip Augustus for Anjou, Maine and Touraine, now lost to John.

John headed north and was welcomed in Normandy, despite their fractious history during Richard's reign. He was invested as Duke of Normandy in Rouen Cathedral on 25 April, with Walter of Coutances 'placing a coronet worked with golden roses on the new duke's head.'[2] In the meantime, having heard reports of increasing lawlessness in England, William Marshal and Hubert Walter were despatched there to keep the peace and to receive the oaths of loyalty from the barons and prelates. The time between the death of one king and coronation of the next was always an uneasy period; a new regime invariably brought uncertainty and, quite possibly, a change in fortunes for some. Magnates had started strengthening their fortifications and gathering their men. Many wanted to make their oaths conditional on the king accepting their rights but had to settle for a promise that John would at least give them a hearing.[3]

John then led a punitive expedition into Anjou, to punish the disloyalty of Le Mans, as his mother did similar in other areas of the region; a demonstration of Angevin might. John and Eleanor then went their separate ways, with Eleanor heading south to secure her own Aquitaine, and John departing for England and his coronation at Westminster Abbey on 27 May, two days after he arrived in England:

> On Ascension Day 1199 John, under a canopy held by four barons, was led in procession into Westminster Abbey. On his knees before the high altar he swore, as his brother had ten years earlier, a triple coronation oath: to observe peace, honour and reverence towards god and the Church all the days of his life; to do good justice and equity to the people entrusted with his care; to keep good laws and destroy bad laws and evil customs that had been introduced into the land.[4]

John was then stripped to his underclothes and anointed with holy oil on his head, chest and hands, before being dressed in royal robes, crowned, given the sceptre and virge (a rod of office) and seated on his throne.[5] The ceremony was followed by Mass before John was led out of the abbey to his coronation banquet. One cloud presented itself at John's coronation, and that was the ambassadors from Scotland, who informed him that King William the Lion would recognise John as king, if John returned the earldom of Northumbria. John offered to meet the king of Scots at Northampton ten days later to discuss the situation. However, King William failed to appear, but sent more ambassadors who issued John with an ultimatum: return Northumbria or William would take it by force. John, however, was keen to get back to Normandy, still under threat from Philip Augustus, and so left William de Stuteville to deal with the defence of the north. On 20 June 1199 he sailed back to Normandy with 'a mighty English host'.[6]

John's strength in Normandy lay in the alliances forged by his brother, Richard, before his death. Thanks to Richard's help, John's nephew, Otto of Brunswick was now Holy Roman Emperor, and ready to support his uncle against France. In an assembly at Rouen, held in August 1199, fifteen French counts, led by Flanders and Boulogne, pledged to support

John. It was in August, too, that John and Philip met face-to-face on the border between their lands. Philip complained that John had not paid him homage for the French lands held by the English king, he demanded the Vexin and that John relinquish Anjou, Maine and Touraine to Arthur. Anjou, Maine and Touraine were at the centre of the vast Angevin empire and relinquishing them was never an option. According to Gervase of Canterbury, John, with his mighty army and imposing collection of allies 'made up his mind to resist the French king like a man, and to fight manfully for the peace of his country.'[7]

By September, John was winning the war. William des Roches, Arthur's seneschal in Anjou, offered to defect to John. He was bitter that Philip Augustus had destroyed the Angevin fortress of Ballon after capturing it from John, rather than handing it to Arthur. This high-profile defection was followed by the submission of Arthur himself, he and his mother met John at Le Mans. However, they received a warning that the king was planning to arrest and imprison them, and fled Le Mans in the dead of night, making their way to the French court. Whether the intelligence was true or not, John's past record of betrayal was obviously enough to sew distrust in the minds of Arthur and his mother and make the threat credible. Soon after, despite a truce with Philip Augustus, John's coalition collapsed; many of his French allies were preparing to go on crusade and news of his proposed betrayal of Arthur saw more deserting his side.

When the truce ended in January a more permanent peace was agreed, although now balanced heavily in Philip's favour. John was to cede to Philip the whole of the Vexin and the towns in south-east Normandy that Philip had taken in the wake of Richard's death. In return, Philip withdrew his support of Arthur, and also persuaded Arthur to withdraw his claims. In addition, Philip recognised John as heir to Anjou, Maine and Touraine while John promised to pay homage to Philip for those territories and Normandy, thus recognising Philip Augustus as his overlord for his French lands. John also granted Philip 30,000 marks (£20,000); he would impose a tax of 3 shillings on each carucate of land in England to make the payment.[8] The peace would be sealed with a wedding, that of Philip's heir Louis with John's niece, Blanche of Castile. Blanche was the daughter of John's sister Eleanor and Alfonso VIII, queen and king of Castile. A five-month truce was agreed to give time for the bride to be fetched from Spain. Now in her late seventies, it was John's mother, Eleanor of Aquitaine, who made the perilous journey across the Pyrenees to select the bride (the choice was originally between Blanche and her sister, Urraca, and it was Eleanor who decided on Blanche) and bring her back to Normandy for the wedding.

Many were satisfied that the war was over, and peace achieved. The chronicler Ralph of Coggeshall praised John as 'a lover of peace, who intended to live a tranquil life free from wars, understanding how many enemies of the kingdom he faced, and what great misfortunes had befallen his father and brothers and all the kingdom from such wars.'[9] However, while the chroniclers, who were invariably monks, were happy at the prospect of peace, John's more martial subjects thought he had given in too quickly, and it is from this time that he earned the soubriquet 'Softsword'.

With the truce in place, John returned to England, intending to deal with William the Lion, whose threatened invasion of Northumbria had so far not materialised. John summoned the king of Scots to a meeting at York. William refused to appear, claiming the safe-conduct provided by John was inadequate, and the matter remained unresolved. While in York, however, John was confronted by several Cistercian abbots who, traditionally exempt from taxation, refused to pay the new tax John had imposed to pay King Philip. Ralph of Coggeshall claimed that John 'wishes to oppress the order with the obligation of the tax.'[10] When the abbots refused to pay, John was incensed and ordered that his sheriffs 'should persecute them, show them no justice in their injuries and law-suits and not help them in their disputes, but refer everything to the king.'[11] Intervention from the archbishop of Canterbury did nothing to placate John, the archbishop 'reproached the king openly for his great harshness, pronouncing him a persecutor of the Holy Church who presumed to impose such great and so many injustices on these most worthy sons of the Church.'[12] The situation remained unresolved as John headed to Normandy once more, having refused a placatory offer of 1,000 marks from the archbishop for being 'so small', John 'crossed the sea, breathing threats and slanders against the disciples of Christ.'[13]

On 18 May 1200, Philip and John met at the border between the French and Angevin lands. The terms of the January treaty were ratified and four days later, the peace was sealed on the island of Le Goulet, in the middle of the River Seine. John did homage to Philip for his French possessions, Arthur did homage to John for Brittany and Louis and Blanche were married, at Port-Mort, on John's side of the river as France was at the time under interdict due to Philip's repudiation of his wife, Ingeborg of Denmark.[14]

Once the treaty was sealed, John moved south with a large army, to subdue Anjou, Maine and Touraine, the territories that had resisted him for the past year. After a show of force, and taking 150 hostages, he moved further south, into Aquitaine, which had declared for him the previous year, but only after generous concessions had been made to the leading magnates. John now called two of them, the count of Angoulême and viscount of Limoges, to meet with him at the castle of a third, Hugh de Lusignan, Count of La Marche. Hugh and Audemar, Count of Angoulême had been locked in a bitter rivalry for many years, but had recently agreed to put it aside in favour of a marriage between Hugh and Count Audemar's daughter and heir, Isabelle.

John had divorced Isabella of Gloucester, his wife of ten years, shortly after ascending the throne. He had ensured that Isabella was not crowned with him in 1199 and a year later persuaded the bishops of Normandy to declare the marriage void; this was done with little difficulty, given the dubious legality of the marriage, the archbishop of Canterbury's objections when John married Isabella, and the lack of papal dispensation. It was also an advantage to John to be rid of an English wife; as king he was now a greater marriage prospect on the international stage and a marriage to a European princess would bring allies and prestige. John was hoping to marry the daughter of the king of Portugal, and in January 1200 he welcomed the Portuguese ambassadors to his court. This idea, however, seems to have fizzled out and by the summer of 1200 John's marriage plans lay elsewhere – in Angoulême.

The stories of John marrying Isabelle invariably describe a lecherous King John being enchanted by the beauty of 12-year-old Isabelle. However, John's marriage to Isabelle was a smart political move; it prevented the union of the county of Angoulême with the Lusignan lands, which would have essentially created a powerful political bloc in the middle of Aquitaine. Moreover, it secured the loyalty of Count Audemar, to the English crown, whilst his daughter was queen. Unfortunately, it also served to alienate the powerful Lusignan family and drove Count Hugh into the arms of Philip Augustus of France, which we will explore in more detail in chapter ten. The marriage was celebrated on 24 August at Angoulême and by October the newlyweds were back in England; they were both crowned in Westminster Abbey on 8 October 1200.

The wedding was a pleasant interlude for John, but he was soon back to business. By November he was in Lincoln, meeting with William, King of Scots, who finally paid homage to King John, kneeling before him and pledging eternal fidelity on 22 November. The matter of Northumbria, however, went unresolved despite William raising the subject. John decided it was a discussion for another time. While still in England, John's dispute with the Cistercian order was also resolved; the abbots were granted an audience where they fell at the king's feet and begged his forgiveness. Much to their surprise, John was inclined to be charitable, cancelled the oppressive edicts and promised his protection in the future. John even went so far as to promise to build a new Cistercian monastery in England, where he hoped he would eventually be buried.[15] The initial crises of his reign all resolved, John and Isabelle celebrated Christmas at Guildford knowing his succession had been secured. Ominously, unbeknownst to the king, the dark clouds arising from his humiliation of Hugh de Lusignan were already gathering over Poitou.

In the early months of 1201, Hugh started causing trouble, attacking John's castles in Aquitaine. Eleanor of Aquitaine, in retirement at Fontevrault Abbey, wrote to John of the deteriorating situation within her domains. In retaliation, John ordered his officials to seize Hugh de Lusignan's county of La Marche, and the territories of Hugh's brother, Ralph, despite the fact he had remained loyal to John and was in England in the king's service at the time of the unrest. War was averted by the intercession of King Philip II Augustus of France, who met John on the Norman–French border to resolve the issue. John promised to restore the Lusignan lands and to give them justice. John's idea of justice, however, was to charge the Lusignans with treachery and challenge them to a judicial duel, rather than taking them to court, with the best fighters from his dominions to act as his champions. The Lusignans refused the challenge and appealed to Philip Augustus once again. And so started a year of toing and froing between John and Philip, with John refusing to meet the summons of the king of France. When John failed to appear in Paris by 28 April 1202, he was declared a contumacious vassal and his lands forfeit:

> At length the French court assembled and judged that the king of England should be deprived of all lands which he and his predecessors had held from the French king, because they had done scarcely any service owed for a long time, and had refused to obey their lord. King Philip, therefore, gladly accepted and approved of the judgement of his court; he gathered his army and immediately attacked the castle of Boutavant, which had been built by King Richard in Normandy, and razed it to the ground. Then he seized all the land of Hugh de Gournay and all the nearby castles. He took the county and castle of Aumâle, the county of Eu and the whole of that land as far as Arques and met with no resistance.[16]

At this point, King Philip brought his trump card into play: Arthur of Brittany. Now 16 years old, the French king knighted Arthur, invested him with Anjou, Maine, Touraine and Aquitaine, and betrothed him to his infant daughter, Mary.[17] A Plantagenet prince, Arthur was the posthumous son of John's brother Geoffrey, fourth son of Henry II of England, and Constance of Brittany. Geoffrey had died in a tournament in August 1186 and Arthur was born several months later. Used as a foil against his uncle John, at one point Arthur had been recognised by King Richard as his heir. However, when Richard died in 1199, it was John who took the English throne.

Ever eager to meddle in English affairs, Philip II Augustus sought to use Arthur as a weapon against John. He gave the young duke a small force and sent him south into Aquitaine to advance his claims as the rightful heir to the Angevin Empire. He was besieging his grandmother, Eleanor of Aquitaine, at Mirebeau, just north of Poitiers, when John came to his mother's aid. Taking Arthur's forces by surprise, John managed to achieve a substantial victory, capturing Arthur in the process. The young duke was imprisoned, first at Falaise and then at Rouen, where he was secretly murdered at Easter 1204, either on John's orders or at the king's own hand, though the former is most likely.

Arthur's mysterious death certainly did nothing to help John's reputation, nor his situation in France. By the summer of 1203 King Philip was again on the offensive, besieging Château Gaillard, the castle that had been the pride of Richard the Lionheart, in August. After failing to break the siege with both land and water-borne troops, John sailed for England on 5 December, leaving the magnificent castle to its fate. According to Ralph of Coggeshall:

> The constable of Chester was in the castle with many famous knights and sergeants, who for a long time strenuously held the castle against the force of the whole army of the French king. But when they urgently needed food supplies they could resist the enemy no longer. King John, indeed, was unwilling to send troops to the besieged because he always feared the treachery of his men, and in the winter in the month of December he crossed to England leaving all the Normans in great worry and fear.[18]

Back on English soil John 'truly oppressed England with many demands for money, hoping to raise a great army and exterminate the forces of King Philip.'[19] Château Gaillard fell on 6 March 1204. During Lent, John sent a delegation to Philip to negotiate for peace, including William Marshal and the archbishop of Canterbury. Philip, however, probably suspecting – or knowing – that Arthur was dead, made the young duke of Brittany's release a condition of any peace settlement: 'For if Arthur was now discovered to be dead, Philip hoped to marry his sister and thus to gain all her continental possessions. King Philip was unwilling to make peace because he was confident that he would soon possess all the lands of the English king.'[20] With John still childless, Arthur's sister was the king of England's heir: if Philip married Eleanor, there was a chance he could have it all.

The fall of Château Gaillard had a devastating effect on morale and was the start of a domino-effect of Norman towns opening their gates to Philip, with Rouen capitulating on 24 June 1204. Eleanor of Aquitaine's death on 1 April 1204 had a similar effect on Poitou, with many Poitevin towns and lords now transferring their homage to Philip; the French king entered Poitiers in triumph in August 1204. To add to John's woes, his brother-in-law Alfonso VIII, King of Castile, invaded Gascony claiming Henry II had promised it as the dowry of his wife, John's sister Eleanor, on her mother's death.[21]

By the end of 1204 John's Continental possessions amounted to the ports of the west coast of France, from Bayonne to La Rochelle, and the fortresses of Chinon and Loches.[22] Matters were not improved in 1205 when John attempted to mount an expedition to the Continent and recover his losses; he was thwarted by the English barons, whose reluctance to follow him led to the campaign being abandoned. Loches and Chinon surrendered to the French, leaving only the main Gascon towns holding out. Some success was achieved in that the Channel Islands were recovered, and Niort in Poitou. In 1206, John landed at La Rochelle, recovered Saintonge and consolidated his hold on his wife Isabelle's county of Angoulême, her father having died in 1202. He also managed to drive the last remaining Castilians from Gascony. On hearing that John was sailing with an army, Philip had moved north to defend Normandy, but now headed south, forcing John to abandon his advance on Anjou. A two-year truce was agreed in October, but the great Continental possessions of the Angevin kings were now, effectively, lost forever, with John retaining only Gascony and south-western Poitou out of an empire that had once controlled half of France.[23]

The loss of Normandy and his vast Continental empire meant that John could concentrate his energies on England, in a way that no king had done since the time of the Norman Conquest of 1066. The next five years saw John raising revenue from taxes and keeping a heavy hand on the administration of the country. His efforts to recover debts and aggressive form of government would see him alienating many of his barons and push the country, inexorably, towards the political crisis that would culminate in Magna Carta. In 1207 he levied a thirteenth, a tax at the rate of 1 shilling raising £57,425, more than twice the usual annual revenue. In the same year he moved against the earl of Leicester, depriving him of his lands for non-payment of debt. In 1208 the lands of William de Braose, once high in royal favour, were confiscated, ostensibly for non-payment of debts, but we will look into this more in the next chapter. In 1210 a tallage on the Jews raised 66,000 marks; the tallage became increasingly unpopular even outside the Jewish community, as John put pressure on those who were indebted to the Jews to pay back what they owed, so that he could be paid. Annual royal revenues rose dramatically after 1209, so that by 1212 it is estimated that John had 200,000 marks in coin stored in his treasuries at Bristol, Corfe and elsewhere.[24]

The first crisis following the loss of Normandy was John's dispute with the pope, Innocent III. As with most rulers of the era, John wanted to have control of church appointments, especially of senior bishops and archbishops. In England, especially, the king's authority over the church was strong. In 1205 John had arranged the election of Peter des Roches as bishop of Winchester. Following the death of Hubert Walter, Archbishop of Canterbury, the pope annulled the election of John de Gray, bishop of Norwich and John's candidate as his replacement, as being uncanonical. In his stead, in July 1205, the monks at Canterbury elected the pope's candidate, Stephen Langton, as their new archbishop. The pope had sanctioned the election and written to John for his approval. John, however, refused to give his consent. Langton's years in Paris making him unacceptable to the king. Nevertheless, Langton was consecrated archbishop in Rome in June 1207 and on 15 July, John expelled the monks from Canterbury. This act saw an exodus to the Continent of many senior church leaders:

> The bishop of London, the bishop of Ely, the bishop of Hereford, the bishop of Chester, the archbishop of York, who was the king's own brother, and numerous others, rich as well as poor, left England unable to bear the king's tyranny. There was not one man in the land who could oppose his will ... Only the bishop of Winchester remained in the king's favour.[25]

Relations with the pope and the church deteriorated further and on 24 March 1208 England was placed under interdict, the church's greatest weapon:

> divine services were suspended throughout England. Great sorrow and anxiety spread throughout the country. Neither Good Friday nor Easter Sunday could be celebrated, but an unheard-of silence was imposed on all the clergy and monks by laymen. The bodies

of the dead, whether of the ordinary folk or the religious, could not be buried in consecrated cemeteries, but only in vile and profane places.[26]

John ordered the seizure of all clerical property in retribution and ordered the arrests of priests' and clerks' mistresses – though they were soon allowed to buy their freedom. John was worried that the election, against his wishes, of Langton would set a precedent for future clerical appointments, a stumbling block that would not be overcome in negotiations with the pope; neither would John's refusal to admit liability and pay compensation. As a consequence, in November 1209, Innocent III excommunicated the king of England. All the bishops of England save Peter des Roches, who stayed in England, and John de Gray, who was despatched to Ireland to act as justiciar, left for exile, leaving seven bishoprics and seventeen abbacies vacant.[27] Although negotiations between John and the papacy continued for a while, they were half-hearted and had broken off altogether by 1211, John being less concerned with his excommunication against the revenues he was receiving from the church lands now under his control.

Relations with the other countries in the British Isles were also deteriorating. In 1209 John, having heard of marriage negotiations between Scotland and France, marched on Scotland. William the Lion, King of Scots was ill and in order to avoid war, was forced to agree to the humiliating Treaty of Norham, in which he promised to pay John 15,000 marks to ensure the king of England's good will. He also agreed to hand over thirteen hostages and his two eldest daughters, for John to arrange their marriages. To be fair to John, he did indeed extend his good will to Scotland when King William was challenged by a rival to his throne, Guthred Macwilliam, in 1211. John knighted King William's son, Alexander, in London before sending him north with a band of soldiers from Brabançon and with them, Alexander 'captured Guthred, called MacWilliam, the leader of the rebels, and hanged him.'[28]

Campaigns in Wales in 1208, and again in 1211, and in Ireland in 1209–1210 saw some successes for John but alienated more barons. His pursuit and eventual destruction of William de Braose, first in Wales and then in Ireland, demonstrated the extent of John's animosity towards his enemies and their families. What was to stop him going against any one of his barons in the same relentless manner? He successfully invaded Gwynedd in 1211, forcing its prince, his son-in-law, Llywelyn ap Iorwerth, to surrender the whole of Gwynedd east of Conwy and to promise that all his lands would revert to king John, should he die without issue by his wife Joan, John's illegitimate daughter.[29] In Ireland, John's whirlwind nine-week campaign in 1210 saw Walter and Hugh de Lacy driven out of Meath and Ulster, the introduction of English laws and currency and an extension of English control. John had little interest in the native Irish lords and kings, and he left Ireland on less-than-friendly terms with the most prominent of Ireland's kings, Cathal Croibhdhearg and Aodh Ō Nēill. Ō Nēill's refusal to hand over hostages led to the Inisfallen annalist's assessment that 'The king of England came to Ireland and accomplished little.'[30] However, on a whole, he left Ireland under greater control of the English government and its justiciar, John de Gray, continued to make some gains, despite being unable to subjugate Aodh Ō Nēill.

John's successes in Scotland, Wales and Ireland were without precedent, as the Barnwell chronicler noted, there was 'no one in Ireland, Scotland and Wales who did not obey his nod – something which, as is well-known, none of his predecessors had achieved.'[31] However, John's successes so close to home gave him an optimism that was to lead to the greatest crisis of his reign and, eventually, to Magna Carta. In 1212, John turned his sights to the Continent, and he set about rebuilding the coalition that had dissolved in 1200, supported by Rainauld, Count of Boulogne and German Emperor Otto IV. In July, plans were well in hand and a combined land and naval force was mustering at Portsmouth when they had to be diverted to Chester to deal with another Welsh revolt, united behind Llywelyn ap Iorwerth. In retaliation for the revolt, on 14 August, John hanged twenty-eight Welsh hostages at Nottingham. Although he would have considered the lives of the hostages forfeit, given they were held to guarantee the good behaviour of the Welsh, it is considered one of the cruellest acts of his reign, and one for which he has been judged harshly.

Whilst at Nottingham, John learned of a plot against his life and the two magnates held responsible, Robert Fitzwalter and Eustace de Vescy, fled to France and Scotland, respectively. Eustace de Vescy is said to have had a personal grudge against John as he had tried to seduce de Vescy's wife. The story goes that 'the baron had cunningly managed to smuggle a prostitute into the king's bedchamber instead. The next day John boasted to de Vesci how good the night had been. But the baron immediately confessed to the deception. He had to flee for his life.'[32] De Vescy was married to an illegitimate sister of the king of Scots and so fled north to Scotland. Another conspirator, Geoffrey of Norwich, an official of the Exchequer, was apprehended and died in prison. According to the Barnwell Chronicler, this was the catalyst of John's increasing paranoia; from this point on, he trusted no one and had an armed bodyguard accompany him everywhere he went:

> The King John's heart was troubled, since it was being said, without authority, that rumours had been heard that the barons who had gathered together were conspiring against him, and that in many ears there were tales of letters absolving the barons from John's allegiance. It was said that another king should be elected in his place and that John should be expelled from the kingdom ... the king began to have misgivings and would go nowhere without either being armed or accompanied by a great force of armed men. Having taken captive some who seemed to be too intimate with the rebels, he quickly seized the castles of the earls and barons, so that there was unrest for some time.[33]

John took hostages and castles from those barons he suspected of disloyalty, being especially thorough in the north. Prophecies, notably by Peter of Wakefield, were predicting John's downfall, preaching 'that King John's reign would not last beyond the next Ascension Day, because it had been revealed to him that King John would reign for fourteen years, and that those things which had begun during those fourteen years would reach a happy conclusion.'[34] According to the Barnwell annalist, Peter's prophecies were added to and distorted in their retelling, and 'Every day false words of the common people were added to his falsehoods.'[35] Peter was arrested and imprisoned; he and his son were hanged on 27 May 1213, four days after Ascension Day and the anniversary of

John's accession. In a bid to increase his popularity across the social spectrum, and especially in the north, John chose this time to tackle the abuses of sheriffs and forest officials. He ordered forest officials to only exact the same amounts as they had under his father and repealed new exactions that had been imposed in the ports. Moreover, he reopened negotiations with Innocent III in November 1212. In a demonstration of his willingness to compromise, John 'exacted from all the prelates of the Church a confirmation of all that he had taken from them ... so that in this way they would greatly modify their claims concerning what he had taken away.'[36]

By 1213 John was planning a new Continental expedition and negotiating with Toulouse and Aragon to open a southern front against King Philip of France. His plans were forestalled, however, when Philip himself announced in April that he was planning to invade England, apparently with encouragement from the pope. John's position was precarious, to say the least, the loyalty of his barons only maintained by a combination of bribery and intimidation. In response to Philip's announcement, the army was gathered with John at Dover, with his fleet just off shore. As a consequence, according to the Barnwell annalist, the majority of John's barons were present to witness John's surrender of the kingdom to Rome, on 15 May 1213, promising to pay 1,000 marks a year to Rome and swearing 'liege homage and fealty to Pope Innocent III and to his successors.'[37] Although this was a humiliation for John, his hold on his country and people was precarious and he had little choice but to submit to the church; it has been seen as 'a master stroke of diplomacy'.[38]

England was now a papal fief, but John was still excommunicate and on 1 July he sent a delegation to Stephen Langton on the Continent, headed by the archbishop of Dublin and the bishop of Norwich, urging the archbishop of Canterbury and his fellow exiles to return to England as quickly as possible. On 20 July, he met the former exiles at Winchester; they led the king to the doors of Winchester Cathedral where, in front of a host of nobles, clergy and commoners, he was absolved. The king swore an oath that he 'would henceforth love and defend the Church and renew the good laws of his ancestors.'[39] The interdict on England would finally be lifted on 2 July 1214, six years, three months and sixteen days after it was imposed.[40] Despite the fact compensation payments would take another year to settle, John's submission to the pope meant that Innocent was now a staunch defender of the king. However, it also meant that John's enemies, including Robert Fitzwalter and Eustace de Vescy, were now able to return from exile, alongside the abbots and clerics.

King Philip's fleet was destroyed by John's half-brother, William Longespée, Earl of Salisbury, on 30 May and in June John ordered his army to sail for Poitou. However, the magnates refused, with the northern barons – 'the northerners' – led by Eustace de Vescy, claiming that their conditions of tenure did not require them to serve in Poitou. Stephen Langton, now restored to his see at Canterbury, thwarted John's attempts to punish the rebels and when the king did finally sail for Poitou in 1214, several barons were absent, including Fitzwalter, Vescy and Geoffrey de Mandeville, the soon-to-be husband of John's first wife, Isabella of Goucester. A two-pronged attack saw John landing at La Rochelle, while Longespée landed in Flanders, joining Otto of Germany, Rainauld of Boulogne and Count Ferrand of Flanders. The idea was to force Philip to divide his forces.

John sought a reconciliation with the Lusignans, agreeing to grant them Saintes and Oléron and to marry his daughter Joan to Hugh X de Lusignan, the son of Hugh IX de Lusignan, who had been betrothed to John's wife, Isabelle d'Angoulême. A similar peace offering, of the earldom of Richmond, to Pierre, Duke of Brittany, was less well received and the duke remained aloof. John's campaign was successful at first, with him entering Angers unopposed before he laid siege to Roche-au-Moine. However, he was forced to retreat on 2 July, with the approach of the army of Prince Louis of France and the refusal of the Poitevins to fight by his side. Although he was able to keep his own army intact, John's fate was sealed on 27 July when Longespée and the allies faced Philip at the battle of Bouvines and were decisively defeated. Otto IV managed to escape, but William Longespée was captured and taken to Paris, along with the counts of Flanders and Boulogne. With the threat in the north neutralised, Philip was now able to join his army to that of his son, Prince Louis, and challenge John in the south. John had no choice but to seek peace and a five-year truce was agreed on 13 October, with Ralph of Coggeshall reporting rumours that it had cost John 60,000 marks.[41] At home, John's policy of reform of the sheriffs and forest officials in 1212–

1213 had resulted in a significant reduction in royal revenue, and the military campaign drained John's treasury. He was no longer a wealthy king. In October 1214 John returned to England following his defeat by the French at the Battle of Bouvines, which ended the king's hopes of regaining the lost empire. After his return from this disastrous campaign on the Continent, baronial opposition to John now gathered pace. The refusal to pay scutage of 3 marks on the knights' fee demonstrating a coordinated effort by the magnates, rather than the individual disobedience that had been seen earlier in the reign. The barons' objections to John were almost beyond number. He had failed to face the French and had lost not only his family's Continental possessions, but also those of his barons. Few had forgotten his treachery against his brother in trying to take the throne whilst Richard was on crusade.

Added to these catastrophes was the character and personality of John himself. By nature, John was paranoid, secretive and distrustful and his cruelty is widely known. He is accused of killing his nephew and rival claimant to the English throne; he had hanged twenty-eight Welsh hostages (sons of rebel chieftains); and he had hounded William de Braose and his family all the way to Ireland and back. De Braose's wife and son died in one of John's prisons, probably from starvation. *The History of William Marshal*, a biography of the great knight and statesman, claimed that John treated his prisoners harshly and with such indignity that it was a disgrace to all involved.[42] His barons even complained that he forced himself on their wives and daughters. With such military losses, accusations and seemingly acute character flaws stacked against him, it is no wonder England's king faced opposition by many of the most powerful in his realm.

In January 1215 John arranged to meet with his challengers in London to hear their demands, and it was agreed that they would reconvene at Northampton on 26 April to hear the king's response. The disaffected barons demanded reform and the confirmation of the coronation charter of King Henry I, in which the king promised; 'Know that by the mercy of God and by the common counsel of the barons of England I have been crowned king of this realm. And because the kingdom has been oppressed by unjust exactions, being moved by reverence towards God and by the love I bear you all, I make free the Church of God ... I abolish all the evil customs by which the kingdom of England has been unjustly oppressed.'[43] Although many of the clauses of this charter, also referred to as the Charter of Liberties, were now outdated, several still resonated with the barons, including that a baron's widow would not be married without her consent, that an heiress would not be married without the consent of her relatives and that, on the death of a baron, his heir would only pay a relief that was 'just and lawful.'[44] Whilst John was ruminating on these demands, both sides were preparing for war. John borrowed from the Templars to pay his mercenaries and on 4 March he took the cross. This latter move was seen as being highly cynical and no one seems to have believed that John would actually go on crusade. His purpose for doing so was political: a crusader's lands and properties were protected by the church and this action firmly identified the king's opponents as the 'bad guys'.

John failed to appear at Northampton. He did, however, send messages to the rebels. According to the Barnwell annalist the king 'tried to win them back through many emissaries, and there was much discussion amongst them, the archbishop, bishops and other barons acting as intermediaries, the king himself staying at Oxford.'[45] On 5 May the rebels formally renounced their fealty. John retained the support of some magnates, such as William Marshal and William de Warenne, but the majority were now standing against him. As was London, which opened its gates to the rebels on 17 May, despite John's granting the city the right to elect its mayor only eight days before. In the Welsh Marches the Braose family had allied with Llywelyn ap Iorwerth and had taken Shrewsbury. The rebels were ready to fight. After occupying London, they made one final attempt to prevent war, presenting the king with a list of their demands.

John had no choice but to make concessions and on 10 June agreed to further discussions of the rebels' terms. Following these negotiations, a long, detailed document was produced, dealing with particular grievances of the time and with injustices in general. It touched on the whole system of royal government. And it was granted to 'all free men of the realm and their heirs forever'.[46] Of its sixty-three clauses (see Appendix A) some terms were asking for immediate remedies, such as the removal of corrupt administrators and the sending home of foreign mercenaries.

The clause stating that fighting outside of the kingdom could not be imposed by the king was a reaction to John's recent attempts to force his English barons to help him recover his Continental domains. Others had long-term aims. The document sought to guarantee the privileges of the church and the City of London. Restrictions were placed on the powers of regional officials, such as sheriffs, to prevent abuses. The royal court was fixed at Westminster, for justice to be obtainable by all, and royal judges were to visit each county regularly. Taxes could no longer be levied without the consent of the church and the barons.

Clauses included the fixing of inheritance charges and protection from exploitation for under-age heirs; the king was to take only what was reasonable from an estate (although 'reasonable' remained undefined). From henceforth a widow was to be free to choose whether or not to remarry and her marriage portion (dowry) would be made available to her immediately on her husband's death. Another clause sought to prevent the seizure of land from Jews and the king's debtors. Magna Carta even went so far as to regulate weights and measures. It also reduced the size of the king's forests and limited the powers of forest justices. Although most of the sixty-three clauses of Magna Carta are now defunct, three still remain as major tenets of British law, including 'to no one will we sell, to no one will we deny or delay right or justice.' That no person would be imprisoned, outlawed or deprived of his lands except by judgement of his peers and the law of the land has remained the cornerstone of the English legal system ever since.

Magna Carta was sealed at Runnymede, Berkshire, on 15 June 1215. John ordered that the charter be circulated around the towns and villages, throughout the realm. As a peace agreement between the king and his rebellious barons, however, it failed miserably. By July John was appealing to the pope for help. Pope Innocent III's response arrived in England in September. The treaty was declared null and void; according to Innocent, Magna Carta was:

> not only shameful and base but also illegal and unjust. We refuse to overlook such shameless presumption which dishonours the Apostolic See, injures the king's right, shames the English nation, and endangers the crusade. Since the whole crusade would be

undermined if concessions of this sort were extorted from a great prince who had taken the cross, we, on behalf of Almighty God, Father, Son and Holy Ghost, and by the authority of Saints Peter and Paul His apostles, utterly reject and condemn this settlement. Under threat of excommunication we order that the king should not dare to observe and the barons and their associates should not insist on it being observed. The charter with all its undertakings and guarantees we declare to be null and void of all validity for ever.[47]

The letter was accompanied by more papal letters, excommunicating rebels, including nine barons and the Londoners. However, by the time the letters arrived in England, the dispute had already erupted into the Barons' War. John laid siege to Rochester Castle with his mercenaries and the castle surrendered on 30 November, after a seven-week siege. Deciding they could no longer deal with John's perfidy, the rebel barons had invited the King of France, Philip II Augustus, to claim the throne. Philip's son and heir, the future Louis VIII, accepted the offer. He sent an advanced guard, which arrived in December of 1215. Louis himself would arrive in the spring of 1216. He landed on the south coast and marched for London, where he was proclaimed King of England on 2 June 1216. In the meantime, while waiting for the French to arrive, the rebels and their allies were not inactive. Following a judgement in his favour from the Twenty-Five barons appointed to oversee the enforcement of Magna Carta, Alexander II, King of Scots, was awarded Northumberland, Cumberland and Westmorland and received the homage of the Northerners. In Wales, eleven Welsh princes united under Llywelyn ap Iorwerth, establishing him as *de facto* prince of Wales and in three weeks they captured seven castles, including Cardigan and Carmarthen.

In December John headed north and chased the Yorkshire rebels all the way to Scotland, where he captured Berwick on 13 January 1216. He then raided the Scottish Lowlands and set fire to Berwick before turning back south and heading for East Anglia in March 1216. While John appears to have held the initiative with his military successes, and he was able to win some rebels over to his side, the leaders remained firmly against him. His failure to take London and prevent the landing of Prince Louis at Sandwich in the spring, was a major setback. John spent the summer campaigning in the west of England as Louis was proclaimed king in the capital, captured Winchester and laid siege to Dover, Windsor and Lincoln, the three strongholds which still held out for King John. By autumn 1216, John was at his lowest point as the earls of Arundel, Warenne and Salisbury (John's own brother) submitted to Louis. Alexander II of Scotland met the French prince at Canterbury and paid him homage for the lands he held from the English crown. Two-thirds of his magnates had abandoned John, as had one third of his household knights.[48]

At Lynn, on the evening of 9 October, John suffered an attack of dysentery. His health deteriorated as he made his way west until he reached Newark. He died there on the night of 18-19 October 1216 and was buried at Worcester Cathedral, 'not because he had asked to be buried there but because that place at that time seemed a safe one where his supporters could gather to deliberate on what was to be done next.'[49]

John was lamented by few, especially among the clergy, who firmly believed he was going to Hell. As Matthew Paris commented, 'Foul as it is, Hell itself is made fouler by the presence of John.'[50] Ralph of Coggeshall was more generous, stating:

John was indeed a great prince but scarcely a happy one and, like Marius, he experienced the ups and downs of fortune. He was munificent and liberal to outsiders but a plunderer to his own people, trusting strangers rather than his subjects, wherefore he was eventually deserted by his own men and, in the end, little mourned.[51]

John's fortuitous death at Newark in October 1216 turned the tide against Louis and the rebels. The highly respected knight and statesman, William Marshal, Earl of Pembroke, was appointed regent for John's 9-year-old son, Henry III. Marshal's staunch loyalty was renowned throughout Europe; he was the embodiment of the chivalric code. Many barons who had previously sided with Louis saw the opportunity to come back from the brink, and rally around the young king.

Marshal reissued Magna Carta in November 1216, then faced and defeated the joint French and rebel army at Lincoln on 20 May 1217. A naval battle off Sandwich on 24 August 1217 saw the English ships under Hubert de Burgh defeat the French fleet and capture their flagship and thus consolidate the Royalist victory over the rebels and their French allies. As a consequence, the English were able to dictate terms to Louis. Peace was signed at Kinston Upon Thames on 12 September and the French went home. Magna Carta was issued a third time, along with a new charter, the Charter of the Forest, issued for the first time (see Appendix C). A newer version of Magna Carta was issued in 1225, on Henry III attaining his majority, and it is this 1225 Magna Carta which made it onto the statute books.

Although John faced the fallout of Magna Carta, many of the injustices targeted by the barons can be seen in the reigns of his predecessors. Heavy taxes, arbitrary fines and the exploitation of wardships were long-established royal revenue earners. However, where Henry and Richard had a whole empire to exploit, John's need for money had to be met by England alone. Even John's disagreement with the church parallels the reign of Henry II and his clashes with Thomas Becket. As we have seen, John opposed the election of Stephen Langton as archbishop of Canterbury and refused to allow his consecration. Pope Innocent III placed England under interdict and excommunicated John himself; in 1213 Philip II Augustus of France was even invited, by the papacy, to depose him.

It is hard to overstate the enduring significance of Magna Carta. Although it was initially a document conceived by rebel barons, the regents of Henry III exploited Magna Carta as a Royalist device to recover their loyalty. However, once it was issued it was used as a curb to all regal excesses and in 1265 it was invoked to create the first parliament. By the late 1200s Magna Carta was regarded as a fundamental statement of English liberties. Although a failure in the short term, in the long term, Magna Carta established defined limitations to royal rights, laying down that standard to be observed by the crown and its agents.

The drawing up and issuing of Magna Carta in June 1215 was only the start of its journey and while its influence and impact on the country in general, and the barons who forced it on John in particular, is widely known, the charter's effect on the lives of the women who were associated with its creation, or affected by its clauses and implementation, has been largely ignored. It is now time to redress that imbalance and examine how this great charter, Magna Carta, influenced and impacted the women of the thirteenth century, who lived through the conflict and the unsettled years which followed.

Chapter 3

The Fall of the Braose Family

The story of the de Braose family is one of the most dramatic falls from favour in English history. William (III) de Braose (also spelt Briouze), fourth Lord of Bramber, was one of the most trusted advisors of King John, and one of his best friends. However, as a result de Braose knew John's greatest secret, what happened to Arthur of Brittany, and this was to cause his spectacular downfall and the sad deaths of his wife and son in one of John's dungeons. William de Braose's dramatic fall from favour contributed considerably to baronial distrust and fear of the king, leading to the heightened tensions of 1212 onwards, and to the drawing up of Magna Carta itself.

The Braose family name comes from the Norman barony of Briouze-St Gervais, near Argentin, where William and his ancestors held three knights' fees.[1] William (III) was the son of William (II) de Braose and his wife, Bertha, the daughter and coheiress of Miles of Gloucester, first Earl of Hereford. The Braose family had held the castle and rape of Bramber, Sussex, since the eleventh century, when it was granted to William's great-grandfather, William (I), by William the Conqueror. It was the first William's son, Philip, who extended the Braose holdings by adding the Welsh lordships of Builth and Radnor and acquiring claims to the baronies of Totnes and Barnstaple, in Devon, through his marriage to Aenor, daughter of Juhel of Totnes. Aenor was coheir of her father and through her William (III)'s father, William (II), acquired a half share in the lordship of Barnstaple. In 1158 William (II) had offered King Henry II a fine of 1,000 marks for twenty-eight knights' fees, as his mother's share of her inheritance. On his death in 1192 or 1193, £430 was still outstanding.[2]

William (II)'s own marriage to Bertha brought the lordships of Abergavenny and Brecon, in south Wales, into the family from Bertha's share of the Hereford estates after the deaths of her two brothers, although her elder sister, Margaret, married to Humphrey II de Bohun, received the bulk of the Hereford inheritance. William (II) concentrated his attentions on his land in the Welsh Marches, serving as sheriff of Herefordshire for Henry II between 1173 and 1175. His daughter, Sybil, married firstly William de Ferrers, Earl of Derby, and secondly Adam de Port, Baron of Basing, Hampshire. William (II)'s son, William (III), married Matilda de Saint Valery, better known to history as Matilda (or Maud) de Braose.[3]

Matilda de Braose

Matilda de Braose was probably born in the early 1150s in Saint-Valery-en-Caux, France, to Bernard IV, Seigneur de Saint-Valery and Lord of Beckley in Oxfordshire, and his first wife, Matilda. Contemporary records describe Matilda as 'tall and beautiful, wise and vigorous.'[4] More famous for her role in the de Braose's spectacular falling-out with King John and the manner of her death, very little is known of Matilda's early years, although it is likely that she spent time at her family's manor of Hinton Waldrist in Berkshire. Sometime around 1166 she was married to William (III) de Braose, fourth Lord of Bramber.

William (II) appears to have withdrawn from public life in the late 1170s, probably retiring to his estates. He is thought to have died around 1192 or 1193.[5] He was succeeded in the administration of his estates and, eventually, in his barony, by Matilda's husband, William (III) de Braose, who was highly favoured by both Richard I and, later his brother King John. William and Matilda continued to expand the Braose holdings acquiring estates until they had an annual income of over £800 through holding as fiefs or custodies a total of 325 knights' fees, and sixteen castles in England, Wales and Ireland.[6] William's career in royal service began in the reign of Richard I; he was sheriff of Herefordshire from 1191 until he was replaced on the orders of King John in 1200. He was active against the Welsh throughout Richard's reign, defending the volatile frontier. He also served on the Continent with King Richard in 1194 and again in 1199, being present at the siege of Châlus when the king was mortally wounded.

After their marriage William and Matilda settled at their main family seat of Abergavenny Castle. William had a particularly ruthless reputation among the Welsh and was known as the 'Ogre of Abergavenny' following an incident in 1175 when he murdered the Welsh prince Seisyllt ap Dyfnwal, in retaliation for the murder of his uncle Henry of Hereford, who had been killed at the Welsh prince's home of Castel Arnallt. Seisyllt and two other Welsh princes, plus other members of the Welsh aristocracy, had been invited to a Christmas feast, supposedly in the spirit of reconciliation. However, having surrendered their weapons at the door the defenceless Welsh princes, their sons and retainers, were locked in the hall and massacred by William and his men. Seisyllt and his eldest son were among the slain. Determined upon the destruction of Seisyllt's entire family, William then rode into the Welsh prince's domains, where he murdered Seisyllt's younger son and kidnapped his wife, who disappears from the historical record thereafter. The boy was just 7 years old.

Matilda was also known as the Lady of Hay, taken from the Castle of Hay, and had her own reputation in Welsh folklore. She appears to have taken on a supernatural persona among the Welsh; one legend arose of Matilda building the Castle of Hay in one night, single-handed, carrying the stones in her skirts.[7] Whilst William was away campaigning in Normandy or in attendance on the king, Matilda would be left to manage their estates in Wales. In 1198, Matilda defended Painscastle in Elfael, just south of Radnor and Builth, against a massive Welsh attack by Gwenwynyn, Prince of Powys. She held out for three weeks until English reinforcements arrived, earning the castle its nickname of Matilda's Castle. Geoffrey fitz Peter, the justiciar, came to her rescue, lifting the siege on 13 August. Ralph of Diceto described the encounter:

> On the Welsh Marches, near what is called "Matilda's Castle" the principal defence forces of the area gathered with hostile intent, equipped for battle. In the first grouping of the Welsh were only foot soldiers; in the second knights and infantry; in the third knights only. In the first grouping of the [king's] army were placed foot soldiers, and knights in the second; but the whole strength of the army was in the third grouping. On the first engagement, the Welsh turned their backs and spoils were seized from them. Many were captured, and very many killed, amounting to as many as three thousand warriors,

so it is said. Thus was the prophecy fulfilled, "The roaring cubs shall cause great slaughter among any who oppose them."[8]

Gerald of Wales described Matilda in 1188, saying 'She was, I say, a prudent and chaste woman, well equipped to rule her household skilled in preserving her property within doors as increasing it outdoors.'[9]

William and Matilda had around sixteen children together, who married into some of the most powerful families of the time. Their eldest son, William, married Maud de Clare, daughter of the earl of Hertford; he died alongside his mother in John's dungeons in 1210. Their second son, Giles, became bishop of Hereford in 1200; he died in 1215. A third son, Reginald, became head of the family on Giles' death in 1215 and married, as his second wife, Gwladus Ddu, daughter of Llewelyn the Great, Prince of Gwynedd in north Wales, and his wife, Joan, illegitimate daughter of King John.

Reginald's son William, by his first wife married Eva Marshal, daughter of the great knight, William Marshal. It was this William de Braose who was ignominiously hanged by Llewelyn the Great, after being found in Llewelyn's bedchamber with the Welsh prince's wife Joan, the Lady of Wales and natural daughter of King John. William had been at the Welsh court to arrange the marriage of his daughter, Isabel, to Llewelyn and Joan's son, Dafydd. Interestingly, after some diplomatic manoeuvring by Llywelyn, the marriage still went ahead, although it was to be childless.

A fourth son of William and Matilda, John, married Mabel de Limesy, coheir to the barony of Cavendish in Suffolk; his father, William de Braose, had offered the king £1,000 for this marriage in 1203. Of their daughters Loretta, married Robert de Breteuil, fourth Earl of Leicester and another, Margaret, married Walter de Lacy, Lord of Meath. A third daughter, Annora, married Hugh (III) de Mortimer, Baron of Wigmore in Herefordshire. Another daughter, Matilda, married Gruffudd ap Rhys, the son of Lord Rhys of Deheubarth.

William's star continued to rise on the accession of King John in 1199. He helped to win support for John over Arthur as his rival claimant and he was an almost-constant companion of the new king in the early years, regularly witnessing John's charters. He was one of the king's staunchest allies as John consolidated his position in England and fought for his possessions on the Continent. William also managed to attend to his duties in Wales and on the Welsh March. He also watched over the marcher barony of his son-in-law, Walter de Lacy, while Walter was occupied with his honour of Meath in Ireland; the reciprocal arrangement saw Walter looking out for the Braose interests in Ireland, as well as his own. William and Matilda de Braose continued to thrive under King John, who sought to use William as a counterbalance to the power of William Marshal, Earl of Pembroke, especially on the Welsh March where both enjoyed significant influence. William and Matilda's family also benefited from John's largesse, with their son, Giles, being promoted to bishop of Hereford in 1200. In the same year, John granted William all the lands he could conquer in Wales to increase his barony at Radnor.

William was also granted several wardships, including that of the heir to the barony of Salwarpe, Shropshire, the Welsh lordships of Glamorgan and Gower in 1202 and the barony of Great Torrington, in Devon, in 1203.[10] In the following year, William was granted the estates of Alan Trenchemer in Surrey, after paying John £100 to have the case heard before the king, and sending the king a gift of 300 cows, thirty bulls and ten horses so the case could be heard swiftly. A further 700 marks would be paid 'if it indeed should be won.'[11] William was pardoned all outstanding debts to the crown in September 1202, including those his father had owed to Henry II and the ones he himself had owed to Richard I. In 1203 he was forgiven a £50 debt to Jewish moneylenders and in 1204 the £825 fine for his son's marriage to a coheir of the barony of Limesy. All these grants were a clear indication of the high favour, in which William was held by the king, in the early years of John's reign.

At the same time, William was expanding his landholdings in Ireland, thus accumulating more debt. William's grandfather had been granted the honour of Limerick by King Henry II, but never taken possession. John regranted Limerick to William de Braose in 1201, with sixty knights' fees, in exchange for 5,000 marks to be paid in annual instalments of 500 marks. In 1210 he still owed £2865 for Limerick and £350 for three Welsh castles.[12] It was this arrangement, a substantial debt on William's part, that would later be used by John to pursue judgement against William and his family. Traditionally, the king was less than rigorous in his pursuit of debts to the crown; such debts were seen as a necessary price of baronial ambition. However, following the loss of his Continental possessions, John broke with tradition, seeing the repayment of such debts as a new source of income. In 1207 John declared the lands of the Earl of Leicester forfeit, for non-payment of his debts. He would turn his sights on William in the following year.

William de Braose's troubles started long before he was aware of them, in the castle at Rouen at Easter 1203. On 1 August 1202 William had been the one to capture Arthur of Brittany at the siege of Mirebeau. As briefly discussed in Chapter One the great William Marshal and Hubert Walter, Archbishop of Canterbury and Justiciar of England, were instrumental in persuading the English barons to accept John as King, reasoning that John knew more of England – and was more experienced – than young Arthur. According to *L'Histoire de Guillaume le Maréchale*, Marshal counselled against giving the crown to Arthur. Arthur was 12 years old at the time, and under the influence of King Philip of France, two factors that were not in the young duke's favour. Marshal successfully pressed for the succession of John, Richard's brother, a grown man, who it was believed was more aligned with the interests of the Anglo-Norman baronage than the young Breton duke. Arthur's claim was revived in the early 1200s when the King of France, Philip II Augustus, confiscated John's possessions in Northern France for failing to acknowledge the French King as his overlord. Philip recognised Arthur as the rightful heir to Normandy and Anjou.

Arthur was knighted by the French king, betrothed to his infant daughter and sent south with 200 knights to join up with the Lusignans in Poitou. He intercepted his grandmother at Mirebeau, where capturing her would have been a significant coup, Eleanor of Aquitaine being a considerable bargaining chip. The dowager queen of England was forced to seek safety in the castle but managed to get a message out to King John at Le Mans. After a forced march of 100 miles in less than forty-eight hours, John and a detachment of his army had fallen on Arthur's troops in the town streets of Mirebeau and achieved a complete victory over his mother's attackers. William de Braose captured Arthur and handed him over to John, who sent him into imprisonment, first at Falaise and then at Rouen. Demanding Arthur's release, 'King Philip of France, with the Bretons, instantly ordered King John of England to release Arthur to them. They took many hostages for him and added fierce threats to these commands. When John refused, Philip again attacked the castles of Normandy.'[13]

Arthur's captivity was probably less than comfortable, despite his rank and familial relationship. According to William Marshal, John 'kept his prisoners in such a horrible manner and such abject confinement that it seemed an indignity and disgrace to all those with him who witnessed his cruelty.'[14] While he was being held at Falaise, John had sent orders for Arthur's castration and blinding while he was in the custody of Hubert de Burgh, but Hubert had refused to carry out the punishment, believing that 'the king would immediately repent of such an order and that ever afterwards would hate anyone who presumed to obey such a cruel mandate.'[15] Hubert de Burgh was partly right and Arthur's survival at that time helped to pacify the rebellious Bretons. However, in 1203 Arthur was moved to the castle at Rouen. King Philip and the nobility of Brittany continued to press for the release of the young duke, but John had other ideas:

The King of the French took the castle of Chinon, and afterwards all the garrisons of Normandy, Anjou, and the city of Poitiers, with other castles, fortified towns and cities, as he so willed it – for this reason; when king John had captured Arthur, he had him kept alive in prison for some time, but finally, in the great tower at Rouen, on the Thursday before Easter, after his dinner and when drunk and possessed by the devil, he killed him by his own hand, and, after a large stone had been tied to the body, threw it in the Seine. It was discovered by a fisherman in his net and recognised when it was brought to the riverbank, and, for fear of the tyrant, secretly buried at the priory of Bec, which is called Notre Dame des Pres.

When the aforesaid king of the French heard the news of this and knew for certain that Arthur had been killed, he had his killer John summoned to the court of France, as was customary with dukes of Normandy, to answer for the murder of such a great man and to defend himself if he could; of such a great man, say I, for he was the legitimate heir of England, the count of Brittany, and the son-in-law of the king of France. John, fully aware of his evil deed, never dared to appear before the court, but fled to England and exercised a most cruel tyranny over his people until he died. When he never came to answer for the death of Arthur or to defend himself, judgement was given against him by the king's court, and he was deprived of all his titles, in all the lands and honours which he held of the French crown; this was an incontrovertible and just sentence.'[16]

The murder was conducted in secret and Arthur's fate was never publicly acknowledged; only a trusted few knew exactly what had happened, including William de Braose. John's complicity in the act, however, seems to be beyond doubt. Arthur had been a hostage to the good behaviour of his Breton subjects. In the short term, his death led to a renewed offensive by King Philip and the loss of most of John's Continental possessions. In the long term it exacerbated the growing mistrust of John among his barons. How could they hand over hostages for their good behaviour if John could not be trusted to keep them safe and alive? It is said that it was Matilda's voicing of these concerns, that caused the spectacular downfall of the Braose family.

It was following Arthur's murder that things started to go wrong for the Lord and Lady of Bramber. John became increasingly suspicious of de Braose's loyalty and turned against him. This could have been for several reasons, not least being de Braose's knowledge of Arthur's fate. Elsewhere, de Braose had fallen behind in his payments to the Exchequer for the honour of Limerick, but he had also sided with his friend William Marshal in his disagreements with the king. In addition, de Braose's son, Giles had been one of the bishops to approve an Interdict against John.

Whatever the reason, King John moved to make a public example of one of his most powerful barons and punish him for his debts to the Exchequer. In December 1207 John granted William's honour of Limerick to Walter de Lacy, hoping to sew dissension between William de Braose and his son-in-law. The following year, the king's persecution of the family continued apace. John appointed one of his mercenary captains, Gerard d'Athée, as sheriff of Herefordshire, in order to threaten William's lordship of Brecon and Giles' own position as bishop of Hereford. William's eldest son, also William, was amerced 300 marks for forest offences. John then demanded William and Matilda give up their sons as hostages. Matilda refused and Roger of Wendover recorded her response to the soldiers sent to collect the boys, as; 'I will not deliver my sons to your lord, King John, for he foully murdered his nephew Arthur, whom he should have cared for honourably.'[17] Knowing that his wife had gone too far, William promised the messengers he would make amends and was heard to rebuke his wife, saying, 'You have spoken like a foolish woman against our lord the king.'[18] The messengers, however, returned to John and related the whole story. The furious king sent more knights, this time to seize William and his entire family.

In an attempt to appease the king, the couple sent John expensive gifts. Matilda is said to have sent a herd of cows to Queen Isabelle, including a fine white bull. William surrendered his castles of Hay, Brecon and Radnor, mortgaged his English lands and handed over hostages. In a public letter of 1210 justifying his actions against the family, John claimed that they were due to the repeated non-payment of the debt owed for Limerick, William had fallen behind on payments and ignored every deadline. As a consequence, John had ordered the sheriff of Gloucester to attack and seize the Braose lands in south Wales. John wrote that when William did hand over his castles and surrender hostages, they were guarantees that he would keep up with his payments in the future.[19]

The king took possession of de Braose's castles and moved to arrest William. Forewarned, the couple fled to Ireland with two of their sons, where they took refuge with Walter de Lacy, their son-in-law and lord of Meath. John was not to be thwarted and launched an invasion of Ireland to capture the fugitives, bringing other recalcitrant barons to heal along the way. While William de Braose tried to come to terms with the king, Matilda and their eldest son, William, escaped by taking ship for Scotland. Nevertheless, Matilda, her daughter Annora and William, along with his wife and children, were captured in Galloway by Duncan of Carrick, who was richly rewarded by his distant cousin, the English king.

John sent two ships, with crossbowmen and sergeants as an escort to bring his prisoners to him at Carrickfergus. When he returned to England, John took Matilda and her family with him, initially imprisoning them in Bristol Castle. King John made an agreement with both William and Matilda that entailed freedom for her and a pardon for William in return for 50,000 marks, a king's ransom, with Matilda remaining imprisoned until the sum had been paid in full. William was allowed to leave court to raise the money, leaving Matilda as hostage. However, he managed to evade his escort and escaped to France, disguised as a beggar, where he joined his son, Giles, who had fled to exile there in 1208. It may be that, despite knowing what had befallen Arthur, William never expected John to impose the same punishment on a woman and hoped that Matilda would be safe in the king's custody.

Informed of her husband's escape Matilda remained defiant, refusing to pay the fine, saying she had only 24 marks of silver, 24 gold coins and 15 ounces of gold left to her.[20] Of Matilda's response, in his 1210 public letter of justification for his actions against the family, John wrote 'So neither then nor afterwards did she, her husband, or anyone else on their behalf, pay me anything of the debt.'[21] Being either unwilling or unable to pay, Matilda and her son were moved from Bristol to imprisonment at either Windsor or Corfe Castle. William (III) de Braose was outlawed in every shire 'according to the laws and customs of England.'[22] He remained in France and died at Corbeil on 4 September 1211 and was buried in the abbey of St Victoire in Paris. Stephen Langton, the exiled archbishop of Canterbury, is said to have assisted in the funeral rites.

Matilda's fate was more gruesome. She and her son were left to starve to death in John's dungeons, whether deliberately or out of neglect by their jailers, it is impossible to say (and whether this was at Corfe or Windsor is unclear). Tradition has it, that when their bodies were found, William's cheeks bore his mother's bite marks, where she had tried to stay alive following his death. Anonymous of Bethune described the scene:

On the eleventh day the mother was found dead between her son's legs, still upright but leaning back against her son's chest as a dead woman. The son, who was also dead, sat upright, leaning against the wall as a dead man. So desperate was the mother that she had eaten her son's cheeks. When William de Braose, who was in Paris, heard this news, he died soon afterwards, many asserting that it was through grief.[23]

John's treatment of the de Braose family did not lead to the submission of his barons as he had hoped and the remainder of his reign was marred by civil war. However, it has gone down in history in that when Magna

Carta was written in 1215, Clause 39 may well have been included with Matilda and her family in mind: 'No man shall be taken, imprisoned, outlawed, banished or in any way destroyed, nor will we proceed against or prosecute him, except by the lawful judgement of his peers or by the law of the land.'[24]

Matilda's daughter, Annora, who had been taken prisoner at the same time as her mother and brother, was held at Windsor, in the custody of John's constable, Engelard de Cigogné, but on 27 October 1214, she was given into the keeping of the papal legate, Nicholas of Tusculum. She was, however, still kept apart from her family and her husband.[25]

In his final days John may have felt some remorse at his relentless pursuit of the destruction of Matilda and her family, as shortly after the onset of his final, fatal illness, on 10 October 1216, the king gave permission to Matilda's daughter, Margaret, to found a religious house in Herefordshire in memory of her father, mother and brother William.[26] John died at Newark on the night of 18/19 October 1216.

Loretta de Braose

A less well-known story of the Braose family is that Matilda may not have been the only Braose to influence the composition of Magna Carta. The experiences of Matilda's daughter, Loretta de Braose, may well have inspired clauses 7 and 8 (see Appendix A), relating to widows' rights. Probably born in the early-to-mid-1180s, Loretta was one of the sixteen children of Matilda and William de Braose. Four of her sisters married prominent Welsh Marcher lords, but Loretta was married to Robert de Breteuil, fourth earl of Leicester, in 1196. Robert was the second son of Robert de Breteuil, third earl of Leicester, and his wife, Petronilla de Grandmesnil. Born, probably, in the early-1160s Robert was closely associated with his elder brother William, as they grew up and entered public life they were linked with the household of their cousin, Robert, Count of Meulan, and they regularly appeared on their father's charters together.[27] William died in 1189, sometime after the accession of King Richard I. A later legend suggests he suffered from leprosy. Robert therefore became heir to the earldom of Leicester when he departed on crusade with the king in 1190 and his adventures in the Holy Land would make a wonderful novel.

Robert's father died on 31 August or 1 September 1190 and so Robert was invested as earl by the king on 2 February 1191, in Sicily. During his time in the Holy Land, Robert was one of the leaders of the assault on Acre on 11 July 1191 and fought in the battle of Arsuf on 7 September. In November he rescued some ambushed Templars at Ibn-Ibrak and then was himself surrounded with his knights by a party of Turks outside the camp at Ramlah. Robert was rescued by his cousin Robert de Neubourg; in the process he nearly drowned in a river and had two horses killed under him. He and his men were prominent among the forces who stormed Deir al-Bela on 22 May 1192 and on 5 August 1192 he was one of the ten knights who helped to thwart an attempt to kidnap the king from his tent at Jaffa and the king himself rescued Robert when he was thrown from his horse. He probably set out for home in September or October 1192, having distinguished himself and earned the king's eternal goodwill.[28]

Following his return from the crusade, Robert was occupied with the defence of Normandy, but was captured by King Philip Augustus' forces in June 1194, after a skirmish outside Gournay. He was imprisoned at Étampes for more than a year and only freed after surrendering his castle and lordship of Pacy-sur-Eure to King Philip. His freedom was achieved sometime around February 1196 and in the same year he was married to the teenage Loretta de Braose. The marriage was an alliance of two of the leading Anglo-Norman families of the Plantagenet world. He was a powerful earl who had made a name for himself on the crusades, whilst she was a daughter of one of the most powerful barons of the Welsh March. As her marriage portion, Loretta was given Tawstock, near Barnstaple in Devon.[29]

Robert de Breteuil was back campaigning in 1197 and 1198 and was with King Richard when he was mortally wounded at Châlus in April 1199. He had had a long association with Richard's brother since John had been Count of Mortain, and so was a firm supporter of John's accession, acting as steward at his coronation on 27 May 1199, claiming the office his grandfather had relinquished in 1153. Robert was highly influential in the early years of John's reign. He also fought for John in Normandy, being one of the major landholders in the duchy, and was rewarded generously for his support; he was granted Richmondshire in Yorkshire in September 1203. The following year he suffered the loss of his Continental estates when Normandy fell and was the biggest loser of the Anglo-Norman barons.

Although he was one of the two barons (the other being William Marshal) who was given a year to decide whether to pay homage to King Philip of France to try to retain his Norman estates, Robert was not punished by John. Indeed, he was given more lands in England, English lands that had belonged to families who had chosen to remain in Normandy, such as the Harcourts.[30] Robert died before King Philip's deadline, and so never did have to decide where and how to share his allegiances in order to keep all his lands. He died on 20 or 21 October 1204; the life of St Hugh of Lincoln reported that he died a leper, although this seems highly unlikely.[31] He was buried in the choir of the Augustinian Abbey in Leicester. His lands were divided between his two sisters. The earldom and the town of Leicester went to his eldest sister, Amice, the wife of Simon de Montfort and therefore grandmother of the Simon de Montfort who would marry King John's daughter, Eleanor. Half of the old earldom, centred around Brackley in Northamptonshire, went to Robert's younger sister, Margaret, wife of Saher de Quincy, Earl of Winchester.

Loretta de Braose, was probably only in her mid-twenties when her husband died. She and Robert had no children, so she had no claims on her husband's estate other than her dower. She received dower lands in Hampshire, Berkshire and Dorset, amounting to £140 per annum in 1205.[32] The downfall of her family, however, was to have a greater impact on Loretta than the death of her husband. King John turned against the Braose family in 1207, calling for the repayment of fines and for hostages to guarantee their debts. There was no going back following Matilda's unguarded words, spoken probably in fear, to John's messengers, refusing to give up her sons as hostages.[34] As we have seen, John's relentless persecution of the family saw Loretta's father, William, flee to exile in France, dying there in 1211, and her mother, Matilda, and oldest brother, another William, dying in John's dungeons in 1210, starved to death either deliberately or by neglect. Given the lengths John had gone to in order to destroy the family, deliberate starvation is a strong possibility. John's ire extended to the whole family and in November 1207, Loretta was obliged to promise not to marry again without the king's consent.

She went into exile in France shortly afterwards, her lands taken into the king's custody.

By winter 1214, Loretta was back in England. A charter was issued on 8 December, witnessed by, among others, Peter des Roches and Loretta's brother, Giles, Bishop of Hereford, whereby Loretta abandoned all claims to seizures from her estates by the king or anyone appointed to their keeping. This quitclaim was accompanied by testimony that she was unmarried, and that she would not marry again without the king's permission. In return for these promises an order was made for the restitution of her dower lands in Devon, Dorset, Hampshire and Berkshire. She was also promised compensation would be paid for any stock or property taken from her lands while they were in the hands of Henry fitz Count.[33] On the one hand, John's willingness to restore Loretta was a sign that he wanted to make peace with the Braose family, who were still a powerful force on the Welsh March, especially with Giles de Braose as bishop of Hereford. On the other hand, this new arrangement risked the alienation of both Henry fitz Count, who had benefited from the fall of the Braose family, and Saher de Quincy, who would lose out on the Leicester lands that made up Loretta's dower.

Opposition to the king was reaching its climax in the winter of 1214. The major crisis of 1215 and the issuing of Magna Carta was just around the corner. The treatment of Loretta's dower and marriage in December 1214 is addressed in two clauses of Magna Carta. Clause 7 dictates:

> After her husband's death, a widow shall have her marriage portion
> and her inheritance at once and without any hindrance; nor shall she
> pay anything for her dower, her marriage portion, or her inheritance
> which she and her husband held on the day of her husband's death;
> and she may stay in her husband's house for 40 days after his death,
> within which period her dower shall be assigned to her.[34]

The treatment Loretta received, whereby she was forced to relinquish all claims to seizures made from her dower, went completely against this provision in Magna Carta. Moreover, the promise made by Loretta that she would not remarry without the king's wish and consent, flaunted Clause 8 of Magna Carta, which stipulates: 'No widow shall be compelled to marry so long as she wishes to live without a husband, provided that she gives security that she will not marry without our consent if she holds of us, or without the consent of the lord of whom she holds, if she holds of another.'[35] This clause effectively allowed widows to choose where and when – and, indeed, if – to remarry, rather than making that choice dependent on the king's will, as Loretta had been forced to do.

Whether Loretta's experiences informed Magna Carta or were among a number of such injustices that had occurred over recent years, the inclusion of these clauses sought to protect other widows from the pressure Loretta had been faced with in biding by the king's will and not claiming against the crown for the losses from her dower. Once Loretta had recovered her lands, she gave some of her manor at Tawstock to the sisters of the Order of St John at Buckland Sororum, Somerset. By 1220, possibly with the encouragement of Stephen Langton, Archbishop of Canterbury, she appears to have decided on the life of a religious recluse or anchorite. In June 1219 she had granted her dower lands to the bishop of Winchester and Philip D'Aubigny for three years, in preparation for her new life; the rent from these grants would finance her life as an anchorite. In 1221 she took a vow of chastity and became a recluse at Hackington, near Canterbury.[36] The life of an anchorite was a strange, solitary existence in which the person was physically cut off from the world, while still being a part of it. It was a life that could be followed by a man or woman, but was one which could not be lightly taken on by the anchorite themselves, or by the church at large. Not all were suited to the life and a person wanting to profess themselves as an anchorite had to go through a rigorous process to assess that suitability. This even included an interview with the diocese's bishop or archbishop, in this case possibly Stephen Langton himself.

Of particular concern was the anchorite's mental capacity to deal with the solitude and limitation on human contact. Once the church had endorsed a person's suitability to become an anchorite, there was a specific ceremony to signify the end of the life they had previously known. An anchorite was, effectively, dead to the world. They would live in a small cell, attached to the church. As they were led to this cell, a requiem Mass would be sung for them and they would receive extreme unction, normally reserved for the dying. They would be sprinkled with dust, to signify their burial, and then the door to the cell bolted from the outside. In some cases, the cell was walled up. The only access to the outside world was a small, curtained window.[37]

Once they had taken their vows, anchorites were forbidden to leave their cell, on pain of excommunication from the church. As an anchoress, Loretta had to adhere to vows of poverty and chastity and to remain in her cell for the rest of her life. She was not allowed to teach young girls or possess valuables. Conversations with men in private were strictly forbidden and communication with the outside world was done from behind a black curtain, through which she could also hear the daily church offices, even if she could not interact with them. She is known to have had a manservant and may well have had two female attendants to see to her daily needs, such as food, laundry, and clearing away waste.[38] However, her daily interactions with her servants would have been restricted to dealing with her physical needs, rather than friendship and companionship. She would also have been allowed to keep a cat, to control the mice and rats.

Anchorites were expected to devote their lives to prayers and contemplation, to be a benefit to their community and to work for it by praying for their souls. They were an integral part of the church, and the parish in which they lived: 'True anchoresses are indeed birds of heaven which fly up high and sit singing merrily on the green boughs – that is, direct their thoughts upwards at the bliss of heaven.'[39] Once Loretta entered her cell, her time was her own. She could manage her own daily routine, although she probably followed the canonical hours and prayed seven times daily.

Taking up the life of a recluse or anchoress was not uncommon for aristocratic women; it allowed them to take some control of their lives and futures. Following Loretta's example, her own sister, Annora, would become a recluse at Iffley in 1232.[40] For Loretta, withdrawing from public life in such a way did not preclude her being able to use her social standing to help the poor and those in need. For instance, she is known to have helped to establish the Franciscan order in England and was described as 'cherishing the friars as a mother does her children.'[41]

Loretta's influence was widely acknowledged, a thirteenth century French manuscript claimed she held a particular devotion to the Virgin Mary. On 29 April 1265, at the height of the Second Barons' War, Simon de Montfort, Earl of Leicester and leader of the rebel barons, called on Loretta to resolve a constitutional issue concerning the 'rights and liberties' of the stewardship of England, the office then held by Simon but formerly held by Loretta's husband, Robert.[42] Her response, if there was one, is unknown.

Loretta de Braose, dowager countess of Leicester, died on 4 March, probably in 1266, though it may have been the year after. She was buried in the church of St Stephen, Hackington. Loretta appears to have outlived all her siblings. Despite the fact we do not know exactly when Annora died, it seems likely to have been in 1241, or shortly after, the last year in which she received annual gifts of firewood from the king (although this could also have been due to her great-nephew attaining his majority and taking over the responsibility for her care).[43] Another sister, Flandrina, was abbess at Godstow Abbey from 1242, but was deposed in 1248 and disappears thereafter.[44]

John's relentless pursuit of Matilda and William de Braose saw the destruction of the couple and their eldest son, and the persecution of their surviving children. John's own apparent desire to make amends is shown in his dealings with Loretta, restoring her dower lands, and in his grant of 10 October 1216, when he was already gravely ill, to Margaret de Braose, wife of Walter de Lacy, to found a religious house in Herefordshire in memory of her parents and older brother. John knew he had gone too far. Given the extent of the family's suffering at the hands of King John, it seems only fair that the dramatic experiences of the Braose women are enshrined in no less than three clauses of Magna Carta, 7, 8 and 39.

Chapter 4

Nicholaa de la Haye

G iven John's actions and reputation, even when he was alive, it is not difficult to understand why so many of his barons rebelled against him. The loss of Normandy, murder of Prince Arthur and persecution of the Braose family is more than enough to justify the mistrust and withdrawn loyalty of the barons. Indeed, it is harder to understand why some barons remained loyal in spite of everything. The most famous of these, of course, is William Marshal, Earl of Pembroke. Another is Nicholaa de la Haye, hereditary castellan of Lincoln Castle.

Nicholaa de la Haye is one of those very rare women in English history. She is renowned for her abilities, rather than her family and connections. In a time when men fought and women stayed home, Nicholaa de la Haye held Lincoln Castle against all-comers, defending it in no less than three sieges. Her strength and tenacity saved England at one of the lowest points in its history. She was also the first ever female sheriff in England, when she was created Sheriff of Lincolnshire by King John just hours before his death in 1216.

The eldest daughter and co-heiress of Richard de la Haye and his wife, Matilda de Verdun, Nicholaa was probably born in the early 1150s. As with many noble families of the time, the La Haye (or La Haie) family had their origins in Normandy and took their name from the honour of La Haie-du-Puits in the duchy.[1] The family had also acquired land in England after the Norman Conquest through their continuing service to the Norman and Plantagenet kings. Nicholaa's father, Richard de la Haye was a minor Lincolnshire lord, holding the barony of Brattleby; in 1166 he was recorded as owing twenty knights' fees, which had been reduced to sixteen by 1172. Nicholaa was the eldest of three sisters and, when her father died in 1169, she inherited his barony of Brattleby in Lincolnshire. Like her father and grandfather before her, she also inherited the position of castellan of Lincoln Castle; a post that she would hold for over thirty years. The initial settlement between Nicholaa and her sisters was later modified; sometime around 1197, agreement was reached at Caen which allowed Nicholaa to take possession of all her father's English lands. The family lands in Normandy were divided between Nicholaa's two sisters, Julia and Isabella, and their husbands.[2]

Nicholaa was married twice, her first husband, William Fitz Erneis, died in or around 1178, but little else is known of him or their relationship. Before 1185 she married Gerard de Canville, son of Richard de Canville, lord of Middleton Stoney in Oxfordshire, and his first wife, Alice. Like the de la Haye family, the Canville's had a long record of service to the crown. Gerard's father, Richard, was a loyal supporter of King Stephen and then served Henry II. He was part of the entourage that accompanied Henry II's daughter, Joanna, to Sicily for her marriage to King William II in 1176. He died in Apulia, in southern Italy, in the same year, having made numerous gifts to religious houses, including the Cistercian abbey of Combe in Warwickshire, which he had founded during the reign of King Stephen.[3] Gerard inherited the majority of his father's estate. Gerard's half-brother, Richard was the son of their father's second wife, Millicent, who was a cousin of Henry I's second wife, Adeliza of Louvain. He inherited his father's land at Stretton and his mother's interest in the manor at Stanton Harcourt. This Richard attended the coronation of King Richard I in 1189 and was a commander of the king's crusading fleet, embarking in the spring of 1190. *En route* to Marseilles, where he met up with King Richard, Richard de Canville negotiated a truce with the king of Portugal at Lisbon. At Messina, he was one of the sureties for a truce between King Richard and King Tancred of Sicily and in 1191 he was appointed joint governor of Cyprus, alongside Robert of Thornham. He fell ill shortly afterwards and, having re-joined the king, died at Acre, in the Holy Land, in June 1191.[4]

Gerard's family originated from Canville-les-Deux-Églises in Normandy, in the same region as the de la Haye honour of La Haie-du-Puits. The leper hospital of Bolleville, near to La Haie-du-Puits, records grants from both families in its cartulary.[5] Gerard's lands were spread across the Midlands and south-west England, but his marriage to Nicholaa gave him a concentrated power base in Lincolnshire, and possession of one of the greatest fortresses in England.

Nicholaa's husbands each claimed the position of castellan of Lincoln Castle by right of his wife, but Nicholaa seems to have been far from the normal subservient wife. When her husband was not in the castle, she was left in charge rather than an alternative, male deputy. On the accession of King Richard I in 1189 Nicholaa and Gerard travelled to Normandy to receive confirmation of their inherited lands 'with the [service of] castle-ward and the constableship of the castle of Lincoln'.[6] The pipe roll for Michaelmas 1190 records that Gerard paid 700 marks for the possession of Lincoln Castle and the shrievalty of Lincolnshire.[7] Gerard was a talented administrator and was sheriff of Lincoln in 1189 and 1190 and again from 1199 to 1205. He was described by one chronicler as a 'factious man, prodigal of his allegiance'.[8] While another chronicler, William of Newburgh described him as 'a man rich and noble'.[9]

The contradictory descriptions probably result from Gerard's own divided loyalties. Although he had sworn allegiance to King Richard in 1191, Gerard paid homage to the king's brother John, then count of Mortain, for Lincoln Castle. For what may have been the one and only time in his life, in 1191 John was on the right side, leading the opposition against the oppression of Richard's chancellor, William Longchamp, whose heavy-handed administration of the country caused much dissent among the barons. Longchamp demanded Canville's allegiance and the surrender of Lincoln Castle, which the chancellor intended to hand to one of his own supporters, William de Stuteville. However, Longchamp had not reckoned on the tenacity of the Canvilles, and of Nicholaa in particular.

Gerard appealed to John, in person, while he was at Nottingham, and Longchamp took the opportunity, presented by Gerard's absence, to lay siege to Lincoln Castle, left in Nicholaa's charge. Despite promises of clemency for the garrison, the formidable Nicholaa refused to yield, holding out for six weeks before Longchamp abandoned the siege, following the fall of the castles at Tickhill and Nottingham to John's forces. Amusingly, Richard of Devizes said of this defence of Lincoln Castle, 'his wife Nicholaa, not thinking of anything womanly, defended the castle manfully.'[10] The siege lasted for forty days, as confirmed in the pipe rolls of 1191, which show that mercenaries were employed for that length of time on the siege of Lincoln Castle.[11]

King Richard, in Sicily *en route* to the Holy Land, having heard of the growing unpopularity of Longchamp, had despatched Walter de Coutances, Archbishop of Rouen, back to England to restore peace. Coutances brought the two sides together at a conference in Winchester in July, though both John and Longchamp each brought a large number of troops with them, just in case. Settlement was reached whereby John would return the castles he had taken, Gerard de Canville was reinstated until his case could be heard in a royal court, and Longchamp would withdraw his support of Arthur as Richard's heir and recognise John as heir presumptive. Longchamp would, however, remain in power; moreover, according to Richard of Devizes, King Richard had sent orders that his brother must obey Longchamp.[12] This uneasy peace was not to last the year, and when Geoffrey, the newly consecrated archbishop of York, was arrested for entering England on 18 September 1191, John exploited public opinion.

Presenting himself as the champion of English liberties, John raised a coalition against the foreign justiciar. The mutual distrust on both sides saw skirmishes between retainers, and in a skirmish on the road to Windsor, one of John's knights was killed. Longchamp accused John of intending to usurp the throne. Within days John was welcomed into London, recognised as heir presumptive and 'declared supreme governor of the realm, and ordered that all castles should be turned over to whomever he wanted.'[13] A conference was held in the Tower of London on 10 October, during which Longchamp resigned as justiciar and was replaced by Walter de Coutances. Coutances was no pushover, however, and John was denied full authority, having to work alongside the new justiciar.

Gerard and Nicholaa benefited from John's largesse; Gerard was appointed keeper of the honour of Wallingford. In return, Gerard was a staunch supporter of the count of Mortain and backed him in his rebellion of 1193. With Richard in captivity in Germany, John saw an opportunity to seize England. In January 1193 he sealed a treaty with Philip Augustus of France, in which he relinquished the Norman Vexin to the French king and agreed to marry his sister Alix, Richard's erstwhile fiancée. While Philip took Gisors and assembled an invasion fleet, John returned to England to gather support for his enterprise.

Even in captivity, Richard was dismissive of his brother's abilities, saying that John 'is not the man to seize any land by force, if anyone meets his attack with the slightest resistance.'[14] The forces loyal to the king besieged John's castles at Tickhill and Nottingham, although some Norman barons refused to join the siege at Tickhill, claiming they were John's liegemen. Richard's ministers were caught in a dilemma; they had to keep John in check in order to protect the king's throne, but always had to keep in mind that John was likely to be Richard's successor, should anything happen to the king. John was keenly aware of the quandary which faced the king's ministers and appears to have taken advantage of the situation whenever and wherever he could.

In July 1193 agreement was reached whereby, if John contributed to the king's ransom and returned to his fealty to Richard, his lands would be restored to him. He was to relinquish the castles of Windsor and Wallingford, but retained possession of Tickhill and Nottingham. By December 1193, Holy Roman Emperor Henry VI declared himself satisfied with the ransom payments and ready to release Richard. Desperate to prevent the English king from returning home, John and Philip Augustus offered to pay the German Emperor in order to keep Richard imprisoned; John had promised King Philip the whole of southern Normandy in return for his support. Despite being tempted by the offer of £1,000 a month, Emperor Henry was forced to adhere to his deal with Richard by the princes and bishops of his empire. King Richard was finally released on 4 February 1194.

On his return to England Richard was quick to re-establish his authority. John was excommunicated and his castles captured even before Richard was back in England; all save Nottingham, which only surrendered when the king appeared before its walls in person. John fled to France. His supporters, however, did not escape Richard's wrath and in 1194, the Canville lands were declared forfeit and Gerard was stripped of his positions as sheriff of Lincolnshire and Castellan of the castle; he was replaced as sheriff by Simon of Kyme. After a time, Gerard was allowed to recover his forfeited lands, and the king's goodwill, on payment of 2,000 marks. He was not, however, reinstated in his offices and he and Nicholaa probably retired to their own lands in Lincolnshire, out in the cold for the remainder of Richard's reign. In 1194 Nicholaa was fined 300 marks by the king, for an agreement that she could marry her daughter, Matilda, to whomever she wished except, of course, to an enemy of the king. Nicholaa was still accounting for this debt until 1212 and had renegotiated the amount with King John in 1200; in 1201 she still owed £20, 40 marks and one palfrey (a horse).[15] Given that this debt was attributed solely to Nicholaa, rather than Nicholaa and Gerard, it seems likely that Matilda was Nicholaa's daughter by her first husband, William FitzErneis.

Gerard and Nicholaa had at least two further children. One son, Thomas, of whom we know nothing beyond his name and who may have died young, and their son and heir, Richard de Canville. In 1200 Richard was married to Eustachia, the daughter and heir of Gilbert Basset, and widow of Thomas de Verdon, after Gerard offered £1,000 for her wardship. The couple was to have one daughter, Idonea, who was the heiress of both Gerard and Nicholaa and who was married to William II Longespée, son and heir of William Longespée, third Earl of Salisbury and illegitimate son of King Henry II, and his wife Ela, Countess of Salisbury in her own right. The marriage would have implications for Nicholaa later on, with Longespée challenging Nicholaa for control of parts of Idonea's inheritance.

King Richard's death in 1199, and John's accession to the throne, saw a dramatic change in circumstance for Nicholaa and Gerard. Not only were they restored to favour, but also to Lincoln Castle and Gerard was again appointed sheriff of Lincoln, a position he held for the next six years. Gerard, and probably Nicholaa, were present when William the Lion, King of Scots, did homage to John at Lincoln, in 1200. Gerard also supported the men of Holland, in Lincolnshire, in their long–running marshland dispute with Crowland Abbey. From 1208 to 1209 Gerard served as itinerant justice for Lincolnshire and Cambridgeshire and in 1208, during the interdict imposed by the pope, Gerard supervised the collection of the revenues for the diocese of Lincoln.[16] Nicholaa and Gerard are among the few barons who stayed faithful to John throughout his reign.

Gerard de Canville died before 15 January 1215, when his son Richard secured possession of Gerard's property at Middleton Stoney.[17] Nicholaa, however, was able to retain Lincoln Castle, despite the fact Richard was obviously old enough to take on the castellan's responsibilities. On Gerard's death, she secured possession of her inheritance as a *femme sole.* Her loyalty to John probably helped her to retain her lands and position, with Nicholaa rendering account for her bailiwick and appearing regularly in the records of the chancery and exchequer and following government orders. Although she received just three royal letters in 1215, between January 1216 and John's death in October of the same year, when Lincoln was at the heart of the struggle against the rebels, Nicholaa was the recipient of, or concern of, no less than twenty-eight royal letters, close and patent.[18]

The duties and responsibilities that John gave to Nicholaa demonstrate the king's continuing confidence in her abilities. Having been entrusted with a large amount of money, in April 1216, John wrote to her from Windsor, with an order for its release:

> The king to Nicholaa de la Haye etc. We command that you cause to be released forthwith to Ralph Ridell, our Sheriff of Lincoln, the money which we sent to be held by him and which you have in your keeping, as the said sheriff should hand over that money to our trusty Philip Marc to do our pleasure, as we have so ordered him.[19]

However, apparently Nicholaa had not acted on this order as promptly as John would have liked, and he sent a reminder to Lincoln when he was at Odiham on 16 April, with some more specifics about the money: 'Money to be paid. The king to Nicholaa de la Haye etc. We command that you send without delay to Philip Marc the sixty-two pounds which Ralph Ridell, our sheriff of Lincoln, has sent to you to enable our orders to be carried out.'[20] The king was obviously keen to gather as much money together as he could and have the money transfer go ahead as quickly as possible, as he also wrote to his sheriff at Lincoln:

> The king to Ralph Ridell, Sheriff of Lincoln, etc. We command that you send without delay to Philip Marc at Nottingham all the money which you have in your possession from the fines made with us when we were in your territory, any from fines made afterwards or from other acquisitions, and also from all other revenues of your county, to enable out orders to be carried out.[21]

King John had managed to upset practically every baron in England, with his despotic and heavy-handed ways. In 1215 open rebellion was thwarted when John put his seal to Magna Carta, a long, detailed document dealing with the barons' particular grievances, but touching the whole system of government and including arbitrary fines and the exploitation of wardship. John 'had broken the spirit of kingship.'[22]

As we have already seen, John was soon writing to the pope to have Magna Carta annulled, plunging England into rebellion. The barons invited the French dauphin, Louis, to join them and make a play for the throne. Louis was the son of John's erstwhile friend Philip II Augustus, King of France, and the husband of his niece Blanche, who was the daughter of his sister Eleanor, Queen of Castile. Louis and his men had landed on the Isle of Thanet on 14 May 1216. The dauphin advanced through Kent and took Canterbury before moving onto Winchester. Louis was hailed as King of England in London in June of 1216. John seems to have been undecided as to how to act; he sent his oldest son Henry to safety at Devizes Castle in Wiltshire. Dover Castle, under the command of Hubert de Burgh, held out against the French and rebel forces, as did Windsor and Lincoln.

Nicholaa de la Haye is often featured in Johns' daily business and on 4 February he wrote to her and the sheriff of Lincoln with an order to hand over the lands of someone named de Kyme – probably Simon. Simon de Kyme was a rebel, who was trying to raise the ransom for his son Philip. He himself would be captured by Royalist forces in 1217 at the Battle of Lincoln, thus adding his own ransom to his rising debts to the crown:

> Nicholaa de la Haye is commanded that she cause Geoffrey de Neville, Chamberlain of the lord king, to have possession of the land that was [...] de Kyme's in her Bailiwick, which the lord king has granted to him. At Guisborough, the fourth day of February. The same is commanded of the sheriff of Lincoln. Witness the same in the same place.[23]

In the same month, another order was made which touched Nicholaa on a more personal level. William Longespée, Earl of Salisbury, was given the right of marriage of Nicholaa's granddaughter by her son Richard,

Idonea. Longespée intended to marry Idonea to his son, William II Longespée. Both children were very young at this point, with Idonea being, possibly, no older than 8, the youngest age that a betrothal was sanctioned by the church, though she could not be married until the age of 12. John ordered:

> The Sheriffs of Oxford and of Berkshire are commanded that they cause William, Earl of Salisbury, to have the right of marriage of the daughter of Richard de Canville, born of Eustacia, who was the daughter of Gilbert Basset and wife of the said Richard, for William his first-born son by his wife Ela, Countess of Salisbury, with all the inheritance belonging to the said Richard's daughter from her mother in their Bailiwicks. Witness myself, at Reigate, the twenty-second day of April.[24]

This order may be the source of Nicholaa's later wranglings with Salisbury, given that it appears to pass all of Idonea's inheritance into the custody of Longespée, regardless of the fact Nicholaa was still very much alive at this time. It also suggests that Richard de Canville may already have been deceased, despite most mentions of him have him dying in the first quarter of 1217.

Strategically placed in the centre of the country, Lincoln was a target for the rebel barons and their French allies. The northern barons, led by Gilbert de Gant and the king of Scots, attacked Lincoln but 'were defeated in their attempts to take Lincoln. A certain lady called Nicholaa, who was the custodian's wife, freed herself from this siege with a money payment.'[25] Essentially, Nicholaa paid the northern barons to lift the siege and go home. On 4 September, John wrote a letter in support of Nicholaa and her efforts to bring the rebels back into the king's peace:

> the King to all those who may look upon these letters, greetings. Know that we have taken into our grace and favour all those of the county of Lincoln who wish to return to our fealty and our service by the hand of our well-beloved Nicholaa de la Haye and our trusty Robert de Gaugy [constable of Newark]; and, indeed, we gratefully welcome the fine which those who shall return to our fealty and

our service have made with the said Nicholaa and Robert for having
our peace. And in testimony hereof we have hereto made for them
these our letters patent. Witness myself, at Oxford, the fourth day of
September, in the eighteenth year of our reign.[26]

John was not so magnanimous, however, with those who had not returned
to his fealty and had fled into the Isle of Axeholme. The king made his way
north to deal with the rebels. John advanced beyond Lincoln, devastating
the Isle of Axeholme in North Lincolnshire 'with fire and sword' before
arriving back in the city in September 1216, just days after the besieging
army had departed with their payment.[27] Nicholaa is said to have met the
king at the eastern gate of the castle. A widow for the last year, she offered
the keys of the castle to the king:

> And once it happened that after the war King John came to Lincoln
> and the said Lady Nicholaa went out of the eastern gate of the castle
> carrying the keys of the castle in her hand and met the king and
> offered the keys to him as her lord and said she was a woman of great
> age and was unable to bear such fatigue any longer and he besought
> her saying, "My beloved Nicholaa, I will that you keep the castle as
> hitherto until I shall order otherwise."[28]

When Nicholaa spoke of her 'great age' she was not exaggerating. She
was probably around 60 years old at the time, a good age for anyone in
those days, but John still had great confidence in her.

As Louis consolidated his position in the south, John made a full
inspection of Lincoln castle. Shortly after the visit Nicholaa de la Haye,
who held the castle for John, even though the city supported the rebels,
was appointed, alongside Philip Marc, sheriff of Lincolnshire in her own
right, a very unusual move in a male-dominated world. Her son Richard
was now a grown man and able to inherit the position his father had
held, but appears to have taken the side of the rebels and so was not in a
position to replace his mother as castellan or sheriff.[29] Marc, who was also
sheriff of Nottingham, seems to have disappeared from the Lincolnshire
records shortly after. He was later replaced by Geoffrey de Serland, who
was appointed as deputy 'under our beloved lady Nicholaa de la Haye'.[30]

Moving south, just two weeks later, the king's baggage train was lost as he crossed the Wash estuary and within a few more days John was desperately ill. He had contracted a violent fever and died of dysentery at Newark on the night of 18/19 October 1216. The new king was now John's 9-year-old son, Henry III, with the famous and redoubtable William Marshal, Earl of Pembroke, acting as reluctant regent. Following the coronation of young Henry, Magna Carta was reissued, alongside the newly-written Charter of the Forest, and some of the rebel barons returned to the fold, not wanting to make war on a 9-year-old king. Although Louis still had some powerful allies and did not seem keen to give up on his dream to rule England, support began to fall away from Louis, and he returned to France to gather reinforcements. In early 1217 he returned to continue the fight.

Louis' forces, under the Comte de Perche, marched north intending to relieve Mountsorel Castle, which was being besieged by the earl of Chester. Chester had withdrawn as the French arrived and Perche's forces diverted to Lincoln. In early 1217, they took the city and laid siege to the castle with a small force. Henry III's regents wrote to Philip Marc, sheriff of Nottingham, on 12 February of hostages sent by Nicholaa's deputy:

> The king to Philip Marc, sheriff of Nottingham, greetings. We command that, when our trusty and well-beloved Geoffrey de Serland shall have sent to you at Nottingham Robert fitz Peter de Pons, Martin fitz Thomas de Paris and the other two hostages who are the children of the said Peter and Thomas, you should receive them; having received them you should forthwith release Thomas de Paris and Richard, first born son of Peter de Pons, whom you have in your custody. And in testimony hereof etc. we send there to you. Witness the earl [William Marshal] at Gloucester the twelfth day of February in the first year of our reign.[31]

William Marshal was also concerned with protecting the property of Nicholaa and her family whilst she was trapped in Lincoln castle, including Richard, who must have returned to the king's peace by this time, and on the same day sent out a letter saying:

The king to all those who may look upon these letters, greetings. Know that we have taken into our protection and defence our trusty and well-beloved lady Nicholaa de la Haye and her son Richard de Canville, and all their lands, affairs and possessions. We therefore command and firmly enjoin that you support, protect and defend the said Nicholaa and Richard, and all that is theirs, neither causing nor permitting to be caused against them any trouble, harm or harassment. If any forfeiture has been made against them or their people, that should be forthwith compensated to them; you should also permit the aforesaid Nicholaa and Richard to have the benefit of the use of their woods as they please. And in testimony, whereof etc … Witness the said earl, at Gloucester, the twelfth day of February.[32]

Now in her sixties, Nicholaa de la Haye took charge of the defences, with the help of her lieutenant, Sir Geoffrey de Serland. Shortly afterwards, Prince Louis personally travelled up to Lincoln to ask for her surrender, assuring her no one would be hurt, but Nicholaa refused to yield and settled in for another long siege. Despite the French army outside her walls, she may have been quietly confident; this was, after all, her third siege and no one had ever managed to breach the castle walls. Lincoln Castle is a rather large fortress, sitting opposite the impressive cathedral and perched on the top of a bluff – the hill going down to the town is not named Steep Hill for nothing! However, this siege was to last longer than the others. From March through to May, Louis' forces battered the walls of Lincoln Castle. The French prince had brought impressive siege engines, leaving them at Perche's disposal when he returned to London, fully expecting to hear of Lincoln's capitulation within weeks, if not days. However, he did not count on the tenacity of Nicholaa and her deputy, Sir Geoffrey de Serland, who rallied their troops and resisted the combined Anglo-French forces of the Comte de Perche, and awaited reinforcements.

For almost three months – from March to mid-May – siege machinery bombarded the south and east walls of the castle. When the small force proved insufficient to force a surrender, the French had to send for reinforcements. This meant that half of Louis' entire army was now outside the gates of Lincoln Castle and provided William Marshal with an opportunity; one decisive battle against Louis' forces at Lincoln could destroy the hopes of Louis and the rebel barons once and for all. Risking all on one battle was a gamble, but one that Marshal was determined to take. Spurred on by the chivalrous need to rescue a lady in distress William Marshal was determined to relieve Lincoln. After all, it would have been 'dishonourable not to help so brave a lady'.[33] While the young king Henry III waited at Nottingham, Marshal's forces prepared for war.

Marshal mustered his forces at Newark on 17 May; the Royalist army was made up of 406 knights, 307 crossbowmen and a large number of followers, including non-combatants. The papal legate, Guala, absolved the Royalist army of all their sins – of all the sins they had committed since their birth – and excommunicated the French forces, before riding to join the king at Nottingham. While at Newark, Marshal set out the order of battle, although not without some argument. The Norman contingent and Ranulf, earl of Chester, both claimed the right to lead the vanguard. However, when Ranulf threatened to withdraw his men, it was decided to acquiesce to his demands. The regent led the relief of Lincoln himself, but was accompanied by the great and the good, including the warrior-bishop, Peter des Roches, Bishop of Winchester, Ranulf, Earl of Chester, William Longespée, Faulkes de Bréauté, John Marshal, Marshals' nephew, and William Marshal the Younger, the regent's son. Marshal was eager to relieve Lincoln before the besiegers could receive reinforcements, which would increase the opposing force to a complement of 600 knights.[34] On the 19 May Marshal's forces crossed the River Trent and set up camp at Torksey, about eight miles to the north of Lincoln, with some troops possibly camped three miles closer to the city, at Stowe.

At various points in the lead up to the battle, William Marshal is known to have made some stirring speeches. When battle was imminent, he made one more:

Now listen, my lords! There is honour and glory to be won here, and my opinion is that we have the chance to free our land. It is true that you can win this battle. Our lands and our possessions those men have taken and seized by force. Shame be upon the man who does not strive, this very day, to put up a challenge, and may the Lord our God take care of the matter. You see them here in your power. So much do I fully guarantee, that they are ours for the taking, whatever happens if courage and bravery are not found wanting. And, if we die … God, who knows who are his loyal servants, will place us today in paradise, of that I am completely certain. And, if we beat them, it is no lie to say that we will have won eternal glory for the rest of our lives and for our kin. And I shall tell you another fact which works very badly against them: they are excommunicated and for that reason all the more trapped. I can tell you that they will come to a sticky end as they descend into hell. There you see men who have started a war on God and the Holy Church. I can fully guarantee you this, that God has surrendered them into our hands. Let us make haste and attack them, for it is truly time to do so![35]

As with all battles, the information gets confusing as fighting commences, timings get distorted and facts mixed. No two sources give exactly the same information. It follows, therefore, that the story of a battle is a matter of putting the pieces together and making sense of various snippets of information – much as it would have been for the commanders on the day. William Marshal decided not to attack Lincoln from the south, which would have meant heading up the Fosse Way (the old Roman road) and forcing a crossing of the River Witham, before climbing the steep slope to the castle and cathedral. Instead he chose to take a circuitous route, so he could come at the city from the north-west and attack close to the castle and cathedral, directly where the enemy troops were concentrated.

In the dawn of 20 May, the English Royalist army marched south towards Lincoln. Marshal had hoped that, on reaching the plain in front of the city walls, the French would come out and meet him and a pitched battle would be fought outside of the city. Marshal was resting everything – the very future of England – on the outcome of that one battle. However, it seems that, although the French leaders did come out and take a look at the forces arrayed before them, they then chose to stay inside the city walls and wait for the Royalists to come to them. Although Louis was in charge of the French forces in England, those in Lincoln were led by Thomas, Comte de Perche, himself a grandson of Henry II's daughter Matilda, and therefore a cousin of King Henry

III; the commanders, of the English rebels in the city included Robert FitzWalter and Saer de Quincy, Earl of Winchester. They led over 600 knights and several thousand infantry.

Lincoln is an unusual city. Its castle and cathedral sit at the top of a hill, with the rest of the city to the south, at the hill's base. In the twelfth century it was enclosed in a rectangular wall, which had stood since Roman times, with five gates, and the castle abutting the wall at the north-west corner. William Marshal's nephew, John Marshal was sent to the castle, to ascertain the situation within the city, but as he approached, Nicholaa's deputy, Geoffrey de Serland, was making his way out to report to the English commanders that the castle was still in Nicholaa's hands. It is not hard to imagine Nicholaa or her deputy climbing the tallest towers of the castle, to watch out for an approaching relief force. Seeing the Marshal's banners appearing in the north must have been an amazing feeling. The castle itself had two main gates, one in the eastern wall and one in the west, with postern gates in the Lucy Tower to the south-east of the castle and the Cobb Hall to the north-east corner. On ascertaining that the castle still held, Peter des Roches then made his way inside, probably by the postern gate in Cobb Hall. The *Histoire de Guillaume le Maréchal* tells how Peter des Roches managed to sneak into Lincoln Castle by a secret entrance; he had been sent by William Marshal to reassure Nicholaa that relief was on its way.[36] Nicholaa was delighted to hear the news and it must have bolstered the morale of the men under her command; all they had to do was sit tight and wait. Having met with Nicholaa de la Haye in the Lucy Tower, it seems Roches then made his way into the town via the postern, to check the defences and try to find a way into the city.

Des Roches' reconnaissance proved successful and he reported to Marshal that there was a gate within the north-west wall of the city, which, although blockaded, could be cleared. As Marshal set men to clearing the blockaded gate, the earl of Chester was sent to attack the North Gate as a diversion and Faulkes de Breauté took his crossbowmen into the castle via the West Gate and set them on the ramparts above the East Gate, so their bolts could fire down on the besiegers. They were positioned on the castle walls, looking into the town, and rained a deadly barrage of crossbow bolts into the Anglo–French army. It must have been a fine sight for Nicholaa and her garrison to watch their relief march straight through the castle and engage the enemy in battle. The siege engines were destroyed, and fierce hand-to-hand fighting ensued.

De Breauté fell into disgrace in 1224 and so the major source for the Battle of Lincoln – the *Histoire de Guillaume le Maréschale* – plays down his role in the battle. However, his crossbowmen managed to keep the French forces focussed on the castle, rather than Marshal's forces outside the city. De Breauté did make a sortie out of the East Gate, to attack the besiegers, but was taken prisoner and had to be rescued by his own men; although at what stage of the battle this happened is uncertain.

It took several hours, it seems, for Marshal's men to break through the gate, but when they did, the 70-year-old William Marshal was so eager to lead the charge that he had to be reminded to don his helmet. Once safely helmeted, he led his men down West Gate, turning right to approach the castle from the north, his men spilling into the space between castle and cathedral, where the main force of the besiegers were still firing missiles at the castle. The English forces took the enemy so totally by surprise that according to the *Histoire*, one man, the enemy's 'most expert stonethrower', thought they were allies and continued loading the siege machinery, only to have his head struck from his shoulders by one of Marshal's men.[37] Almost simultaneously, it seems, the earl of Chester had broken through the North Gate and battle was joined on all sides. Vicious, close-quarter combat had erupted in the narrow streets, but the fiercest fighting was in front of the cathedral. In the midst of the melee, William Longespée took a blow from Robert of Roppesley, whose lance broke against the earl. The aged Marshal dealt a blow to Roppesley that had the knight crawling to a nearby house 'out of fear, [he] went to hide in an upper room as quickly as he could'.[38]

The Comte de Perche made his stand in front of the cathedral, rallying his troops; and it was there he took a blow from Reginald Croc which breached the eye slit of his helmet. Croc himself was badly wounded and died the same day. The Comte continued to fight, striking several blows to the Marshal's helmet (the one he had almost forgotten to don), before falling from his horse. It was thought the Comte was merely stunned until someone tried to remove his helmet and it was discovered that the point of Croc's sword had pierced the count's eye and continued into his brain, killing him. With the death of their leader, the French and rebel barons lost heart and started pulling back. They fled downhill, to the south of the city. Although they briefly rallied, making an uphill assault, the battle was lost and there was a bottleneck at the South Gate and the bridge across the Witham as the enemy forces fled. The rebel leaders, Saher de Quincey and Robert FitzWalter were both taken prisoner, as were many others. In total, about half of the enemy knights surrendered.

Marshal's army advanced down the hill into the town itself and the Anglo–French encampment. The Battle of Lincoln, on 20 May 1217, raged through the streets, the fierce fighting followed by looting and sacrilege in the medieval city. Sacking the city and attacking citizens who had collaborated with the French was considered a just punishment by the Royalist forces. The city, which had supported the rebels, was pillage, churches included; the excommunication pronounce by Guala seen as permission that everything was fair game. The battle earned the name 'The Lincoln Fair', probably because of the amount of plunder gained by the victorious English army. A sad story is related that, after the battle, women took to the river with their children, in small boats, to escape the attentions of the victorious army. However, not knowing how to control the overloaded craft, many capsized and the women and children drowned.

Immediately after the battle was won, William Marshal, Earl of Pembroke, rode to Nottingham to inform the king of the victory. The Second Battle of Lincoln (the first being in the time of the Anarchy, the war between King Stephen and Empress Matilda) was one of two decisive battles that ended French hopes of winning the English throne. It turned the tide of the war. On hearing of the battle, Louis immediately lifted his siege of Dover Castle and withdrew to London. Support for Henry III grew, and the young king's forces were soon marching on London to blockade Louis within the capital city. Louis' situation became desperate, his English allies bristled against the idea of Louis giving English land as reward to his French commanders and were beginning to see the young Henry III as rightful king – after all, the son could not be blamed for the actions of the father. In August of the same year Louis was soundly defeated at sea in the Battle of Sandwich, off the Kent coast. The sea battle prevented Louis from receiving much-needed reinforcements and on 12 September, the two sides came to terms, with Louis being paid 10,000 marks to go home.[39]

The Battle of Lincoln turned the tide of the war. The French were forced to seek peace and returned home. The battle had been a magnificent victory for the 70-year-old regent, William Marshal, Earl of Pembroke, and is a testament to his claim to the title 'The Greatest Knight'. He staked the fate of the country on this one battle and pulled off a decisive victory, saving his king and country. Magna Carta was soon reissued and Henry III's regents set about healing the country.

Nicholaa de la Haye also earned praise for her actions, though the French chronicler Anonymous de Béthune, probably bitter at the defeat meted out at Lincoln, described her as 'a very cunning, bad-hearted and vigorous old woman.'[40] In one of the most remarkable examples of ingratitude ever, and surely worthy of King John himself, Nicholaa was relieved of her duties as sheriff of Lincolnshire just four days after the Battle of Lincoln. The position was handed to the king's uncle, William Longespée, Earl of Salisbury. Salisbury immediately took control of the city and seized the castle. Not one to give up easily Nicholaa travelled to court to remind the king's regents of her services, and request her rights be restored to her. Salisbury had a keen interest in Lincoln and Lincolnshire through his son. Nicholaa's son, Richard, had died in about February 1217 and his daughter, Idonea, was now the aged widow's heir. Idonea was married to Salisbury's son, William II Longespée and the couple inherited the de la Haie and Canville lands on Nicholaa's death. A compromise was reached whereby Salisbury remained as sheriff of the County, while Nicholaa held the city and the castle. The settlement was not ideal, however, and some wrangling seems to have continued until Salisbury's death in 1226.

A staunchly independent woman, Nicholaa issued charters in her own name, of which some twenty-five have survived. She made grants to various religious houses, including Lincoln Cathedral, and even secured a royal grant for a weekly market on one of her properties. A most able adversary for some of the greatest military minds of the time, and a loyal supporter of King John, she was unique among her peers. Although praised by the chroniclers, they seemed to find difficulty in describing a woman who acted in such a fashion; the Dunstable Annals refer to her as a 'noble woman', saying she acted 'manfully'.[41] It is impossible not to feel admiration for a woman who managed to hold her own in a man's world, who fought for her castle and her home at a time when women had so little say over their own lives – and at such an advanced age. Her bravery and tenacity saved Henry III's throne. Not surprisingly, Henry III referred to her as 'our beloved and faithful Nichola de la Haye'.[42]

By late 1226 she had retired to her manor at Swaton in Lincolnshire. Having lived well into her seventies, Nicholaa died there on 20 November 1230 and was buried in St Michael's church. Her granddaughter Idonea succeeded to Nicholaa's lands in Lincolnshire, although her manor of Duddington in Northamptonshire reverted to the king.[43]

Nicholaa's steadfast hold on Lincoln Castle against an Anglo–French force saved England and turned the tide in favour of the regents of Henry III. Nicholaa's actions are remarkable, not only because she was a woman but also in view of her advancing years. At an age when even men would expect to be allowed to sit by the fire and reminisce about their past exploits, Nicholaa stood firm, holding a key stronghold against an invading army.

Nicholaa de la Haye's bravery and tenacity saved Henry III's throne and has earned her a place in history as one intricately linked to the struggles of King John and the fight for the creation of Magna Carta. The fact she was appointed sheriff of Lincolnshire, on 18 October 1216 just hours before John's death, is testament not only to the high esteem in which John held her, but also to her singular abilities which made her well suited to the role.[44] Her actions thereafter, in the lead up and execution of the Second Battle of Lincoln, only served to justify John's trust in Nicholaa and her unique abilities. William Marshal's approval of her and belief in her abilities are demonstrated in the *Histoire de Guillaume le Maréchal*'s description of her as 'the good dame' and the prayer for Nicholaa 'whom God preserve both in body and in soul.'[45]

Nicholaa's place in the Magna Carta story, and her relevance to it, is unique. She is not here because of her influence on its clauses, nor because of its effect on her and her life. She is in *Ladies of Magna Carta* because she is an integral and essential part of the story of its creation, of the violent struggles in England that saw the emergence of Magna Carta and its increasing importance to the survival of the country and its king.

Chapter 5

Ela of Salisbury

Another lady caught up in the struggle that defined the end of King
John's reign is Ela, Countess of Salisbury. Ela's husband was
John's half-brother, William Longespée, and as an illegitimate
son of King Henry II, his fortune and position in society were inextricably
linked with the fortunes of his royal half-brothers, King Richard I and
King John.

Ela was born at Amesbury in Wiltshire, probably in 1187.[1] She was
the only surviving child – and sole heir – of William Fitzpatrick, Earl
of Salisbury, and his wife, Eleanor de Vitré, daughter of Robert III de
Vitré, Baron of Vitré in Brittany. Ela's father was a descendant of Walter,
an ally of William the Conqueror, who had been rewarded for his
support at Hastings with great estates which eventually passed to Ela.
Her grandfather, Patrick of Salisbury, had been created earl of either
Wiltshire or Salisbury (there seems to be some confusion as to which)
by Empress Matilda before 1147, but was styled Earl of Salisbury.[2] As
earl, Patrick witnessed the 1153 peace treaty between King Stephen and
Henry of Anjou, which would see Henry succeed Stephen as king. He
served as sheriff of Wiltshire in 1160 and was leading the king's troops
in Aquitaine when he was killed by the Lusignans in 1168. Earl Patrick
had been escorting Eleanor of Aquitaine when their party was ambushed
in an attempt to kidnap the queen of England. Patrick suffered a fatal
spear wound during the ensuing skirmish and was buried in Poitiers.
A younger member of the party, William Marshal, the future earl of
Pembroke, was wounded and taken prisoner during the encounter; Queen
Eleanor would later negotiate his release. William Marshal was the son of
Patrick's sister, Sybil, making him a cousin of Ela. Patrick's son William
eventually succeeded to the earldom.

Ela's father, William, Earl of Salisbury, had carried the sceptre at
Richard I's coronation, but when the king was taken prisoner in Germany,

William supported his brother John, Count of Mortain. In 1194 he served as high sheriff of Somerset and Dorset and in 1195 served with King Richard in Normandy. In the same year, he was one of the four earls who supported the canopy of state at Richard's second coronation, and attended the great council, called by the king, at Nottingham. He died in 1196, leaving his only child, Ela, as his sole heir. Ela became Countess of Salisbury in her own right, and the most prized heiress in England. There is a story that little Ela, only 9 years old at the time of her father's death, was kidnapped by her uncle, her father's brother, and hidden away in a castle in Normandy, so that he could gain control of the vast Salisbury inheritance. According to the mid-fourteenth-century Book of Lacock: 'when Ela was deprived of both her father and her mother she was secretly taken into Normandy by her relations and there brought up in close and secret custody.'[3]

Another version of the story has Ela taken to Normandy by her mother, in order to protect her from her grasping uncle; this suggestion 'would account for her daughter's confinement by an anxious and affectionate mother, that she might be placed out of reach of those who perhaps might have meditated worse than confinement.'[4] The story has obvious inconsistencies, but it may be that the countess thought her daughter would be safer being raised among her own family on the Continent, away from her brother-in-law who would have inherited the earldom had anything happened to Ela. She may also have preferred the security of her family in Normandy to the court of King Richard I, where Ela would be under the prying eyes of those who would seek an advantageous marriage with the little heiress.

As the tale goes, an English knight, named William Talbot toured the Norman castles in search of poor Ela singing ballads beneath castle windows in the hope that the little countess would hear him and join in with his singing. He is said to have wandered Normandy for two years, dressed as a pilgrim, in search of the little countess. When he found her, he exchanged his clothing with that of a troubadour in order to gain entry to the castle in which she was being held. He engineered her escape, took her back to England and presented Ela to King Richard, who promptly married her to his half-brother, William Longespée. It is a story that closely resembles that of the legendary Blondel, who was said to have toured the castles of Germany, singing ballads beneath windows in an attempt to find King Richard during his imprisonment. Whether a romantic legend or a true story, the distance of time makes it difficult to be certain, but there appears to be little basis in truth. William Talbot, however, was a faithful retainer of the Salisbury family and witnessed several of the earl's charters.[5]

Whether Ela was rescued, or never kidnapped in the first place, we do not know. However, what we do know is that, on her father's death, Ela's wardship passed into the hands of the king himself, Richard I, the Lionheart. The king saw Ela as the opportunity to reward his loyal, but illegitimate, brother, William Longespée (or Longsword), by offering him her hand in marriage. The Salisbury lands were a suitable reward for a king's son, especially one born out of wedlock, and would give him a power base in England. Ela and Longespée were married in the same year her father died, 1196, so if Ela had been spirited away to Normandy, she was soon recovered, and the story of William Talbot wandering Normandy for two years in search of her is an exaggeration, to say the least. It may also be that Ela was quickly married off to prevent any further kidnap attempts, although they would not have lived as husband and wife until Ela was 12 years old, the church's legal age of marriage for a girl. Her husband was an experienced soldier and statesman and would be able to protect Ela, her lands and interests. William acquired the title Earl of Salisbury by right of his wife and took over the management of the vast Salisbury estates.

William Longespée was the son of Henry II by Ida de Tosney, wife of Roger Bigod, Earl of Norfolk, from a relationship she had with the king before her marriage. For many years, it was thought that Longespée was the son of a common harlot, called Ikenai, and a full brother of another of Henry's illegitimate sons, Geoffrey, Archbishop of York. There were also theories that his mother was Rosamund Clifford, famed in ballads as 'the Fair Rosamund'. However, it is now considered beyond doubt that his mother was, in fact, Ida de Tosney, with two pieces of evidence supporting this. There is a charter in the cartulary of Bradenstoke Priory, made by William Longespée, in which he refers explicitly to his mother as 'Countess Ida, my mother'.[6] There is also a prisoner roll from after the Battle of Bouvines, in which a fellow captive, one the sons of Ida and the earl of Norfolk, Ralph Bigod, is listed as 'Ralph Bigod, brother [half-brother] of the earl of Salisbury'.[7] Ralph was a younger son of Earl Roger and Ida and had been fighting under Longespée's command in the battle in which both were taken prisoner.

Ida was probably the daughter of Roger (III) de Tosney, a powerful Anglo-Norman lord, and his wife, also called Ida.[8] She was made a royal ward after her father's death and became mistress of King Henry II sometime afterwards. She gave the king one son, William Longespée, who was born around 1176, making him ten years younger than the king's youngest legitimate son, John. Ida was married to Roger Bigod, Earl of Norfolk around Christmas 1181. Through his mother's Norfolk family, Longespée had four half-brothers, Hugh, William, Ralph and Roger and two half-sisters, Mary and Margery.[9] Despite the misunderstandings over his mother, the identity of William Longespée's father was never in doubt. He was Henry II's son and acknowledged by his father; he served two of his half-brothers, Richard I and King John. He adopted the coat of arms of his paternal grandfather, Geoffrey Plantagenet, Count of Anjou, of azure, six leoncels rampant or [gold], to emphasise his descent from the Angevin counts.[10] The moniker of Longespée (also Lungespée or Longsword) harkens back to his Norman forebear and namesake William Longsword, second Duke of Normandy (reigned 928–942), from whom he was descended through his father, the king. Little is known of Longespée's childhood, upbringing or education, though a letter of 1220 that Longespée sent to Hubert de Burgh reminds the justiciar that they were raised together, probably fostered in a noble household.[11] In 1188 he had been given the manor of Appleby in Lincolnshire by his father, but he did not come into prominence until the reign of his half-brother Richard I.

At the time of his marriage to Ela, Longespée was in his early-to-mid-twenties, while his bride was not yet 10 years old, although she would not have been expected to consummate the marriage until she was 14 or 15. William (I) Longespée had an impressive career during the reigns of his half-brothers. He first served in Normandy with Richard between 1196 and 1198, attesting several charters for his brother at Château Gaillard, and taking part in the campaigns against King Philip II of France, gaining essential military experience. He took part in John's coronation on 27

May 1199 and was frequently with John thereafter. The half-brothers appear to have enjoyed a very cordial relationship; the court rolls record them gaming together and John granting Longespée numerous royal favours, from gifts of wine to an annual pension.[12] By 1201 Longespée, along with William Marshal and Geoffrey fitz Peter, Earl of Essex 'were seen by John at this stage in his reign as the main props to his rule, and lavish gifts followed.'[13]

Although Longespée's marriage to Ela of Salisbury gave him rank and prestige, it was not a wealthy earldom. The barony commanded fifty-six knights' fees and gave the earl custody of the royal fortress of Salisbury, but Longespée had no castle of his own. He was made sheriff of Wiltshire on three separate occasions, 1199–1202, 1203–1207 and 1213–1226, but was never granted the position as a hereditary right by the king. As sheriff, it was Longespée's task to hunt down the famous outlaw Fulk Fitzwarin, whom he besieged in Stanley Abbey in 1202. Fitzwarin and his band of about thirty men were pardoned in 1203, Longespée was among those who secured the pardon from the king.[14] During his career, William was also entrusted with several important diplomatic missions. In 1202 he negotiated a treaty with Sancho VII of Navarre and in 1204 he and William Marshal escorted the Welsh prince Llywelyn to the king at Worcester. He was also sent to Scotland on a diplomatic mission to King William the Lion in 1205 and was with John at York in November 1206 when the two kings met. The earl was also involved in the election of his nephew, Otto, as German emperor, heading an embassy to the princes of Germany which resulted in Otto's coronation.

William Longespée's most prominent role during the reign of King John, however, was as a military leader. He was a commander of considerable ability. In August 1202 he had fought alongside William Marshal and William de Warenne, Earl of Surrey, hounding the retreating forces of King Philip of France. The French king had withdrawn from the siege of Arques following news of John's victory over his nephew, Arthur, at Mirebeau. Longespée and his lightly-armed fellow earls, however, narrowly escaped capture from a counterattack led by William de Barres. Following the fall of Normandy, Longespée was given command of Gascony in May 1204. In September of the same year he was also given custody of Dover castle and made warden of the Cinque

Ports; he retained both offices until May 1206.[15] In 1208 Longespée was appointed warden of the Welsh Marches and in 1210 he joined King John on the Irish expedition which had been prompted by William de Braose fleeing to Ireland to escape John's persecution. In 1213 he allied with the counts of Holland and Boulogne, led an expeditionary force to the aid of Count Ferrand of Flanders against King Philip II and on 30 May he achieved a significant naval victory when his forces destroyed the French fleet off the Flemish coast near Damme, burning many enemy ships and capturing others. The victory forced King Philip to abandon plans for an invasion of England.

In 1214 William Longespée commanded an army in northern France for the king, while John was campaigning in Poitou. He managed to recover most of the lands lost by the count of Flanders. In July of the same year, however, he commanded the right-wing of the allied army at the Battle of Bouvines, alongside Renaud de Dammartin, Count of Boulogne. William fought bravely but was captured, after being clubbed on the head by Philippe, the bishop of Beauvais. According to the *Histoire de Guillaume le Maréchal* the battle had been fought against the earl's advice, and if it were not for Longespée's own heroic actions, Emperor Otto would have been taken prisoner or, worse, killed.[16] The battle was a military disaster for the English forces in France and ended John's hopes of recovering his Continental possessions. William Longespée was held prisoner for almost a year. He was eventually ransomed and exchanged in March 1215, for John's prisoner, Robert, son of the count of Dreux, who had been captured at Nantes in 1214.

William Longespée was back in England by May 1215 and appointed to examine the state of royal castles. However, England was reaching crisis point by this time with the rebellion gathering pace. Although unable to prevent rebels from gaining control of London, he was effective against the rebels in Devon, forcing them to abandon Exeter. He was named among those barons who had advised John to grant Magna Carta, though whether he was actually present at Runnymede, when the charter was sealed, is unknown. He was granted lands from the royal demesne in August 1215 in compensation for the loss of Trowbridge, which had been returned to Henry de Bohun, one of the twenty-five barons appointed to the committee to oversee the enforcement of the terms of Magna Carta.[17]

Also in 1215, following the fall of Rochester, Longespée was given the task of containing the rebels in London, while John led the rest of his forces north. Alongside Faulkes de Bréauté and Savaric de Mauléon, he led a punitive *chevauchée* through Essex, Hertfordshire, Middlesex, Cambridgeshire and Huntingdonshire. However, in the early weeks of 1216, when Walter Buc's Brabançon mercenaries ravaged the Isle of Ely, it was Longespée who protected the women from their worst excesses.

Longespée was still supporting John when Louis, the Dauphin, landed on 21 May 1216; however, Louis' rapid advance through the southern counties led the earl of Salisbury to submit and ally with Louis after Winchester fell to the French, in June 1216. He remained in opposition to his half-brother for the rest of John's life.[18] Unfounded rumours, recorded by William the Breton, suggested that Longespée's desertion of John was caused by the king's seduction of Ela while the earl was a prisoner of war in France.[19] It seems more likely that, like so many others, he saw John's cause as lost and decided to cut his own losses. With Longespée's defection, and that of William de Warenne, Earl of Surrey, John's support was severely diminished and in retaliation, John ordered his brother's lands seized in August 1216. The king still had the adherence of William Marshal and Ranulf de Blundeville, Earl of Chester, with only the earls of Derby and Warwick offering additional support.[20]

Despite the death of King John in October 1216, Longespée remained with Louis and even called for Hubert de Burgh to surrender Dover to the French.[21] However, when Louis returned to France in March 1217, Longespée submitted to the king, swearing loyalty to his 9-year-old nephew, Henry III. He was also absolved the sentence of excommunication which had been passed on all those who had defected to Louis. Along with Longespée, William Marshal's eldest son, William (II), and a hundred other men from Wiltshire and the south-west, returned to the king's peace. Longespée was now instrumental in driving the French from England and defeating the remaining rebel barons. He was part of William Marshal's army at the Battle of Lincoln Fair on 20 May 1217, when Lincoln Castle and its formidable castellan, Nicholaa de la Haye, were finally relieved following a three-month siege by the French under the Comte de Perche.

We know little of Ela's whereabouts during Longespée's various adventures, nor how she felt about her husband's defection from John to Louis. We know nothing of their married life, although it appears to have been a happy one. The couple had at least eight children together, if not more; four boys and four girls. Of their three youngest boys, Richard became a canon at the newly built Salisbury Cathedral, Stephen became seneschal of Gascony and justiciar of Ireland, and their youngest son, Nicholas, was elected bishop of Salisbury in 1291; he was consecrated at Canterbury by Archbishop John Pecham on 16 March 1292. Already in his sixties, Nicholas died on 18 May 1297.[22]

In 1216, the oldest son, William II Longespée, fourth Earl of Salisbury, was granted marriage by King John to Idonea, granddaughter and sole heiress of the formidable Nicholaa de la Haye. Both children were very young when the grant was made, with Idonea being, possibly, no older than 8, the youngest age that a betrothal was sanctioned by the church, though she could not be married until the age of 12. John ordered that:

> The sheriffs of Oxford and of Berkshire are commanded that they cause William, Earl of Salisbury, to have the right of marriage of the daughter of Richard de Canville, born of Eustacia, who was the daughter of Gilbert Basset and wife of the said Richard, for William his first-born son by his wife Ela, Countess of Salisbury, with all the inheritance belonging to the said Richard's daughter from her mother in their Bailiwicks. Witness myself, at Reigate, the twenty-second day of April.[23]

This order may be the source of Nicholaa's later wranglings with Salisbury, given that it appears to pass all of Idonea's inheritance into the custody of Longespée, regardless of the fact Nicholaa was still very much alive at this time. It also suggests that Richard de Canville already may have been deceased, despite most mentions of him have him dying in the first quarter of 1217.

Young William and Nicholaa de la Haye would spend several years in legal disputes over the inheritance of Nicholaa's Lincolnshire holdings. William (II) Longespée went on crusade with Richard, Earl of Cornwall, in 1240–1 and later led the English contingent in the Seventh Crusade, led by Louis IX of France. His company formed part of the doomed vanguard, which was overwhelmed at Mansourah in Egypt on 8 February 1250. William's body was buried in Acre, but his effigy lies atop an empty tomb in Salisbury Cathedral. His mother is said to have experienced a vision of her son's last moments at the time of his death.

Of the couple's four daughters, Petronilla died unmarried, possibly having become a nun. Isabella married William de Vescy, Lord of Alnwick, and had children before her death in 1244. Another daughter, named after her mother, married, firstly Thomas de Beaumont, Earl of Warwick and, secondly, Phillip Basset; sadly, she had no children by either husband. A fourth daughter, Ida, married Walter Fitzrobert; her second marriage was to William de Beauchamp, Baron Bedford, by whom she had six children. As a couple, William Longespée and Ela were great patrons of the church, laying the fourth and fifth foundation stones for the new Salisbury Cathedral in 1220. William de Warenne, Earl of Surrey and a cousin to Ela, also laid a foundation stone.[24]

In the first half of the 1220s, Longespée played an influential role in the minority government of Henry III and also served in Gascony to secure the last remaining Continental possessions of the English king. In 1225 he was shipwrecked off the coast of Brittany and a rumour spread that he was dead. While he spent months recovering at the island monastery of Ré in France Hubert de Burgh, first Earl of Kent and widower of Isabella of Gloucester, proposed a marriage between Ela and his nephew, Reimund. Ela, however, would not even consider it, insisting that she knew William was alive and that, even if he were dead, she would never presume to marry below her status. It has been suggested that she used clause 8 of Magna Carta to support her rejection of the offer: 'No widow is to be distrained to marry while she wishes to live without a husband.'[25] However, as it turned out, William Longespée was, indeed, still alive and he eventually returned to England and his wife, landing in Cornwall and then making his way to Salisbury. From Salisbury he went to Marlborough to complain to the king that Reimund had tried to marry Ela whilst he was still alive. According to the *Annals and antiquities of Lacock Abbey* Reimund was present at Longespée's audience with the king, confessed his wrongdoing and offered to make reparations, thus restoring peace.[26]

Unfortunately, Longespée never seems to have recovered fully from his injuries and died at the royal castle at Salisbury shortly after his return home, on 7 March 1226, amid rumours of being poisoned by Hubert de Burgh or his nephew.[27] He was buried in a splendid tomb in Salisbury Cathedral. Although the title earl of Salisbury still belonged to his wife, his son, William (II) Longespée was sometimes called Earl of Salisbury, but never legally bore the title as he died before his mother.

Ela did not marry again. On her husband's death, she was forced to relinquish her custody of the royal castle at Salisbury, although she did eventually buy it back. Importantly, she was allowed to take over her husband's role as sheriff of Wiltshire, which he had held three times in his career and continuously from 1213 until his death in 1226. Ela herself served twice as sheriff of Wiltshire from 1227 until 1228 and again from 1231 to 1237. Nicholaa de la Haye's appointment as sheriff of Lincolnshire in 1216 may have aided Ela in attaining the post, serving as a precedent.[28] She also appeared in person at the Exchequer to render accounts, demonstrating her personal involvement in the management of her household and estates.[29]

In 1225, William Longespée had been given the wardship of the heir to the earldom of Norfolk, Roger Bigod. When young Roger was married to Isabella, sister of Alexander II, King of Scots, that same year, however, his wardship was transferred to the Scottish king as he was still underage. Two years later, when Ela was early in her widowhood, debts concerning Bigod's wardship and her status as the countess of Salisbury were taken into account:

1227 29 Oct. Rochester. To the barons of the Exchequer. The king has granted to Ela, countess of Salisbury, formerly the wife of William Longespée, former earl of Salisbury, uncle of [the earl of] Salisbury (sic.), that the 550 m. which the executors of the testament of the aforesaid earl of Salisbury ought to render to the king of the fine that Alexander, King of Scots, made with them for having custody of the land formerly of Earl Hugh Bigod , which was in the hand of the aforesaid earl of Salisbury, are to be allowed to the same countess of Salisbury in the debt of £1075 12s 3d which is exacted from her at the Exchequer for the debts that the aforesaid earl of Salisbury owed to the king. The king has also granted to the countess that she may render 100 m. of the residue of the same debt each year at two terms, namely 50 m. at Easter in the twelfth year and 50 m. at Michaelmas in the same year, and 100 m. thus from year to year at the same terms until the rest of the aforesaid debt is paid in full. The king has further granted to the countess that if death befalls her before the rest of the debt is paid to the king, the heirs of the aforesaid earl of Salisbury and the countess are to render the aforesaid debt each year at the same terms, namely 100 m., until the debt is paid to the king. Order to cause this to be done and enrolled thus.[30]

It is a testament to Ela's own considerable abilities, in the management of her money and estates, that the crown dealt directly with her in relation to the debts of her husband. When Roger Bigod was in the earl's wardship, the revenues from his estates passed directly to William. However, when his wardship was handed over to his brother-in-law, King Alexander, accounting had to be taken of the revenues of Roger's lands and Ela had to renegotiate the debt her husband had incurred in purchasing the Bigod wardship.

Ela was also known as a great patron of religious houses; she and her husband had co-founded Salisbury Cathedral and Ela herself founded two Augustinian religious houses. She managed to lay the foundation stones of both, at Hinton and Lacock, sixteen miles apart, on the same day in 1232. The abbey at Hinton, Somerset, was endowed for monks, in memory of her husband, after the original house, founded by Longespée at Hathorp, proved to be unsuitable. The foundation of Lacock Abbey had been three years in the planning; in 1229 Ela's charter, granting the manor and church of Lacock to the abbess and nuns of the newly-founded abbey of Lacock, was confirmed by her son, William (II) Longespée and witnessed by many of the leading nobles of the kingdom, including, among others William (II) Marshal, Earl of Pembroke, Hubert de Burgh, Earl of Kent and justiciar and William de Warenne, Earl of Surrey.[31] On April 3 of the same year an indented agreement was made between Ela and John, rector of the church at Lacock, whereby John gave his assent to the building of Lacock Abbey and Ela, in return, promised that she and her heirs would preserve the indemnity of the church. The agreement was witnessed by many of the leading officers of Salisbury Cathedral, including the bishop of Salisbury, Robert de Bingham.[32]

Lacock Priory was established in 1232 as a house for Augustinian canonesses at the village of Lacock in Wiltshire. Ela herself entered the priory in 1237 and became its first abbess when it was upgraded to an abbey in 1239. As abbess, Ela was able to secure many rights and privileges for the abbey and its village, including a charter from Henry III, granting the right to hold a fair for St Thomas of Canterbury, a grant to hold a market on Tuesdays, permission for the nuns to host a fair on the vigil and feast of Saints Peter and Paul, including the six days following, and a charter permitting Lacock's abbess to take a cart through the forest of Melksham to collect dead wood for firewood.[33] All these grants, and the establishment of a village with reeve, ploughmen, shepherds, fishermen and others, ensured that the abbey was self-sufficient.

As abbess of Lacock, Ela obtained a copy of the 1225 issue of Magna Carta, which had been given to her husband for him to distribute around Wiltshire. Despite her seclusion, she did retain contact with her family and with her lands. Held in the National Archives at Kew one grant is made by her son, William (II) Longespée to Ela as 'abbess of Lacock, of all the lands which had belonged to her daughter Ela, countess of Warwick, his sister, held in marriage in Chitterne [Wiltshire], which she has quitclaimed to him, as well as the homage and service of Robert de Holta, clerk, for the tenement which he holds of him in the same vill.'[34] The grant is witnessed by William of York, Bishop of Salisbury and Richard Longespée, Ela's son, and others. The grant must have been made sometime after 1256, when William of York became bishop of Salisbury, but before 1259, when Ela resigned as abbess after twenty years in that position.

Ela remained at Lacock Abbey after she retired as abbess and, having eventually outlived both her eldest son and grandson, died there on 24 August 1261. On her death Ela was succeeded as countess of Salisbury by her great-granddaughter, Margaret, who was the daughter of William (III) Longespée. Margaret was married to Henry de Lacey, third earl of Lincoln and grandson of John de Lacy and Margaret de Quincey. Margaret was the mother of Alice de Lacey, fourth Countess of Lincoln and the unfortunate, unloved wife of Thomas, Earl of Lancaster, who was killed in rebellion against Edward II, at the Battle of Boroughbridge in 1322.

Ela, third Countess of Salisbury, was described in the *Register of St Osmund* as 'a woman indeed worthy of praise because she was filled with the fear of the Lord.'[35] Ela was not buried alongside her husband in Salisbury Cathedral, but was given a funeral fit for a countess and laid to rest within the abbey church of Lacock that she had founded and ruled – and had called her home for the last twenty-four years of her life. Her tombstone demonstrates the high esteem in which she was held and records the words: 'Below lie buried the bones of the venerable Ela, who gave this sacred house as a home for the nuns. She also had lived here as holy abbess and Countess of Salisbury, full of good works.'[36] Still a young woman when she lived through the Magna Carta Crisis, Ela had no influence on the Great Charter's creation but may well have used it to avoid an unwanted marriage when her husband was presumed dead. A generous patron of the church and influential in her political connections as sheriff and countess, Ela is described by Linda Elizabeth Mitchell as having been 'one of the two towering female figures of the mid-thirteenth century'.[37]

Chapter 6

The Daughters of the Earl Marshal

I t is impossible to talk about anything related to Magna Carta without mentioning the man who has come to be known as 'the Greatest Knight', William Marshal, Earl of Pembroke, and his family. Marshal was one of the few nobles to stay loyal to King John throughout the Magna Carta crisis. That is not to say that John and Marshal did not have their differences, nor that their relationship was always smooth sailing. However, William Marshal was famed for his loyalty and integrity and maintained his oaths to King John throughout his reign, regardless of the distrust of the king. To tell the story of his daughters, we must first tell the story of William Marshal, this fourth son who rose from being a humble hearth knight on the tournament circuit to being regent to King Henry III and the most powerful man in the kingdom.

William Marshal was the second son of John FitzGilbert, hereditary royal marshal, by his second wife, Sybil, sister of Patrick, Earl of Salisbury, whom he had married around 1145. The marriage was part of a peace deal between the two neighbouring lords, an act of conciliation. Marshal also had two sons from his first marriage to Aline Pipard, whom he repudiated in 1141, Gilbert and Walter; Walter died before his father, and Gilbert died within a year of John's death in 1165. The Marshal lands and title, as a result, passed to William's older brother, John Marshal, which he held until his death in 1194. The *Histoire de Guillaume le Maréchal* addresses John Marshal's humble origins by highlighting his merits: 'Though he was no earl and no baron with fabulous wealth, yet his generosity so increased that all were amazed by it.'[1] Evidence from the *Histoire* suggests that William was born sometime around the year 1147.[2]

Unlike most medieval characters, who remain elusive until they reached adulthood and joined the political stage, William's story was already a part of legend by the time he attained his majority. After initially accepting King Stephen in 1135, by 1141 John Marshal had switched his allegiance to Empress Matilda during her conflict with King Stephen, in the period now known as The Anarchy, when the two rivals battled for control of England – and the crown –between 1139 and 1153. Marshal was badly injured in a desperate rearguard action at Wherwell; he took refuge in the abbey church, but his pursuers set the church alight and Marshal refused to surrender to save his life. He lost an eye and his face was badly disfigured by molten lead falling from the roof of the church tower in which he was hiding. He only emerged from the church after his pursuers had given him up for dead and left. Marshal then walked the twenty-five miles home to his castle at Marlborough where he finally received treatment for his wounds.[3]

In 1152, aged only 4 or 5, William was given as a hostage by his father to King Stephen as a pledge of good faith during a truce. Stephen was blockading John Marshal's new castle at Newbury and expected the truce to be used in order to negotiate the castle's surrender. John Marshal, however, used it to buy himself some time to provision and reinforce the castle with more men, apparently in reckless disregard of the risk this held for young William's life. King Stephen's advisers wanted young William hanged in front of the castle, a ruthless warning of what would happen to anyone who broke the terms of truce. When John Marshal was made aware of this intention, he is said to have replied that he 'still had the hammers and anvils to make more and better sons.'[4]

While this statement at first appears the words of a heartless father, it is more likely that John Marshal, who had served King Stephen in the early years of his reign, knew the king well enough to know that William was never in any real danger. Indeed, Stephen's refusal to execute William for the actions of his father is often cited as an example of the king's lack of that ruthless streak that was needed to put an end to the civil war once and for all. It was, however, a gamble on John Marshal's part, and may have appeared as one he had badly miscalculated when the story continues that young William was escorted to the gallows and placed on a siege catapult, which the child took for a swing. When Marshal refused to react, the child was then dangled from a wicker shield before the castle gate. Apparently young and innocent William asked what kind of strange toy was being hung out of the castle window, causing 'the king to smile and have him taken back to safety.'[5] After this, threats against William's life ceased, but the king kept him as a ward at court and kept him close, despite the fact William was too young even to act as a page in the royal household. William himself later told the story of how Stephen would play a game of 'knights' with him.[6]

We do not know when young William was returned to his family, it may not have been until after Matilda's son, Henry, and Stephen came to an agreement in November 1153, whereby Stephen recognised the young count of Anjou as his heir, rather than his own eldest son, Eustace. Before 1160, William had been fostered into the household of William de Tancarville, chamberlain of Normandy, with whom he stayed for six years as a squire. Little is known of his education in this time, though it is known that he was never taught his letters. One story handed down from William's time in Tancarville's household was that he earned the nickname 'Gaste-Viande' (the Glutton), and it was said that when there was nothing to eat, he slept.[7] William first appears in a charter in or just before 1156, where he was included as consenting to John Marshal's sale of the Somerset manor of Nettlecomb to Hugh de Ralegh. The price of the sale was 'the service of one knight, a horse, two dogs and 80 marks in cash (£53 6s 8d).'[8] William was knighted in 1166, just after his father's death. John Marshal had left his son no share in the family lands, which first went to William's half-brother Gilbert and then to his full brother, John.

Shortly after his knighting, William saw his first action when he was involved in a border dispute between Henry II and the counts of Flanders, Ponthieu and Boulogne, which led to an invasion of the Pays de Caux. William was among de Tancarville's household knights who garrisoned the castle of Neufchâtel-en-Bray.[9] He distinguished himself in a skirmish, though he earned a scolding from de Tancarville who chastised him for being too headstrong; 'Get back, William, don't be such a hothead, let the knights through!'[10] William then lost his horse in a skirmish in the streets of Neufchâtel and failed to redeem his loss by taking ransoms and harness from the defeated enemy. De Tancarville refused to offer William further maintenance, which forced the young knight to sell his clothes in order to finance the purchase of a new horse. However, de Tancarville did allow William to accompany his household to a tournament in Maine, in which William distinguished himself by capturing, among others, a prominent courtier of the king of Scots. For the next year, with the consent of William de Tancarville, William Marshal followed the tournament circuit. In 1167 or 1168 he left de Tancarville's service to join the household of his uncle Patrick, Earl of Salisbury.

William accompanied Patrick to Poitou where the earl had been given joint responsibility for the province, alongside his queen, Eleanor of Aquitaine. William was a younger member of the escort for Queen Eleanor when it was ambushed by the troops of Guy de Lusignan. The queen escaped, but in the ensuing skirmish, Earl Patrick was mortally wounded and William was taken prisoner after being wounded by a strike from behind during the encounter. He had to endure an uncomfortable period of captivity, wounded and half-starved; he was only released after Queen Eleanor paid his ransom. The queen then took the young knight into her retinue.

In 1170 he was placed in the household of Henry II's young heir Henry, known as the Young King after his recent coronation; William was to act as Henry's tutor in arms and infused the young man with a love of the tournament.[11] William Marshal is named by Roger of Hoveden as having joined the Young King in his rebellion against his father in 1173 and of knighting his charge in the first days of the campaign.[12] Although, Hoveden must have been confused as Henry II himself knighted his son shortly before the boy's coronation in 1170. William was in constant attendance on the Young King, even witnessing the 1174 agreement between Henry II and his sons, which ended the conflict. The two men parted ways, however, in 1182, after William's enemies spread rumours that he held nothing but contempt for the Young King by promoting his own interests on the tournament circuit, and that he had committed adultery with young Henry's wife, Queen Margaret of France. Although the accusations were unfounded, they caused a breach between the Young King and William Marshal and William left Henry's service in the last days of 1182, his attempts to receive justice from Henry II being dismissed at Caen at Christmas of that year.[13]

William Marshal then went on pilgrimage to Cologne, to visit the relics of 'the three kings' before going into service with the count of Flanders, 'from whom he accepted a large money fee in the city of St Omer.'[14]

After continuing difficulties between Henry II and his heir, Marshal returned to the Young King's service sometime after February 1183. His renewed service was short-lived, however, as Henry the Young King died on 11 June near Limoges. William was at Henry's deathbed and asked by Henry to take his cloak to Jerusalem and lay it before the altar of the Holy Sepulchre as a fulfilment of the vow of pilgrimage to the Holy Land that the Young King had made. After escorting the Young King's body to its burial in Rouen, William was given permission by Henry II to fulfil his son's dying wish and he arrived in Jerusalem in 1184, staying there for nearly two years, though practically nothing is known of his experiences there.

On his return in 1186, William joined the Angevin royal household, after which he received rewards for his service, including the wardship of the lordship and heir of William of Lancaster, and the royal estate of Cartmel.[15] By the end of Henry II's reign William was one of the commanders of the royal household guard, fighting with distinction against Philip II Augustus of France. He was in command of the rearguard at Le Mans as the king escaped to Angers, opposing Richard, the king's oldest surviving son, who was leading the pursuit of his father. Richard and William came face-to-face, with Richard lightly armed and unsupported, having ridden ahead of his troops. The *Histoire* recounts that Richard begged William to spare him.[16] William was back with the king in time to witness the conference at Azay and Henry II's death at Chinon on 6 July 1189.

In spite of his earlier run-in with Marshal, as the new king Richard I appreciated William Marshal's abilities and even confirmed Henry II's offer of the marriage of Isabel de Clare, the heiress of Striguil (now Chepstow), whose father was the late earl Richard de Clare (later known as Strongbow) who died in 1176. Isabel's mother was Aife (Eva), daughter of Diarmait Mac Murchada, King of Leinster. In August 1189, after arriving in London, Isabel and William were married even though Isabel may have been as much thirty years William's junior, having been born in the early to mid-1170s. Nevertheless, the early death of Isabel's brother, Gilbert, when still a child, meant Isabel was the sole heir to her father's estates in England, Normandy, south Wales and Leinster.[17] In addition to Striguil, marriage to Isabel also brought William a half-share in the Giffard honour of Longueville in Normandy and some Giffard manors in England, including Caversham, as well as the lordship of Leinster, conquered by Strongbow in 1170–71.[18] And to consolidate his power in the southern Welsh March, William was granted the shrievalty of Gloucester and created keeper of the Forest of Dean.

William's star continued to rise in the reign of King Richard I. He was in constant attendance upon the king until his departure on crusade, and William was appointed as one of the four men tasked with monitoring the conduct of the justiciar, William Longchamp. William cooperated with the king's brother, John, in his attempts to have Longchamp removed from office, and fully supported Walter de Coutances, the man sent by Richard to resolve the tensions in England. With Longchamp removed, William worked alongside John and his fellow justiciars to govern the country until news of Richard's capture and imprisonment in Germany reached England, in December 1192. The justiciars were forced to confront John and thwart his attempts on the throne, a delicate task given John was Richard's heir and may one day be their king. John fled England, however, in 1194 when news arrived that Richard was free and on his way home. John's lands in England were confiscated by the justiciars. As the king returned in March 1194, William's older brother, John Marshal, died at Marlborough, without a legitimate heir, leaving William to succeed to the Marshal lands, supplementing an already impressive power base in the west country and southern Welsh March.

William Marshal played a prominent part in Richard's successful conclusion of the siege at Nottingham Castle, which held out for John in 1194. However, his relationship with Richard was not without its hitches Although he paid homage to the king for his English lands, he refused to do so for Leinster reasoning that John, lord of Ireland since his father's reign, was overlord there. It was noted at the time that William was keeping his options open with John. Longchamp accused him, 'Here you are planting vines!',[19] as Marshal obviously had one eye on the future. Richard accepted William's reasoning and allowed him to carry a sword of state at his solemn crown-wearing at Winchester on 17 April 1194.[20] From then until the end of Richard's reign, William spent much of his time in Normandy and elsewhere in France, campaigning. In the summer of 1197, it was William who was sent to negotiate with the counts of

Flanders and Boulogne and in August he took part with Count Baldwin of Flanders, in the action at Arras, in which King Philip was trapped and forced to surrender to terms. The *Histoire* relates a story of William leading the attack on the castle of Milly-sur-Thérain in 1198, which clearly demonstrates his leadership style and stamina, where he climbed a scaling ladder and defended a section of the wall, knocking out the castle's constable as they met on the wall walk. William was already in his fifties at the time, and apparently had to rest by sitting on the constable's prone body.[21]

When King Richard was fatally wounded on 6 April 1199, William was acting as ducal justice at Vaudreuil. He made his way to Rouen after receiving instructions to secure that city and it was there that he heard the news of Richard's death. Despite the late hour, William met with Hubert Walter, Archbishop of Canterbury, and a keen debate followed over the merits of the two contenders for the throne, John and his nephew, Arthur of Brittany. According to the *Histoire*, while the archbishop backed Arthur as having the greater right, William gave his full support to John, arguing that Arthur's overbearing attitude, treacherous advisers and French leanings would act against the interests of the realm.[22] More with a nod to hindsight (the *Histoire* was written in the 1220s), than the skill of prophecy, the archbishop cautioned: 'This much I can tell you, you will never come to regret anything you did as much as what you're doing now'.[23]

William Marshal was rewarded for his loyalty to John by being invested with the earldom of Pembroke, previously held by his father-in-law Richard Strongbow but taken from him in 1154 and held by the English crown, shortly before John's coronation on 27 May 1199. By 1201 William held the lands as well as the title of Pembroke, and had also visited his lands in Leinster, Ireland, to take the homage of his men there.[24] William was again made sheriff of Gloucester and given the keeping of the royal castles at Gloucester and Bristol. By 1202 it looked as if William's star had reached its zenith. He was also entrusted with the protection of Upper Normandy, but the king's political misjudgements compromised his efforts. His unsuccessful attempt to relieve Château Gaillard with river-borne and land forces led to his being decisively defeated by the French commander, Guillaume de Barres. William Marshal left Normandy with

King John in December 1203, after which the duchy soon fell to the French king.

The loss of Normandy was a severe blow to the Anglo–Norman barons of England, with many of them losing half their patronage. When William was sent to negotiate with King Philip in May 1204, along with the earl of Leicester, the two barons secured a private agreement from the French king whereby they were given a year's grace before they would have to pay homage to him for their Norman lands. King John was understanding of William Marshal's predicament and appears to have continued to be supportive of the earl of Pembroke, granting him the lordship of Castle Goodrich and looking the other way when Marshal gained the Dorset manor of Sturminster by taking advantage of the count of Meulan's desperate need for money.[25]

In spring 1205 William returned to France on another diplomatic mission and agreed to do homage to King Philip for his Norman lands. John was still sympathetic, although clearly unhappy that the homage Philip had extracted also obliged William to do military service for the French king when in France. To John, this was treason and he demanded the magnates pass judgement on William. However, they refused, William's warning probably ringing in their ears: 'Be on alert against the king: what he thinks to do with me, he will do to each and every one of you, or even more, if he gets the upper hand over you.'[26] King John basically washed his hands of William Marshal, he had had enough of helping William recover from his Norman losses and demanded the earl give up his eldest son and heir as a sign of good faith while the steady stream of royal favours ceased. William remained at court and was among the earls tasked with escorting King William of Scotland from the Scottish border to his meeting with John at York in November. However, when John left for Poitou in June 1206, William left court and did not return once the king was back in England in September.

William Marshal spent the next seven years in the political wilderness, mainly by choice. His plans to travel to his Irish estates fuelled John's growing distrust of the Marshal, which was demonstrated in the king's demand that William hand over his second son, Richard, as an extra hostage to his good behaviour, thus strongly hinting that the king would rather that William did not leave England. When William failed to heed the warning, and left for Ireland with his family and household, John retaliated by relieving William of his responsibilities in the Forest of Dean and as sheriff of Gloucester, as well as taking the fortress of Cardigan.[27] As such, William spent much of the following nine years in Ireland, in the honour of Leinster. He came into conflict with the king's justiciar, Meiler Fitz Henry, who was not only a tenant of William's in Leinster but had also laid claim to William's lands at Offaly. When William was recalled by John, the king came down on the side of Fitz Henry and William's isolation increased. The conflict eventually ended when John recognised his need for William Marshal's support and Meiler Fitz Henry was offered up as a scapegoat and disinherited. William's lands at Offaly were returned and Leinster restored on new terms. William lived in Ireland, in isolation from the court for several more years, his two eldest sons still in John's custody as hostages.

The Marshal crossed paths with the king again in 1210, when John was preparing an expedition to Ireland in pursuit of his erstwhile friend and now bitter enemy, William de Braose. King John suspected William Marshal of sheltering de Braose and his family, who stayed briefly with the earl at Leinster before moving on to stay with their own daughter Margaret and son-in-law, Walter de Lacy, in Meath. William Marshal crossed to Pembroke to face the king and protest his innocence. He was sent back to Ireland, his punishment being no more than a few harsh words from the king and the loss of the fortress of Dunamase, Ireland[28]

Relations between the monarch and William Marshal began to thaw in 1212 when William made a significant demonstration of loyalty in Ireland as John was facing baronial conspiracy at home. William's two sons were released from custody and, in May 1213, William was recalled to court and restored to his lands and position in south Wales; William Marshal's famed loyalty was now badly needed by the king against the rise of the rebellious barons. He remained in England, watching over the Welsh March as John undertook his final Continental campaign, which ended with the disastrous Battle of Bouvines. The military defeat was a catalyst for the emergence of the rebel baronial party. As the crisis came to a head in 1215, William Marshal was John's chief lay negotiator, first at London in January and again at Oxford in February. When war broke out William was entrusted with the security of the Welsh Marches, against the rebels and their ally Prince Llywelyn of Gwynedd (John's own son-in-law). Following John's defeat, William again took on the role of negotiator, aided by the fact his eldest son, William (II), had sided with the rebels. This may have been a cynical move by the Marshals providing them with the chance to have one foot in each camp, and there was certainly suspicion of this at the time according to the Worcester annals.[29]

When Louis of France arrived to take up the fight on the side of the rebels, landing in Kent on 22 May 1216, it was William Marshal who advised King John against meeting the French prince in the field, gambling with the fate of the entire nation in pitched battle.[30] John heeded the advice, perhaps also unsure of the loyalty of his mercenaries, and retreated. As John took the fight north, facing down the northern contingent of the rebel barons in Lincolnshire and the Isle of Axeholme, William again guarded the Welsh March. King John's death in October 1216, however, brought William Marshal from the Welsh border to the forefront of English politics and the struggle against the rebel barons and their French allies.

John's final testament appointed William as one of the council of thirteen executors tasked with assisting in the recovery of 9-year-old Henry III's inheritance, England. Though yet to be appointed regent, William Marshal immediately took control of the situation, arranging John's funeral at Worcester Cathedral, taking responsibility for the young king and having him brought to Gloucester from Devizes, then convening a council at Gloucester for November, in order to ratify the arrangements for a protectorship. At a council at Bristol in November 1216, William Marshal's role was decided on, he was to be 'guardian of the king and the kingdom'; his new title was first used on 12 November 1216.[31] He was probably in his seventieth year by this time. From this point on, all royal acts were carried out in William Marshal's name; it was his own seal that was affixed to chancery writs.[32] In 1217 Magna Carta was reissued, alongside the newly created Charter of the Forest.

In May 1217, William Marshal and the Royalist forces defeated the rebel barons and their French allies at the battle of Lincoln; this victory was consolidated with victory at sea, in a battle off the coast of Sandwich in August. Louis sued for peace and left England in September in return for a general amnesty and an indemnity of 10,000 marks, a generous settlement for a defeated prince. William Marshal ruled England for nineteen months, with some success; the exchequer was re-established, peace returned to the Welsh March and an accommodation reached with Prince Llywelyn of Gwynedd at Worcester in March 1218. By January 1219, however, the great man, now into his seventies, was suffering his final illness, although he managed to soldier on for several more months. He held a council in his sickroom at his manor of Caversham on 8 and 9 April, where he relinquished his power. The *Histoire* depicts a touching deathbed scene with William taking leave of Isabel, his '*belle amie*', embracing his wife one last time and crying with her.[33] He died on 14 May 1219, his head supported by his eldest son and heir, William (II) Marshal. He was laid to rest in the church at the New Temple, London, where the effigy from his tomb can still be seen.

William Marshal, Earl of Pembroke, was survived by his wife, Isabel de Clare, by only a year. Isabel and William had been married in August 1189, William having collected her from the household of Ranulf de Glanville in London, where she had been residing.[34] The *Histoire* gives us a glimpse of Isabel, depicting her as a personality in her own right when the family resided at her estates in Ireland, between 1207 and 1213.[35] Isabel had taken part in the council of Marshal's men at Chepstow, prior to their departure for Ireland, when she argued against sending their second son, Richard, into John's custody to be yet another hostage. And when William was forced to be in attendance upon the king in this period, it was Isabel who took over the running of the family's Irish estates. During William's absence, a number of his retainers sided with John's justiciar, Meiler Fitz Henry, in return for lands from King John. According to the *Histoire*, Isabel opposed William's decision to pardon these rebellious vassals on his return to Ireland.[36] Although it is unusual for a woman of her time, Isabel appears to have enjoyed some measure of authority and personal independence. She had her own chaplain, named Walter, her own clerk, a man named Robert, and her own seal. This seal depicts her in a standard contemporary pose: 'full face, standing, in tight-fitting dress, pointed headdress, and long cloak, with a falcon on her left wrist.'[37] In his final will, William Marshal left all the lands to Isabel that he had held from her and Isabel would continue to administer these lands, personally, until her death. Their eldest son, William, was to receive all the Marshal lands and those that William had acquired throughout his career and would only inherit the lands William held in his wife's name on Isabel's death. It is a mark of the authority and independence that Isabel enjoyed as a widow that she was able to make her own agreement with the king of France, whereby the family were allowed to retain their property in Normandy. It should come as no surprise, therefore, that her daughters were themselves strong, remarkable women. Isabel died in 1220 and was buried at Tintern Abbey in Wales.[38]

Isabel and William Marshal had ten children together, five sons and five daughters. Of the sons the eldest William (II) succeeded his father as earl of Pembroke. He married King John's daughter, Eleanor, but died childless in 1231 and was succeeded in the earldom by his brother, Richard, who had inherited the Norman lands in their father's will. Richard died in captivity in Ireland from wounds received at the battle of the Curragh in 1234. He was succeeded as earl by Gilbert Marshal, who married Margaret, sister of King Alexander II of Scotland. Gilbert died in 1241, leaving only an illegitimate daughter, Isabel. He was succeeded as earl by Walter, William and Isabel's fourth son, who married Margaret de Lacy, Countess of Lincoln, but he died in November 1245, also childless. The fifth and final son, Ancel, briefly succeeded as earl, but died on 22 December 1245. The earldom was then divided among the five Marshal daughters, with the title of Marshal passing through William and Isabel's eldest daughter, Matilda, into the Bigod family and the earls of Norfolk.

Matilda Marshal

The children of William and Isabel cannot fail to have benefited from William Marshal's rise through the ranks from fourth son and humble hearth knight, to earl of Pembroke and, eventually, regent for Henry III. Their father's position as a powerful magnate on the Welsh Marches and the most respected knight in the kingdom saw William's daughters make the most advantageous marriages in the highest echelons of the nobility. Although we do not have a birth date for Matilda Marshal, also known as Maud or Mahelt, given that her parents married in 1189 and she had two elder brothers, she was probably born in 1193 or 1194.[39] She was the third child and eldest daughter. The *Histoire* praises Matilda saying she had the gifts of 'wisdom, generosity, beauty, nobility of heart, graciousness, and I can tell you in truth, all the good qualities which a noble lady should possess.'[40] The *Histoire* goes on to say; 'Her worthy father who loved her dearly, married her off, during his lifetime to the best and most handsome party he knew, to Sir Hugh Bigot.'[41] Of William and Isabel's five daughters, it is only Matilda who is mentioned in the *Histoire* as being 'loved dearly' by her father.

In 1207 when the Marshal family moved to Ireland, William looked to settle Matilda's future. Now aged 13 or 14, Matilda was old enough to be married and William approached Roger Bigod, second Earl of Norfolk, to propose a match between Matilda and Roger's son and heir, Hugh Bigod. Hugh was Roger's son by his wife Ida de Tosny, former mistress of King Henry II and the mother of the king's son, William Longespée, Earl of Salisbury. Roger and Ida had married at Christmas in 1181 and so Hugh was probably in his mid-twenties when the marriage with Matilda was suggested. According to the *Histoire* William asked Roger Bigod 'graciously, being the wise man he was, to arrange a handsome marriage between his own daughter and his son Hugh. The boy was worthy, mild-mannered, and noblehearted and the young lady was a very young thing and both noble and beautiful. The marriage was a most suitable one and pleased both families involved.'[42] The match was a good one. The Bigods were loyal servants of the king, with royal connections through Ida's son, Longespée, who was also half-brother to King John. Through his marriage to Ela of Salisbury, Longespée was also related to William Marshal, Ela's grandfather and William's mother being brother and sister. After the marriage, Matilda lived with her husband at the earl of Norfolk's magnificent thirteen-towered castle at Framlingham. In 1209 she gave birth to a son, Roger, who would succeed his father as fourth Earl of Norfolk. Another son, Hugh, was born in 1212, and a daughter, Isabelle in 1215. A third and final son, Ralph, was probably born in 1216 or 1217.

Matilda's family was deeply divided by the Magna Carta crisis and subsequent civil war. Her husband and father-in-law had joined the ranks of the baronial rebellion in 1215, as had her brother, William Marshal the Younger, whilst her father remained a staunch supporter of the king, holding the Welsh Marches for the Royalist cause during the civil war.

In 1216 the war touched Matilda personally, with Framlingham Castle being besieged by King John, who demanded the castle's surrender:

> The King to his well-beloved men, William le Enveise, constable of Framlingham, and all the knights presently with him in that castle, greetings. We command that you deliver up to our trusty and well-beloved William de Harcourt and Elias de Beauchamp the castle of Framlingham. And in testimony hereof we thereto send you these our letters patent. Witness myself, at Framlingham, the thirteenth day of March, in the seventeenth year of our reign.[43]

We do not know whether Matilda was in residence at the castle at the time of the siege; her father-in-law was in, or on his way to, London and her husband Hugh's whereabouts are unknown, but he was not at Framlingham. The king allowed the constable, William le Enveise, to send messengers to the earl and seek advice on what they should do.[44] The earl probably advised the constable to surrender as the castle capitulated to the king without a fight two days later. One of Matilda's sons, most likely the eldest, Roger, was taken as hostage. It is not hard to imagine what thoughts and feelings – and fears – must have gone through Matilda's mind, knowing that her young son, only 6 or 7 years of age, was in the custody of King John. The king's treatment of Matilda de Braose was common knowledge, and rumours of what had happened to Arthur of Brittany were rife. Her own two older brothers, William and Richard, had also been held for several years as hostages to their father's good behaviour. It must have been a comfort to Matilda, however, to know that King John depended on the loyalty of her father, and so would treat the boy well, if only to avoid alienating the man whose support he sorely needed.

Despite King John's death in October 1216, Matilda's husband and father-in-law remained in rebellion, supporting the claims of Louis of France. The earl of Norfolk only came to terms with the Royalist government when the French prince returned home in September 1217 and when he was finally restored to the earldom of Norfolk and Framlingham Castle was returned to him. It was probably also at this time that his grandson, Roger, was returned to his mother. His last year as a hostage would have been when his own grandfather, William Marshal, was in power as regent, which must have let Matilda rest easier and allayed her fears for her son.

Matilda spent time with her father while he was dying in April and May 1219. The *Histoire* says of Matilda at her father's deathbed: 'My lady Mahelt [Matilda] la Bigote was so full of grief she almost went out of her mind, so great was her love for him. Often she appealed to God, asking Him why He was taking from her what her heart loved most.'[45] It goes on to tell the story of the ailing William Marshal calling for his daughters to sing to him. William asked Matilda to be the first to sing: 'She had no wish to do so for her life at the time was a bitter cup, but she had no wish to disobey her father's command. She started to sing since she wished to please her father, and she sang exceedingly well, giving a verse of a song in a sweet, clear voice.'[46]

Matilda's husband, Hugh, succeeded to the title of earl of Norfolk when his father died sometime between April and August 1221, probably aged well into his seventies. The new earl, however, only enjoyed his title for four years; he died suddenly in 1225, aged only 43. He was succeeded by their eldest son, Roger, then only 16 years old and therefore still a minor. His wardship was given to William Longespée, Earl of Salisbury, and the young earl's half-uncle, but when Longespée died the following year, the wardship was transferred to Alexander II, King of Scots.[47] The *Fine Rolls* of Henry III record in great detail the transfer of wardship:

> 1226: 27 Oct. Westminster. *For the King of Scots.* To the sheriff of Norfolk and Suffolk. The king's faithful and beloved brother, Alexander, King of Scots, has made fine with him by 500 m., to be rendered at Mid-Lent in the eleventh year, for having to himself or to his assigns, until the full age of the heirs of H. Bigod, formerly earl of Norfolk, the wards, marriages and escheats that escheated from the lands and knights' fees and all other things that were held of the same earl by knight service and that the king has retained in his hand, which lands and aforesaid fees the king has granted to the aforesaid king. Also, the king [of England] has granted 50 m. to the king [of Scots] or his assigns, by the same fine, to be received annually from the county of Norfolk until the full age of

the aforesaid heirs, which the aforesaid earl used to receive each year from the county of Norfolk in the name of the same county. The king [of England] has further granted to the king [of Scots] or his assigns, until the full age of the aforesaid heirs, the presentations of the churches that pertain to the same heirs, so that the king or his assigns are to present to them whenever they fall vacant. Order to cause the same king or his assigns to have the wards, marriages and escheats when they escheat, and the presentations to churches when they fall vacant, in his bailiwick, as aforesaid. He is also to inquire diligently by trustworthy and law-worthy men of those parts what lands and fees pertain to the heirs of the same earl, and who holds them, and what lands and fees pertain to W. earl Warenne and Matilda, his wife, in the name of dower of the same Matilda, and who holds them, and which presentations to churches pertain to the same heirs when they fall vacant, and who holds those churches, and which presentations to churches pertain to the aforesaid W. earl Warenne and Matilda, his wife, in the name of dower of the same Matilda. The inquisition having been taken, he is to cause Thomas son of Ranulf, bailiff of the same king, to have it under his seal and the seals of those by whom etc. was taken. Order also to cause to come on a suitable day and place before the aforesaid Thomas or other bailiffs of the aforesaid King of Scots, if the same Thomas will not be present, all knights and free tenants of the lands and fees that are in the hand of the King of Scots by the king's grant in his bailiwick, in order to perform their fealty to the same Thomas, or to other bailiffs of the aforesaid King of Scots if Thomas will not be present, for their lands and tenements, to be observed until the full age of the same heirs, saving fealty to the king. The king has also granted to the same king or to his assigns, by the aforesaid fine, those 50 librates of land which he retained in his hand for the custody of Framlingham castle. The king has ordered Herbert de Alençon to cause the same king or his assigns to have full seisin thereof. Before the justiciar.[48]

It was also ordered in writing:

to the sheriffs of Yorkshire, Leicestershire and Essex [that] The king has granted to A. King of Scots, until the full age etc., by a fine that he made with the king, the wards, marriages and escheats, which escheated in the aforesaid writ, etc., except for that clause "concerning the 500 m. that he used to receive from the county of Norfolk", and the other clause addressed to Herbert.[49]

Essentially, custody of the young earl of Norfolk, and of all his lands, was handed to Alexander II, king of Scots, who would marry Roger to his sister, Isabella of Scotland. The only lands not granted to the king of Scots were those which Matilda held in dower as Hugh Bigod's widow. Matilda was still only 32 when Hugh died, with four children to care for. As a valuable marriage prize she, or her family, acted quickly to secure her future and safety and within three months of her husband's death, she was married once more. Her second husband was William de Warenne, fifth Earl of Surrey, also known as Earl Warenne. William was the only son of Isabel de Warenne, Countess of Surrey in her own right, and her second husband, Hamelin de Warenne, half-brother of King Henry II. Matilda was the earl's second wife, his first wife, Matilda, daughter of William d'Aubigny, second Earl of Arundel had died childless on 6 February 1215 and was buried at Lewes Priory, Sussex.[50] William de Warenne was a neighbour of the Bigods, having lands centred in Castle Acre in Norfolk, and he had joined the rebellion against King John at about the same time as Roger Bigod, although William was back in the Royalist camp by March 1217 and was a prominent participant in the negotiations which ended the war in August 1217.[51]

Probably born in the late 1160s, William was considerably older than his new wife and the marriage appears to have been one of practicality, rather than affection. The earl had purchased Matilda's marriage, essentially meaning her dower in Norfolk, before July 1225.[52] Matilda continued to style herself as 'Matildis la Bigot' in charters, with 'Matildis de Warenne' added only as an afterthought, or not at all. For example, a charter from the early 1240s, following the death of William de Warenne, has the salutation, '*ego Latilda Bigot comitissa Norf' et Warenn.*'[53] This may be an indication that this marriage was not of Matilda's own choosing and may even have preferred to remain a widow, rather than entering into this second marriage. The continuing use of her name from her first marriage being her own mark of rebellion against her new situation.

After the resolution of the crisis of 1216/1217 William de Warenne served the crown faithfully, save for his brief involvement in the confederation against it led by Henry III's brother Richard of Cornwall, between July and October 1227. He was forced to surrender Tickhill Castle, but his disgrace was only temporary and in 1228 he was confirmed in possession of the manors of Grantham and Stamford for life, as well as the receipt of the third penny for the county of Surrey for the first time, an honorary payment previously denied to William and his father. In 1230 William de Warenne was appointed keeper of the east-coast ports of England during the king's expedition to Brittany. In 1236 he was cup bearer at the coronation of Eleanor of Provence and in 1237 he witnessed the reissue of Magna Carta, one of the few surviving barons who were witness to the original charter in 1215.[54]

In his early seventies, William de Warenne died in London on 27 or 28 May 1240; he was buried before the high altar at his family's foundation of Lewes Priory in Sussex. In his memory, the king ordered that a wayside cross be erected on the road between Carshalton and Merton, in Surrey.[55] Matilda bore her second husband two children, a boy and a girl, John and Isabel (later Isabel d'Aubigny). John would succeed his father as earl and attained his majority in 1248, when he succeeded to the Warenne estates. He would pursue a martial career and was one of Edward I's fiercest generals. Matilda did not marry again after William's death. In 1246, as the last surviving child of William Marshal, and with neither of her five brothers leaving a son, Matilda was granted the Marshal's rod by King Henry III. She did, at this point, change her name on charters, to '*Martill marescalla Angliae, comitissa Norfolciae et Warennae.*'[56] Emphasising her Marshal name as her father's eldest surviving child, Matilda was, significantly, claiming the title Marshal of England as her right, thus increasing her power and prestige, and taking the authority of the marshal as her own. Matilda appears to have acted independently during her second marriage, purchasing land in the Don Valley in South Yorkshire, close to the Warenne stronghold of Conisbrough Castle. After the queen she was 'undoubtedly the most powerful and wealthy woman in England from 1242 onwards.'[57]

Matilda died in 1248, in her mid-fifties. Choosing to be laid to rest with her Marshal family, rather than either of her husbands, Matilda was buried at Tintern Abbey, Monmouthshire. Her three Bigod sons and their Warenne half-brother carried their mother's bier into the church, where she was laid to rest close to her mother, Isabel, two of her brothers, Walter and Ancel, and her sister, Sybil. It is through Matilda's marriage to Hugh Bigod, Earl of Norfolk, that the present duke of Norfolk also bears the title of Earl Marshal.

Isabel Marshal

Matilda had been the eldest of the five Marshal sisters; her next sister, Isabel Marshal, was at least six years her junior, born in 1200. She was married to Gilbert de Clare, Earl of Gloucester and Hertford, who was twenty years her senior. Gilbert was the son of Richard de Clare, Earl of Hertford, and Amicia, coheiress of William, Earl of Gloucester. His aunt, Amicia's sister, was Isabella of Gloucester, the discarded first wife of King John, who had held the earldom of Gloucester until her death on 14 October 1217, when it passed to Gilbert. Both Gilbert and his father were named among the twenty-five barons appointed as Enforcers of Magna Carta in 1215; as a consequence, father and son were excommunicated at the beginning of 1216.

After the death of King John, Gilbert sided with Prince Louis of France and was only reconciled with the Royalist cause after the battle of Lincoln in May 1217, despite having married Isabel, the second daughter of the regent, William Marshal, in 1214.[58] Like her older sister, Matilda, Isabel had found her husband's family on the opposing side to her father in the Magna Carta crisis and the civil war that followed. Gilbert's political career was during the minority of Henry III, his position owed mainly to his landed status and his marital connections, rather than his abilities or capacity for leadership. In 1225, he was present at the confirmation of Magna Carta at Westminster, but in 1227 he sided with the king's brother Richard, Earl of Cornwall, in his dispute with Henry III, demanding a renewal of the forest acts and campaigning against Hubert de Burgh. In 1230 Gilbert accompanied the king on his expedition to Brittany, but died there, at Penros, on 25 October 1230. He had made his first will before his departure to the Continent, at Southwick, on 30 April 1230, and made a second will on 23 October, two days before he died.[59]

Gilbert's body was brought back to England and laid to rest in Tewkesbury Abbey, before the great altar, in the presence of an 'innumerable gathering.'[60] Isabel, his widow, set up a memorial stone dated 28 September 1231.[61] Gilbert was succeeded in his earldoms by his eldest son by Isabel, Richard de Clare, who was only 8 years old on his father's death. Richard had been born on 4 August 1222 and was the eldest of five children. Two other sons, William and Gilbert, were born in 1228 and 1229 respectively, but remained unmarried. Gilbert and Isabel also had two daughters. Amicia was their eldest child, born in 1220, she married firstly Baldwin de Revières, Earl of Devon, and secondly Robert de Guines. A second daughter Isabel, born in November 1226, married Robert (V) de Brus, fifth Lord of Annandale; her grandson, Robert the Bruce, would be crowned King of Scots in 1306.[62] On Gilbert's death, wardship of young Richard de Clare and his lands was given to Hubert de Burgh, the king's justiciar, but was passed to Peter des Roches, Bishop of Winchester, when de Burgh fell from power in 1232.

Only just turned 30, Isabel Marshal was not a widow for long. In March 1231, apparently without the king's permission or knowledge, she married Henry III's 22-year-old brother Richard, Earl of Cornwall. Despite the nine-year age difference, it was a good match; Isabel already had five healthy children by her first husband and was yet young enough to bear more. She also brought with her the Marshal name and, eventually, a share in the Marshal inheritance. The marriage with Richard was put under immense strain when their first two children died in infancy and in 1235 Richard attempted to put Isabel aside. He wrote to Rome asking for an annulment, but the pope advised him to persevere with the marriage. Isabel fell pregnant for a third time and gave birth to a healthy son, Henry, known as Henry of Almain in November 1235.[63] The appalation Almain was in reference to his father being named King of the Germans in 1256. Henry would survive into adulthood and was a friend and ally of Lord Edward, son and heir of Henry III, but was to meet a tragic end in March 1271, when he was murdered by his own cousin, Guy de Montfort, while attending mass at church in Viterbo, Italy.

In 1234 Richard had been involved in the rebellion of his brother-in-law, Richard Marshal, Earl of Pembroke, and in August Richard had his wife warn her brother, approaching court to try to settle the dispute, of a possible trap and told him to flee or face arrest.[64] However, he was persuaded to abandon Marshal by his brother the king, and the short-lived rebellion ended with the death of Richard Marshal, while a prisoner in Ireland, and the fall of the Poitevin faction at court. Isabel died in childbirth on 17 January 1240 at Berkhamsted Castle, the child – a boy – died with her. She had asked to be buried at Tewkesbury Abbey, with her first husband, but was, in fact, interred at Beaulieu Abbey, her baby son with her; her heart was sent to Tewkesbury to be interred with Gilbert de Clare.

Following his wife's death, Richard, having taken the cross at Winchester in June 1236, finally began his preparations to leave on crusade. Isabel's brother, Gilbert, had sworn to accompany him but had fallen out with Henry III and decided to resolve his issues with the king before his departure. Despite the fact Gilbert was grieving for his sister, the king was not in a conciliatory mood. King Henry had levelled accusations against Gilbert that were so demeaning that Matthew Paris, the chronicler, refused to record them. Unfortunately, no one else thought to record them, either, so we do not know what transpired between Gilbert and the king. It took a year for Gilbert to resolve his issues with the Henry, by which time Richard of Cornwall had left on crusade without him.[65]

Sibyl Marshal

Isabel was survived by her next-youngest sister, Sibyl, who was born around 1201. Sibyl was married to William de Ferrers, fifth Earl of Derby. The couple played little part in national affairs, Ferrers had been plagued by gout since his youth and took little interest in public matters. He was regularly transported by litter and never fully recovered from an accident that occurred sometime in the 1230s while crossing a bridge at St Neots in Huntingdonshire, whereby he was thrown from his litter into the water. He succeeded to the earldom of Derby on his father's death in 1247 but died in 1254. Sibyl gave birth to seven children, all daughters: Agnes,

Isabel, Maud, Sibyl, Joan, Agatha and Eleanor. Sibyl died sometime before 1247 and was laid to rest at Tintern Abbey, alongside her mother.

Eva Marshal

William and Isabel Marshal's fourth daughter, Eva, was born in about 1203 in Pembroke Castle, and so was only 16 when her father died – and 17 when she lost her mother. As a child, she spent several years with her family in exile in Ireland, only returning to England when her father was finally reconciled with King John in 1212. Sometime before 1221, Eva was married to William (V) de Braose, Lord of Abergavenny, son of Reginald de Braose and grandson of Matilda de Braose, who died of starvation in King John's dungeons.

William de Braose was a powerful Marcher baron who was hated by the Welsh. Having been a prisoner of Prince Llywelyn of Gwynedd in 1228, he returned to the Welsh prince's court in 1230 to arrange the marriage of his daughter to Llywelyn's son, Dafydd. De Braose caused a public scandal by being found in Llywelyn's chamber with the Welsh prince's wife, Joan. Llywelyn's immediate reaction was one of anger and William de Braose was publicly hanged in Wales on 2 May 1230. This rage, however vicious, was remarkably brief. Despite William de Braose's betrayal of Llywelyn, and subsequent violent death, the marriage between William's daughter, Isabella, and Llywelyn's son, Prince Dafydd, was not derailed.

Llywelyn was anxious that the wedding should go ahead and wrote to his 'esteemed friend' Eva Marshal, Isabella's mother, shortly after her husband's execution, with warm greetings and asking

in so far as you might inform us regarding your wish, whether you would want to persist with the alliance made between David [Dafydd], our son, and I. [Isabella], your daughter; because she will never remain with us except that the alliance will stand. And if you would not want this, lest any worse harm might be able to happen, you would want to make known soon your will regarding that alliance and regarding the authority of your daughter with us. And you may know that in no way might we have been able to avert what judgement the magnates of our land might not do, considering what revenge they have done because of the scandal and our outrage. And whatever you will have done from there you might take the trouble to make known to us.[66]

The letter suggests that Isabella had accompanied her father on the mission to negotiate her marriage to Dafydd. It must have been a dreadful time for the young woman, to see her father hanged from the nearest tree and then have to remain at the court of the man who had ordered the execution. However, Llywelyn's letter suggests that he was truly hoping that her mother, Eva, would still allow the marriage to go ahead. Llywelyn also wrote to Isabella's uncle, William Marshal, the second Earl of Pembroke, addressing him as 'friend and dearest brother' and continuing with:

Your grace will know that the magnates of our land might in no way control what they might not do regarding William de Breuse [Braose], the judgement which they will have made on him who engineered our deceit, by deceitfully entering our chamber, bringing shame to us in the highest way. Whereby we ask your grace resolutely, concerning which we show the greatest trust, in so far as you may wish to show to us your will, whether you might have wished the alliance made between your niece and our son Dafydd; which, if you might have wished, on our part that alliance steadfastly and persistently stands firm. Farewell.

You may take the trouble to show to us your pleasure over this and other matters and for certain you may know that never might anything happen in us but that the friendship made between you and us is guarded steadily and invariably forever, neither on account of the king nor on account of anything in the world. Again farewell.[67]

Llywelyn's letters do seem to have healed any possible rift before it became unsurmountable; Dafydd and Isabella were married in 1232, although they remained childless and Dafydd was eventually succeeded by his nephew, Llywelyn, as prince of Gwynedd and, eventually Wales, when he died in 1246.

William and Eva had four daughters together, including Isabella, who was born in 1222. A second daughter, Maud, born in 1224, married Roger Mortimer, first Baron Wigmore, and died in 1301. Eva de Braose, born in 1227, died 28 July 1255 and married William de Cantilupe. The youngest daughter, born around 1228, Eleanor, married Humphrey (IV) de Bohun, Earl of Hereford, and was the mother of Humphrey (V) de Bohun, Gilbert and a daughter, Alianore. Eleanor died sometime in 1251 and her husband remarried to Joan de Quincy. Eleanor's substantial lands in the Welsh Marches passed to her son, Humphrey. However, the younger Humphrey predeceased his father, and the earldom passed to his son, another Humphrey (VI), on the old earl's death in 1275.

Following her husband's execution, Eva kept hold of the Braose lands and castles and continued to administer them in her own right.[68] She is listed as the holder of Totnes in 1230, but it was confiscated by the king in August 1233, during her brother's rebellion, when the king ordered 'the sheriff of Devon to take the castle of Totnes, which is in the hand of Eva de Braose into the king's hand, with all appurtenances, and to keep it safely until the king orders otherwise.'[69] Eva is also recorded in a pledge of 12 June 1237 'for the 800 m. in which she is bound to the king for G. [Gilbert] Earl Marshal, concerning which 800 m. letters were directed to the barons of the Exchequer.'[70] In 1242 Eva also paid a fine to be able to decide the marriage of her youngest daughter, Eleanor:

30 Jan. Westminster. *For Eva de Braose.* To the barons of the Exchequer. The king has betaken himself to H. earl of Hereford and Essex for the 650 m. which still remain to be paid to the king from the fine of 800 m. by which Eva de Braose made fine with the king for having the custody and marriage of Eleanor, her daughter, and he has granted him that he may render the aforesaid 650 m. at the below-written terms, namely 50 m. at Easter in the twenty-sixth year, 50 m. at Michaelmas in the same year, and 100 m. thus from year to year at the same terms until the aforesaid 650 m. are paid to the king in full. Order to cause this to be done and enrolled thus.[71]

Eva was also granted 12 marks by the king to strengthen Hay Castle, which had been granted to her as part of her dower.[72] In 1234 she was somehow involved in the rebellion of her brother, Richard, and probably acted as one of the arbitrators between the king and her surviving brothers, following Richard's murder in Ireland (he died while in custody, his wounds untreated after a battle). She received a safe conduct in May 1234, allowing her to speak with the king; her lands and castles, including Totnes, were restored to her before the end of the month. Eva also received a formal statement from the king, declaring her back in 'his good graces'.[73] She died in 1246.

Joan Marshal

The youngest Marshal sister was Joan, who was still only a child when her father died in 1219. As with her sister Matilda, she is mentioned in the *Histoire* as having been called for by her ailing father, so that she could sing for him.[74] Joan was married before 1222 to Warin de Munchensi, a landholder and soldier who was born in the mid-1190s. When his father and older brother died in 1204 and (possibly) 1208, respectively, Warin was made a ward of his uncle William d'Aubigny, Earl of Arundel. He was ill-treated by King John, who demanded 2,000 marks in relief and quittance of his father's Jewish debts on 23 December 1213. He was ordered to pay quickly and pledged his lands as a guarantee of his good behaviour. However, this harsh treatment drove him to ally with the rebel barons and he was captured fighting against the Royalist forces at the battle of Lincoln, on 20 May 1217.[75] He was reconciled with the crown and served Henry III loyally on almost every military campaign of the next forty years.

His marriage to Joan Marshal produced two children; John de Munchensi and a daughter, Joan, who would marry the king's half-brother, William de Valence, fourth son of Isabelle d'Angoulême and her second husband, Hugh X de Lusignan, Count of La Marche. It was through his wife and, more accurately her mother, that de Valence was allowed to claim the title Earl of Pembroke. Joan Marshal died sometime before November 1234, as Warin married for a second time shortly after that, to a widow, Denise, daughter and heir of Nicholas of Anstey of Hertfordshire.[76]

When the last Marshal son, Ancel, died without heirs in December 1245, the Marshal lands were divided equally between Matilda, the sole surviving Marshal, and the heirs of her four sisters. The legacy of the great William Marshal continued through the female line, but this branch of the Marshal name had died out just one generation after the death of the great knight and regent. His posthumous reputation was permanently established by the *Histoire de Guillaume le Maréchale*, commissioned by William, his son and heir, in the early 1220s. Having had a father of such integrity and fame cannot have failed to rub off, not only on his sons, but also his daughters. Matilda, Isabel, Sibyl, Eva and Joan all showed the strength and determination for which their father was famous, holding together their families in times of hardship and adversity. It seems ironic that, despite William's firm adherence to King John, his daughters were all married to men who fought against him in the Magna Carta crisis; a testament to how much opposition John faced.

Chapter 7

The Princesses of Scotland

There is only one clause in Magna Carta that mentions particular women. Although they are not identified by name, they are easily identifiable due to their positions. These two women were the sisters of Alexander II, King of Scots, who had been hostages in England since the treaty of Norham in 1209. Clause 59 of Magna Carta agrees to negotiate for their release, alongside a number of other Scottish hostages:

> We will treat Alexander, king of Scots, concerning the return of his sisters and hostages and his liberties and rights in the same manner in which we will act towards our other barons of England, unless it ought to be otherwise because of the charters which we have from William his father, formerly king of Scots; and this shall be determined by the judgement of his peers in our court.[1]

The king of Scots' two sisters referred to in the clause were Margaret and Isabella, the oldest daughters of William I (the Lion), King of Scots, and his wife, Ermengarde de Beaumont. The two girls had been caught up in the power struggle between their father and the Plantagenet kings. William I was the second of three sons of Henry, Earl of Northumberland, and his wife, Ada de Warenne. He was, therefore, a grandson of David I and great-grandson of Malcolm III Canmor and St Margaret, the Anglo-Saxon princess. William had succeeded his father as earl of Northumberland in June 1153, when he was about 11 years old. He lost the earldom, however, when his brother, Malcolm IV (known as Malcolm the Maiden) surrendered the northern counties of England to Henry II; he was given lands in Tynedale, worth £10 per annum, in compensation. This loss of Northumberland was never forgotten and was to colour William's future dealings with the English crown throughout his reign.

William was probably knighted in 1159, when he accompanied his brother Malcolm on an expedition to Toulouse and in 1163 he was in attendance in a meeting with King Henry II at Woodstock where the Scots king did homage to the English king. William and Malcolm's younger brother, David, was to remain in England as a hostage. William ascended the Scottish throne on Malcolm's death on 9 December 1165, aged about 23; his coronation took place at Scone on Christmas Eve, 24 December. In 1166 William travelled to Normandy to meet with King Henry II and, although we do not know what they spoke of, it was reported that they parted on bad terms.[2]

Nevertheless, in 1170 William and his brother David were at the English court, attending Henry II's council at Windsor on 5 April 1170 and were in London on 14 June, when Henry's eldest son, also Henry, was crowned king of England in his father's lifetime. He would be known as the Young King, rather than Henry III, and died in 1183, six years before his father. Both William and his brother David did homage to the Young King after the coronation.[3] In 1173 when the Young King and his brothers, Richard and Geoffrey, rebelled against their father, Henry II, the younger Henry promised that he would give the northern counties of England to the Scots king, and the earldom of Huntingdon with Cambridgeshire to the king's brother, David, in return for their support in the rebellion. William considered the offer, consulting his barons in the summer of 1173. It was decided to ask Henry II to return Northumberland, and to renounce homage if he refused. Henry II refused and William joined the Young King's rebellion.

William formed an alliance with Louis VII of France and Count Philippe of Flanders, who both promised mercenaries would be sent to England in support. This was the start of the long Scottish tradition of alliances with France, against England, which would become known as the Auld Alliance. On 20 August 1173 the Scottish forces moved south, to Alnwick, Warkworth and Newcastle. Although they devastated the countryside, the Scots were unable to take the castles. They moved on to Carlisle, in the west, but having again failed to take the castle, they pulled back to Roxburgh after receiving news that a new English force was advancing. This force, under Ranulf de Glanville, the justiciar, burned Berwick. A truce was agreed until 13 January 1174, before the English returned south to deal with an invasion from Flanders. The truce was later extended to 24 March 1174, after a payment of 300 marks by the bishop of Durham to King William.[4]

At the end of the truce, the Scots, accompanied by Flemish mercenaries, again advanced into England. They ravaged the Northumberland coast and besieged both Wark-on-Tweed (on the Northumberland–Scotland border) and Carlisle castles, but failed to take either. The castles at Appleby and Brough surrendered to them, but they were resisted at Prudhoe Castle, near Newcastle, from where they moved north to Alnwick after hearing of an approaching English army. On 13 July, while much of the Scottish army was spread out in raiding parties, the Scots were the victims of a surprise attack. King William's horse was killed, the king trapped underneath.

William surrendered to Ranulf de Glanville and was taken first to Newcastle and then to Northampton, where he appeared before Henry II on 24 July.[5] He was sentenced to imprisonment at Falaise in Normandy and the price of his freedom was to submit himself, his kingdom and the castles of Berwick, Roxburgh and Edinburgh to King Henry II.[6] The Convention of Falaise on 1 December 1174 also granted that 'the church of Scotland shall henceforward owe such subjection to the church of England as it should do.'[7] It was a humiliating treaty for the Scots, which also required twenty Scottish noble hostages be handed to the English in return for their king's freedom. King William arrived back in Scotland in February 1175, having spent two months in England until the handover of the Scottish castles had been completed.

He returned to a revolt in Galloway, which he managed to quash, but in 1179 the king of Scots was forced to go north, to answer the threat of Donald Ban Macwilliam, grandson of Duncan II, who was gaining support for a challenge to the throne and a return to the royal line of Duncan II. William built two new castles at Redcastle and Dunskeath and confirmed to his brother David the earldom of Lennox and lordship of Garrioch, thus controlling the roads to Moray and Ross. Things quietened down for a time, but in April 1181, when the king and David were in Normandy Donald Ban Macwilliam led an uprising in Moray and Ross, apparently gaining full control of the two earldoms. One royal retainer, Gillecolm the Marischal, surrendered the castle of Auldearn and then joined the rebels.[8]

The king was also faced with unrest in Galloway, where Gilbert of Galloway had failed to pay the money he had owed to Henry II since his earlier uprising. Gilbert died on 1 January 1185 and shortly after King William invaded Galloway, alongside Gilbert's nephew Roland, son of Uhtred of Galloway, who had been murdered by Gilbert, his own brother, in 1174. On 4 July 1185 William and his allies defeated the main force of Gilbert's followers and in July 1186, King William presented Roland to King Henry at Carlisle. By 1190 Roland had been granted the lordship of Galloway by King William while Gilbert's son, Duncan, was made lord of Carrick.[9] As a result, Galloway remained at peace well into the thirteenth century, until the death of Roland's son, Alan, in 1234. With Galloway subdued, in 1187 King William was finally able to quash the rebellion in the north, leading his considerable army as far as Inverness. On 31 July, at the now-lost site of 'Mam Garvia', Roland of Galloway faced the rebels in battle where over 500 of them were killed, including Donald Macwilliam, whose head was sent to King William.

The overlordship of Henry II caused additional problems for King William in the Scottish church; the archbishops of York and Canterbury both claimed the homage of the Scottish clergy. William also had a long-running dispute with the papacy, with five successive popes, in fact, over the appointment of a bishop of St Andrews, with none approving the other's candidate. The English king sided with the popes on the matter and in 1181 King William was excommunicated by the archbishop of Canterbury; the Scottish people, as a whole, were subsequently excommunicated by the bishop of Durham. Within two years, however, the papacy and the Scots king were on such good terms that the pope sent William the Golden Rose as a tribute to 'a king of exceptional religious zeal'.[10] On 13 March 1192 Pope Celestine III issued the papal bull, *Cum universi*, recognising the Scottish church as a 'special daughter' of the apostolic see and subject to Rome without an intermediary. Thereby denying the claims to superiority of both York and Canterbury.[11]

Unusually for a king in this period, by 1180 William had been on the throne for fifteen years and was still unmarried. He had several illegitimate children, including a daughter, Isabella, who was married to Robert de

Detail of a miniature of King John. Matthew Paris. Royal 14 C VII f9. (*Courtesy of the British Library Catalogue of Illuminated Manuscripts*)

The meadow at Runnymede, where Magna Carta was sealed on 15 June 1215. (*Photo courtesy of Jayne Smith*)

The Magna Carta memorial, Runnymede. (*Photo courtesy of Jayne Smith*)

'Charta de Foresta;' Westminster, 11 Febr. 9 Hen. III. [1225]. With great seal. – Shelfmark: Add. CH24712. (*Courtesy of the British Library Catalogue of Illuminated Manuscripts*)

The 1215 Magna Carta. Cotton MS Augustus ii.106. (*Courtesy of the British Library Catalogue of Illuminated Manuscripts*)

Newark Castle, Notts, where King John died on the night of 18/19 October 1216. (*Author's collection*)

The Great Hall and Gatehouse of Abergavenny Castle, home of the Braose family. (*Photo courtesy of Rachael Rogers and Abergavenny Museum, Monmouthshire County Council*)

Christmas Day Massacre by Frances Baines, showing the great hall of Abergavenny Castle moments before the murder of Seisyllt ap Dyfnwal by William de Braose at Christmas 1175. (*Reprinted courtesy of Abergavenny Museum, Monmouthshire County Council*)

Windsor Castle, Berkshire, one of the two possible sites for the death of Matilda de Braose and her son, William. (*Author's collection*)

St Michael's Church, Swaton, final resting place of Nicholaa de la Haye. (*Author's collection*)

The Temple Church, London, final resting place of William Marshal, first Earl of Pembroke. (*Author's collection*)

Conisbrough Castle, South Yorkshire, built by Hamelin de Warenne, Earl of Surrey and visited by King John in 1201. (*Author's collection*)

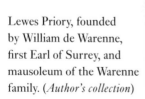

Lewes Priory, founded by William de Warenne, first Earl of Surrey, and mausoleum of the Warenne family. (*Author's collection*)

The gatehouse to Canterbury Cathedral, where Isabella of Gloucester, first wife of King John, was buried in 1217. (*Author's collection*)

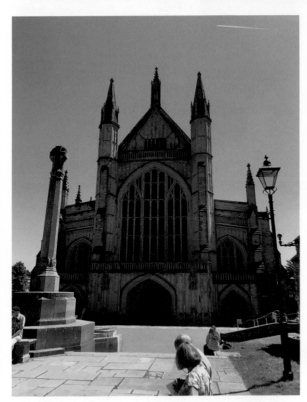

Winchester Cathedral. Isabelle d'Angoulême stayed with John's first wife, Isabella of Gloucester, at Winchester in the early years of her marriage to King John. (*Photo courtesy of Anne Marie Bouchard*)

The Tour Jeanne d'Arc, surviving part of Rouen Castle, where Arthur of Brittany was murdered, Easter 1203. (*Photo courtesy of Kristie Dean*)

Westminster Abbey, London, where Isabelle d'Angoulême was crowned Queen of England. (*Photo courtesy of Daniel Gleave*)

Bowes Castle, North Yorkshire, one of the residences in which Eleanor of Brittany resided. (*Author's collection*)

York Minster, where Henry III's sister Joan married Alexander II, King of Scots. (*Author's collection*)

Detail of a marginal drawing of the marriage of Frederick II to Isabella of England. Matthew Paris. Royal 14 C VII f123v. (*Courtesy of the British Library Catalogue of Illuminated Manuscripts*)

Memorial to the 1265 Battle of Lewes, fought between King Henry III and his brother-in-law, Simon de Montfort, Lewes Priory Gardens, Sussex. (*Author's collection*)

Lincoln Cathedral, owner of the original copy of Magna Carta housed in Lincoln Castle. (*Author's collection*)

The Observatory Tower, Lincoln Castle. Lincoln Castle is the site of the 1217 Battle of Lincoln and home to one of the four surviving copies of Magna Carta. (*Author's collection*)

The Tower of London. (*Author's collection*)

Brus, heir to the lordship of Annandale, in 1183. Another daughter, Ada, was married to Patrick, Earl of Dunbar and a son, Robert of London was endowed with royal lands. However, until he married, William's heir was his younger brother, David. With this in mind, in 1184, William was at King Henry's court to discuss a possible marriage with Henry's granddaughter, Matilda of Saxony. The match was forbidden by the pope on the grounds of consanguinity. In May 1186, during a council at Woodstock, King Henry suggested Ermengarde de Beaumont as a bride for King William.

Ermengarde was the daughter of Richard, Vicomte de Beaumont-sur-Sarthe, who was himself the son of Constance, one of the many illegitimate daughters of King Henry I of England. With such diluted royal blood, she was hardly a prestigious match for the king of Scots, but he reluctantly accepted the marriage after consulting his advisers. The wedding took place at Woodstock on 5 September 1186, with King Henry hosting four days of festivities and Edinburgh Castle was returned to the Scots as part of Ermengarde's dowry.[11]

Although we do not know Ermengarde's birth date, at the time of the marriage, she was referred to as 'a girl', suggesting that she may have only just reached the age of 12.[12] King William agreed to provide Ermengarde with £100 of rents and forty knights' fees in Scotland, for the financial maintenance of her household; she also had dwellings and lands at Crail and Haddington, lands which had previously been held by William's mother, Ada de Warenne.[13] After the wedding, King William accompanied King Henry to Marlborough whilst the new Scottish queen was escorted to her new home by Jocelin, Bishop of Glasgow, and other Scottish nobles. Between 1187 and 1195 Queen Ermengarde gave birth to two daughters, Margaret and Isabella. A son, the future Alexander II, was finally born at Haddington on 24 August 1198, the first legitimate son born to a reigning Scottish king in seventy years; a contemporary remarked that 'many rejoiced at his birth.'[14] A third daughter, Marjorie, was born sometime later.

On the death of King Henry II in 1189, King William again went south, and met with the new king, Richard I, at Canterbury, where he did homage for his English lands. Desperate for money for his crusade, on 5 December 1189, Richard abandoned his lordship of Scotland in the quitclaim of Canterbury; King William was released from the homage and submission given to Henry II, the castles of Roxburgh and Berwick were returned and the relationship between the kingdoms reverted to that in the time of Malcolm IV. The cost to the Scots was to be 10,000 marks, but Scotland was independent once again.[15]

Richard, however, refused to sell Northumberland back to William; instead he sold a life-interest in the earldom to the bishop of Durham. The Scots king remained on good relations with King Richard, paying 2,000 marks towards his ransom in 1193 and meeting him at Nottingham in April 1194, where William asked for two favours. The first, to be granted an honourable escort and daily subsistence allowances during his visits to the English court, was granted but not put into effect until the reign of King John. For the second favour, William asked to be granted the earldom of Northumberland, the lordships of Cumberland and Westmorland and the earldom of Lancaster, last held by the Scots in the 1140s. This second favour was, unsurprisingly, refused by Richard.[17] The Scots king carried one of the three swords of state at Richard's solemn crown-wearing at Winchester on 17 April 1194. Two days later, the bishop of Durham surrendered the earldom of Northumberland; William offered 15,000 marks for it and Richard made a counteroffer saying that William could have the earldom but not its castles, which William refused, and the matter remained unresolved.

In the spring of 1195 King William fell gravely ill at Clackmannan, causing a succession crisis, the sum of his legitimate children being one, possibly two, daughters at this time. The Scottish barons appear to have been divided, between recognising William's oldest legitimate daughter, Margaret, as his heir, or marrying Margaret to Otto, Duke of Saxony, grandson of Henry II, and allowing Otto to succeed to the throne. The earl of Dunbar led a faction who claimed that either solution was contrary to the custom of the land, so long as the king had a brother who could succeed him.[18] In the event, the king recovered from his illness and three years later the queen gave birth to Alexander, the much-desired son and heir. For the last years of the century, William was again occupied with unrest in the north. Before going on campaign in October 1201, he had the Scottish barons swear fealty to his son, Alexander, now 3 years old, a sensible precaution, given that he was approaching his sixtieth birthday.

Relations with England had changed in 1199, with the accession of King John. During the reign of King Richard, William had agreed with the justiciar, William Longchamp, and backed Arthur of Brittany as the king's heir. John may well have remembered this. Soon after John's accession, King William asked for the return of Northumberland. The two kings met at Lincoln in 1200, with William doing homage for his English lands and John asking for the discussion over Northumberland to be deferred until Whitsun 1201. The matter was deferred again when John sailed for Normandy in 1201, and again in 1204 after John's return. The two kings finally met for formal talks at York from 9 to 12 February 1206 and again from 26 to 28 May 1207, although we have little record of what was discussed. William was confirmed in his lands in Tynedale and John granted Arbroath Abbey trading privileges in England.[19] However, John appears to have been prevaricating, suggesting another meeting in October 1207, which the Scots rejected. In the meantime, the death of the bishop of Durham meant John took over the vacant see and set about building a castle at Tweedmouth. The Scots, seeing this as a direct threat to Berwick, destroyed the building works and matters came to a crisis in 1209.

After many threats, and with both sides building up their armies, the two kings met at Norham, Northumberland, in the last week of July and first week of August 1209. The Scots were in a desperate position, with an ailing and ageing king, and a 10–year-old boy as heir, whilst the English, with their Welsh allies and foreign mercenaries, had an army big enough to force a Scottish submission. The subsequent treaty, agreed at Norham on 7 August, was humiliating for the Scots. They agreed to pay 15,000 marks for peace and to surrender hostages, including the king's two oldest legitimate daughters, Margaret and Isabella. As a sweetener, John promised to marry the princesses to his sons; although Henry was only 2 years old at the time and Richard was just 8 months, whilst the girls were probably in their early-to-mid teens. John would have the castle at Tweedmouth dismantled, but the Scots would pay an extra £4,000 compensation for the damage they had caused to it. The king's daughters and the other Scottish hostages were handed into the custody of England's justiciar, at Carlisle on 16 August.[20] How the girls, or their parents, thought about this turn of events, we know not. Given John's proven record of prevarication and perfidy, King William may have hoped that the promised marriages would occur in good time, but may also have expected that John would find a way out of the promises made.

There is no mention of Queen Ermengarde being present for the treaty at Norham, although she did act as mediator in 1212, when her husband was absent, in negotiations with John at Durham. A contemporary observer described the Scottish queen as 'an extraordinary woman, gifted with a charming and witty eloquence'.[21] It seems likely that King John was not immune to the queen's charms, as he did not ask for more hostages and agreed that the Scottish heir, Alexander, would be knighted and one day marry an English princess. Alexander was knighted at Clerkenwell on 4 March 1212.[22] King William I, later known as William the Lion, died on 4 December 1214, aged about 72, having reigned for a total of forty-nine years, almost to the day. He was succeeded by Alexander, his only legitimate son, who was proclaimed king at Scone on 6 December 1214, aged just 16.

King Alexander II sided with the English barons in their struggle against the tyranny of King John, making an alliance with the northern barons, who agreed to press for a decision on the future of Alexander's sisters, and a resolution of the lordship of the northern counties.[23] He raided the northern English earldoms, exploiting the unrest in England to renew Scottish claims to these counties, besieging Norham in October 1215 and receiving the homage of the leading men of Northumberland on 22 October 1215.[24] In the summer of 1216 Alexander took the castle and town of Carlisle and in September the Scots king marched his army the length of England, from Scotland to Dover to pay homage to the dauphin, Louis, for his English lands.

Following John's death in October 1216 and the defeat of the French-rebel army at Lincoln in May 1217, Alexander's position in England became precarious. England's status as a papal fief saw Alexander and Scotland put under interdict. The Scots king surrendered Carlisle Castle at Berwick on 1 December 1217 and submitted to Henry III at Northampton later in the same month.[25] With King Alexander's submission, there followed an unprecedented almost eighty years of unbroken peace between England and Scotland. In June 1221, Alexander married Henry III's sister, Joan, in York Minster.

Margaret of Scotland

It took a little longer to resolve the futures of the king's two sisters who had been held hostage in England since 1209. Margaret, the eldest daughter of William I and Ermengarde de Beaumont, had been born sometime between her parents' marriage in 1186 and 1195, unfortunately we cannot be more specific. We do know that she was born by 1195, as she was mooted as a possible heir to King William I in the succession crisis of that year, when the king fell gravely ill. Several options were proposed at the time, including marrying young Margaret to Otto of Saxony, nephew of King Richard I. However, it was also proposed that Margaret should not even be considered as heir, that the kingdom should pass to her father's younger brother, David. In the event, King William recovered and none of the options were pursued, but at least it means that we know Margaret was born before 1195. And when her brother, Alexander, was born in 1198, Margaret's position as a possible heir was diminished further.

When she was taken as hostage, therefore she may have been as old as 22 or as young as 14. Given the apparent youth of Ermengarde on her wedding day, Margaret's date of birth is more likely to have been 1190 or later. John's demand of Margaret and Isabella as hostages, with the sweetener that they would be brides for his own sons, may well have been to prevent Margaret marrying elsewhere. King Philip Augustus had proposed a marriage between himself and Margaret, a union John would be keen to thwart.[26] Thus, John's control of the marriages of Margaret and Isabella would mean that they could not marry against the king of England's own interests. It also meant that King William had lost two useful diplomatic bargaining chips; marriage alliances could be used to cement political ones, and these had been passed to John, weakening William's position on the international stage. According to the chronicler Bower, the agreement specified that Margaret would marry John's son, Henry, while Isabella would be married to an English nobleman of rank.[27]

While hostages in England, Margaret and Isabella were kept together, and lived comfortably, although John's promise of arranging marriages for the girls remained unfulfilled. One can imagine the frustration of the Scots, to see their princesses languishing in the custody of the English, however comfortably, with their futures far from decided. There must have been considerable pressure from the Scots for a resolution to the situation, to the extent that the princesses are the only women to be identified in Magna Carta; clause 59 of the charter specifically mentions the king of Scots' sisters and promises to seek a resolution to their situation. Unfortunately, King John tore up Magna Carta almost before the wax seals had dried, writing to the pope to have the charter declared void, leaving Alexander to join the baronial rebellion.

When Alexander came to terms with the government of Henry III in December 1217, he pressed for a resolution to the marriages of himself and his sisters, Margaret and Isabella, still languishing in English custody. King John had promised that Alexander would marry one of his daughters and Henry III finally fulfilled this promise in June 1221, when his sister, Joan, was married to the Scots king at York. It was probably at this event, when the Scottish and English royal families came together in celebration, that Margaret's own future was finally resolved. It was decided that she would marry Hubert de Burgh, the king's justiciar and one of the leading figures of Henry III's minority government. They were married in London on 3 October 1221, with King Henry himself giving the bride away.[28] It was a major coup for Hubert de Burgh, who came from a gentry family rather than the higher echelons of the nobility. He had been married twice previously; his first wife was Beatrice de Warenne, daughter of William de Warenne, Baron of Wormegay, a minor branch of the Warenne earls of Surrey. His second wife was Isabella of Gloucester, Countess of Gloucester in her own right, King John's discarded first wife and widow of Geoffrey de Mandeville.

Each of his previous marriages had given de Burgh social and political advancement, and valuable familial connections. Marrying Margaret of Scotland was no less a valuable match, but would later be used against him by his enemies, who accused de Burgh of marrying Margaret while the king was still too young to decide if he might want to marry the Scottish princess himself, as his father had proposed. Clause 6 of Magna Carta, guarding against marriage without disparagement, meaning that a woman could not be forced to marry below her station, was conveniently sidestepped as Magna Carta did not apply in Scotland. The Scottish preferred to view Hubert de Burgh as the royal justiciar he had become, rather than the member of the minor noble family into which he had been born. Margaret was at least 26 years of age when she married Hubert de Burgh and may even have been over 30. De Burgh was in his early fifties. Due to Margaret's high status as a Scottish princess, many of the grants of lands and privileges were made to the couple jointly, rather than solely to Hubert de Burgh. De Burgh was made earl of Kent in 1227, with the title specifically entailed on his children by Margaret, rather than on his children by his first marriage to Beatrice de Warenne.[29]

The couple had one child, a girl named Margaret but known as Megotta, who was probably born in the early 1220s. There were rumours that de Burgh was planning to divorce Margaret in 1232, but he fell from royal favour before such a move could be pursued.[30] From relatively humble beginnings, Hubert de Burgh had risen through the ranks of King John's administration to the highest echelons of power in the minority government of Henry III. However, with the king attaining his majority and taking up the reins of government, Hubert de Burgh's hold weakened. With the king's administration divided by powerful factions, de Burgh fell from favour; he was stripped of his offices and imprisoned. Margaret and her daughter, deprived of all their belongings, sought sanctuary at Bury St Edmunds, from where they were forbidden to leave by the king's own order. Margaret humbled herself before the king when he visited Bury St Edmunds, perhaps softening Henry III somewhat as the king then allowed her to visit her husband so they could discuss their situation. Relations between the king and de Burgh thawed slightly in 1234. In February Margaret was given possession of Hubert de Burgh's hereditary lands and in May of the same year de Burgh was finally pardoned and the king 'undertook to do what grace he will.'[31]

Whilst in sanctuary Margaret secretly arranged the marriage of Megotta to Richard de Clare, Earl of Hertford and Gloucester, the son of Isabel Marshal and Gilbert de Clare, who was of similar age to Megotta. The young couple may have known each other as Richard was a ward of Hubert de Burgh until his disgrace in 1232. Hubert de Burgh may not have known of his wife's activities and the discovery of the arrangement in 1236 reignited tensions between the king and his former justiciar, who was attempting to regain the king's trust. The discovery of the marriage was a devastating blow to de Burgh; he had lost the king's confidence completely and retired from public life. The death of Megotta in 1237 was a further blow but did not ease the tensions with the king. Hubert de Burgh and Margaret were finally pardoned for the marriage in October 1239, de Burgh surrendering his three castles in Upper Gwent and Hadleigh Castle in Essex as part of the agreement.[32] De Burgh did not return to office, despite the pardon, and remained in retirement until his death. He died at his Surrey manor of Banstead in May 1243 and was buried at the Blackfriars in London, a monastery of which he was a benefactor.[33]

Margaret succeeded to those lands which they had held jointly and remained in possession of them until her own death in the autumn of 1259, at a considerable age, possibly even over 70. She was buried at Blackfriars in London, just like her husband, many miles from Scotland, the land that she had left fifty years before. It is a strange twist of fate that three Scottish princesses, the daughters of William the Lion, King of Scots, found their resting place together at Blackfriars in London, rather than their native land. Margaret's younger sister, Marjorie, had also been buried there after her death in 1244. Her sister and fellow hostage, Isabella, would also be laid to rest at Blackfriars on her own death in 1270

Isabella of Scotland

Isabella had come south as a hostage with her older sister, Margaret, in 1209. In the treaty of Norham, King John had agreed to arrange the marriage of Isabella to an English nobleman of rank, possibly even his second son, Richard, who was only a baby at the time. Isabella's date and year of birth is unknown; she was older than her brother, Alexander, who was born in 1198, but may have been born any time in the ten years before. She is not mentioned in the succession crisis of 1195, but that does not mean that she was born after, just that, being the younger daughter, she was not a subject of discussions. Jessica Nelson, in her article for the Oxford Dictionary of National Biography, suggests that Isabella was born in 1195 or 1196.[34] When the sisters were brought south, they were housed comfortably, as evidence demonstrates. Payments for their upkeep were recorded by sheriffs and the king's own wardrobe, which suggests the two princesses spent some time at court.[35] In 1213 Isabella was residing at Corfe Castle in the household of John's queen, Isabelle d'Angoulême; John's niece, Eleanor of Brittany, held captive since the failed rebellion of her brother, Arthur of Brittany in 1202, was also there.

Despite the fact that John had agreed to arrange the marriages of both Margaret and Isabella, no move had been made to find suitable husbands for the princesses before the king's death in October 1216. As the younger sister, Isabella could not expect to be wed before Margaret, but the fact that Margaret's wedding was still not on the horizon meant that Isabella's was even further in the future. In June 1220, at a meeting of King Henry III's minority council, it was agreed that Margaret and Isabella would be married by October 1221 or allowed to return to Scotland. In the event, Margaret was married to Hubert de Burgh on 3 October 1221; a controversial marriage given the disparity in rank between the Scottish princess and her self-made husband. Isabella, however, remained unmarried and returned to Scotland in November 1222. Isabella's own marriage prospects may have been damaged by the relatively lowly marriage of her older sister. Nevertheless, Alexander II was keen to look after his sister's interests and continued to search for a suitable husband. A letter from Henry III alludes to a possible match between Isabella and William (II) Marshal, Earl of Pembroke but the earl was, instead, married to the king's own younger sister, Eleanor.[36]

Isabella's future was finally settled in June 1225, when she married Roger Bigod, fourth Earl of Norfolk, at Alnwick in Northumberland. On 20 May, the archbishop of York was given respite from his debts in order to attend the wedding of the King of Scots' sister:

> Order to the barons of the Exchequer to place in respite, until 15 days from Michaelmas in the ninth year, the demand for debts they make by summons of the Exchequer from W. archbishop of York, because the archbishop has set out for Alnwick where he is to be present to celebrate the marriage between Roger, son and heir of Earl H. Bigod, and Isabella, sister of the King of Scots.[37]

Roger was the young son of Hugh Bigod, Earl of Norfolk, who had died earlier in the year, and Matilda Marshal, eldest daughter of William Marshal, Earl of Pembroke. Roger was still a minor, aged about 13, and possibly as much as seventeen years his wife's junior. In 1224 King Alexander II had levied an aid of 10,000 marks towards the costs of his sisters' marriages, as well as contributing £1,000 towards Henry III's 1225 expedition to Gascony, suggesting the Scots king was eager to see both his sisters comfortably settled.[38] At the time of the marriage, Roger's wardship was in the hands of Henry III's uncle, William Longespée, Earl of Salisbury, but it was transferred to King Alexander II in 1226, after Longespée's death. Now in the custody of the king of Scots, Roger and Isabella moved to Scotland, living at the Scottish court until Roger attained his majority in 1233 and entered into his inheritance.

Roger Bigod was knighted by Henry III in the same year and took his place at Henry's court. He was friendly with his uncle, Gilbert Marshal, Earl of Pembroke, who became Roger's brother-in-law when he married Isabella and Margaret's much youngest sister, Marjorie, in 1235 at Berwick; 'with the [English] king's good will and licence ... and the marriage is well pleasing to the king.'[39] Her given name was Margaret, but she was called Marjorie to distinguish her from her older sister with the same name; she was born around 1200. In 1227 Richard of Cornwall, Henry III's younger brother, had considered Marjorie as a possible bride and had even travelled to Scotland to speak with Queen Ermengarde about the match. However, neither the Scottish court nor King Henry were keen on the union and negotiations were abandoned. Unfortunately, Marjorie and Gilbert Marshal remained childless and the earl died in 1241. The friendship of their husbands suggests that Isabella and Marjorie were also able to spend time in each other's company.

Isabella appears to have remained in the shadows for much of her life. Her marriage to Roger was not the happiest of unions; the lack of children and the seventeen-year age difference probably causing tensions. In need of an heir, the couple separated, and Roger made numerous, ultimately unsuccessful, attempts to have the marriage annulled on the grounds of consanguinity, as they were closely related by blood. Roger even visited Rome to plead his case, but the final decision went against him and in 1253 he was ordered to return to his wife. The chronicler Matthew Paris noted that Roger accepted the judgement with good grace, blaming his attempts to repudiate Isabella on 'evil counsel'.[40] Roger and Isabella were reconciled and lived together until Isabella's death in 1270. A writ of February 1270 shows that she was still living then, but she had died before Roger's death on 3 or 4 July 1270. Isabella was buried at Blackfriars in London, with her sisters, while Roger was interred at his family's mausoleum at Thetford in Norfolk. Their hearts were buried together in the parish church at Framlingham, the Bigod family seat.[41]

It is interesting to note that while only two of the three sisters were hostages of the English crown following the treaty of Norham, all three of them were married to notable magnates of England. The fact that Margaret, Isabella and Marjorie all chose to be laid to rest in the same religious house, Blackfriars in London, suggests that the sisters, despite their different paths, remained close throughout their lives. The status of Margaret and Isabella, not only as hostages of King John and, later Henry III, but also as a clause in Magna Carta, has meant that their stories have been passed down through history, and serve as an example that, often, princesses had no more power in determining their own lives and freedoms than women of other ranks.

Chapter 8

De Warenne

The Warenne earls of Surrey had been stalwart supporters of the crown since William de Warenne, the first earl, had fought alongside William the Conqueror at the Battle of Hastings. The family held a total of sixty knights' fees in England. They had lands stretching from Lewes in Sussex to Sandal Castle in West Yorkshire, with their main landholdings at Castle Acre in Norfolk; they also had extensive estates in Normandy, including Mortemer and Bellencombre.[1] In January 1148 the third earl had been killed at Laodicea, fighting in the rearguard of France's King Louis VII during the Second Crusade.[2] He left a teenage daughter, Isabel de Warenne, as his sole heir and one of the most prized heiresses in England and Normandy. The earl had been a strong supporter of King Stephen; he fought alongside the king during the Anarchy – Stephen's battles with his cousin, the Empress Matilda, to control England – and supported his wife, Queen Matilda, after King Stephen was captured at Lincoln. This affinity with Stephen's regime helps to explain why, in the same year that her father died, and as part of Stephen's attempts to control the vast Warenne lands, Isabel was married to Stephen's younger son, William of Blois, who became Earl of Surrey, by right of his wife. William, it seems, was a little younger than his Isabel, having been born in 1137. Isabel was probably in her early teens. William was removed from the succession to the crown, by his own father when Stephen made a deal with Empress Matilda's son, Henry of Anjou, that the crown would go to him on Stephen's death.[3]

The agreement, sealed at Winchester in 1153, guaranteed William's position as the foremost magnate in the realm, with the lands from Isabel's earldom and the inheritance of his mother's county of Boulogne. Isabel and William had been married for just over ten years when he died in October 1159, while he was returning home to England after King Henry II's expedition to Toulouse. William was buried at the Abbey of

Montmorel, in Poitou. Their marriage had been childless, and Isabel was again an important heiress, so she had little respite from the marriage market. By 1162 Henry II's youngest brother, William X, Count of Poitou, was seeking a dispensation to marry her. The dispensation was refused by Thomas Becket, Archbishop of Canterbury, on the grounds of consanguinity. The objection was not due to a blood relationship between Isabel and William, but between William and Isabel's first husband, William of Blois, who were second cousins. It has often been suggested that this was a love-match rather than an arranged marriage. We will, of course, never know how Isabel felt but William died shortly afterwards, at Rouen on 30 January 1164, supposedly of a broken heart. One of William's knights, Richard Brito, was among the quartet who murdered Thomas Becket in 1170, and is said to have cried as he struck his blow 'for the love of William, the King's brother'.[4]

Henry II was not to be thwarted, however, in his plan to bring the de Warenne lands into the royal family. His illegitimate half-brother, Hamelin, a son of Henry's father, Geoffrey of Anjou, by an unnamed woman, was married to Isabel in 1164. The couple wed in April; Isabel's trousseau cost an impressive £41 10s 8d.[5] Hamelin became the fourth Earl of Surrey by right of his new wife and, in an unusual step for the time, took his wife's surname, so that he was known as Hamelin de Warenne, rather than Hamelin Plantagenet.

The marriage appears to have been highly successful. Hamelin was loyal to his brother, Henry II, and supported the king during the conflict with his sons in 1173. He was among the nobles chosen to escort Joanna, the king's daughter, to her marriage to William, King of Sicily; the nobles were ordered not to return home until they had seen 'the King of Sicily and Joanna crowned in wedlock'.[6] Hamelin continued his support of the crown when his nephew Richard I succeeded in 1189. He played a prominent part in English politics while Richard was absent on the Third Crusade, supporting the chancellor during the chaos caused by the intrigues of the king's brother, John. He was one of the treasurers for the collection of the king's ransom, and carried one of the three swords at Richard I's second coronation at Winchester on 17 April 1194. He was also present at John's coronation on 27 May 1199. Isabel was widowed for a second time when Hamelin died on 7 May 1202; in the same year, she granted sixty beasts to St Katherine's Priory at Lincoln, for the soul of her husband, 'namely 40 as of his gift and 20 as of hers'.[7] Isabel herself died the following year, possibly in her seventieth year; she was buried in the chapterhouse at Lewes Priory, beside Hamelin.

Isabel and Hamelin had four surviving children. Their son and heir was William, who would become the fifth Earl of Surrey. William was born in the late 1160s and was probably raised in Normandy; five days after his father's death, William was allowed to do homage for his father's estates.[8] He witnessed a charter issued by King Richard I at Rouen in September 1197 and witnessed several of his father's charters in the years before Hamelin's death in 1202. In the first eighteen months after his succession to the earldom, William was in Normandy, playing a major role in the defence of the duchy against King Philip II Augustus of France. When King John lost the majority of his Continental possessions, in 1204, Warenne was refused permission to do homage to King Philip for his Norman lands, despite promising that he would remain loyal to John. In compensation for the loss of his Norman estates, Warenne received Stamford and Grantham in Lincolnshire. In 1206, Warenne served on the king's expedition to Poitou and in the following year took part in the peace negotiations with Scotland. During the build up to the baronial rebellion, Warenne was supportive of his cousin, King John, taking charge of baronial hostages and acting as a guarantor for the terms of peace with the church in order to get the papal interdict lifted.

With the outbreak of civil war Earl Warenne sided with the crown, he negotiated with the rebels at Northampton in May 1215. He was named as one of the Royalists present at the issue of Magna Carta on 15 June in the same year and was at the siege of Rochester in the November. On 26 May 1216, Warenne was given the charge of the Cinque Ports. However, on 6 June the rebel army led by Louis of France was allowed to enter the earl's castle at Reigate unopposed and later in the month, Warenne submitted to Louis at Winchester, alongside his cousin, William Longespée, Earl of Salisbury, and the earl of Arundel. It has been suggested that Warenne defected due to a personal grievance after John seduced one of his sisters in the 1190s, but it seems more likely that the earl had seen the way the wind was blowing and thought King John's cause doomed. Warenne's personal rebellion lasted less than a year. By March 1217 he was taking instructions from the new king, Henry III, over his lands at Stamford and on 17 April, at Chichester, he was reconciled with the Royalists, after a truce was negotiated by Guala, the papal legate.[9] On 17 June, eager to safeguard his interests in France, Warenne sent formal letters to Louis to notify the French prince of his decision to return to the Royalists.

William de Warenne had three sisters, Ela, Isabel and Matilda; however, it is possible Matilda was Hamelin's illegitimate daughter by an unknown woman. Ela married twice, firstly to a Robert de Newburn, of whom nothing else is known, and secondly to William Fitzwilliam of Sprotborough, a village just a few miles from the Warenne stronghold of Conisbrough Castle, Yorkshire. After she was widowed for the second time, Ela issued a charter mentioning both of her husbands by name, and all of her children. In this charter, Ela granted to Roche Abbey, just a few miles south of Conisbrough, 'five virgates of land in Rottingdean [Sussex], together with three villeins and their sequels'. Her gift was confirmed by her brother after her death.[10]

A second sister, Isabel, was given land in Sowerby and Sowerbyshire, Yorkshire, in frank-marriage, by her father, Hamelin. Isabel married, firstly, to Robert de Lascy, who died in 1193; after his death, Isabel rendered account at Michaelmas 1194 of 80 marks for her reasonable dower from his land. Payment was completed at Michaelmas 1196.[11] Isabel was married for a second time, to Gilbert de Laigle, Lord of Pevensey, no later than the spring of 1196. In 1200 she was involved in a dispute with Roger de Lascy, constable of Chester and lord of Pontefract, cousin of Isabel's first husband, Robert. Isabel complained that Lascy had disseised her of part of her dower from her first marriage, whereas Lascy claimed that Isabel's dower was excessive. In 1201, Gilbert de Laigle stated that Isabel had been married in another county in the time of Robert de Lascy's father, Henry de Lascy, and that Robert had dowered Isabel with a third of his prospective inheritance and that, after his father's death in 1177 or 1178, Robert had assigned Isabel's dower in a third of 100 librates of land. Roger de Lascy stated that she was dowered in specified lands and the service of five knights' fees.[12] I was unable to discover the final outcome of the legal proceedings. However, it seems that the two families resolved their disagreement with a marriage between Roger's son, John de Lacy, and Alice de Laigle, the daughter of

Gilbert, in 1214. Isabel also held the manor of Northease in the rape of Lewes from her brother, William, and, as a widow after the death of her second husband, she gave a third of it to Michelham priory, which she had founded with Gilbert de Laigle in 1229; the priory later held the same land from earl Warenne, who, as Isabel's brother, was also her heir.

Earl Warenne looked out for his sisters and when the king confiscated the vills of Westcott and Witley from Gilbert de Laigle when he joined the French after 1204, the earl made a fine on his sister's behalf, as Gilbert's wife, for these vills; Westcott was, in fact, part of Isabel's dower. In 1207 the earl paid 3,000 marks, in instalments, for Gilbert's entire estate, for the use of his sister.[13] Gilbert died shortly before 19 December 1231 and in January 1232 his lands were assessed in Sussex, Surrey and Southampton, in order that a reasonable dower could be assigned to Isabel, who died sometime before 30 November 1234, leaving no children by either marriage and naming her brother, William, as her heir.[14]

One of the sisters of William, fifth Earl Warenne – although it is not clear which – bore an illegitimate son, Richard Fitzroy (also known as Richard de Chilham or Richard of Dover), by her cousin, John (the future King John). Richard was feudal baron of Chilham in Kent and was appointed constable of Wallingford Castle during the baronial revolt. In 1217 he took part in the naval battle off Sandwich that finally put an end to Louis of France's hopes to take the English throne. When William de Warenne, fifth Earl of Surrey, joined the baronial revolt in 1215, it was suggested that he had turned against John because of his earlier seduction of the earl's sister, which resulted in the birth of Richard Fitzroy. However, Richard had been born around 1190, some twenty-five years before Magna Carta, so either William de Warenne liked to hold grudges, or he joined the revolt for other reasons. Various attempts have been made to identify which of the Warenne sisters was Fitzroy's mother, all to no avail. There are few clues, though one is an entry in the *Annales Cestriensis*, or Chester Annals, which has an entry for 1200 stating, 'W. de Warren, the mother of the king's son [Richard] is killed.'[15] However, this may be a misleading, false report, as none of William de Warenne's sisters died in 1200, and none of them had a name beginning with 'W'. The mystery deepens.

Alice de Lusignan

William's third sister, Matilda or Maud, married Henry, Count of Eu and Lord of Hastings, who died around 1190. She then married Henry d'Estouteville, a Norman lord. Matilda had at least one son by Henry d'Estouteville, John, who would be his mother's heir and inherit the lands she held in her own right. It is the story of Matilda's daughter by her first marriage, however, that deserves to be told here. Matilda de Warenne and Henry, Count of Eu and Lord of Hastings, had four children, two sons and two daughters. Alice was the eldest of the daughters, her sister Jeanne being younger. Sadly, both sons, Raoul and Guy, died young and in consecutive years, with Guy dying in 1185 and Raoul in 1186, leaving Alice as heir to her father's lands.[16] Very little is known of Alice's early years; we do not even have a year for her birth. Given that her grandparents did not marry until 1164, her parents would not have married until the early 1180s, which would mean it is likely that Alice was born sometime around the mid-1180s. On her father's death in 1191, she came into possession of lands in both England and Normandy, France and became *suo jure* Countess of Eu and Lady Hastings.

As Alice's mother, Matilda, had married again to Henry d'Estouteville of Eckington, Lord of Valmont and Rames in Normandy, and had a son, John, by d'Estouteville, it was John, Alice's half-brother, therefore, who became the heir to all the Warenne lands Matilda held in her own right. This left Alice solely with the inheritance from her father. The struggle to obtain and hold on to this inheritance would be the driving force in Alice's adult life. Her mother's brother William de Warenne actively supported his niece in her fight to retain her paternal inheritance. In August 1209, Alice officially received the Comté of Eu from Philip II Augustus, King of France, when she also made a quitclaim of all rights to Neufchatel, Mortemer and Arques. Mortemer was a part of the de Warenne ancestral lands in Normandy, given to William I de Warenne by William the Conqueror; suggesting that Alice was renouncing her own rights to the French de Warenne lands, as a granddaughter of Isabel de Warenne, Countess of Surrey.[17]

Alice had been born into two of the noblest families of England and France, and married into a third. The daughter of Henry, Count of Eu and Lord Hastings, and Matilda, daughter of Hamelin and Isabel de

Warenne, Earl and Countess of Surrey, made a prestigious marriage to Raoul de Lusignan, the second son of Hugh de Lusignan, a powerful Poitevin lord. It was Raoul's brother, Hugh IX, who was the intended husband of Isabelle d'Angoulême, until King John married her instead. Raoul had been previously married to Marguerite de Courtney, but the marriage had been annulled by 1213, suggesting Alice and Raoul married around that time. On marrying Alice, Raoul became Raoul I, Count of Eu in right of his wife.

Raoul and Alice had two children together; a son, Raoul and a daughter, Mathilde. Raoul II de Lusignan, Count of Eu and Guînes, was married three times and had one daughter, Marie de Lusignan, by his second wife, Yolande de Dreux. Raoul died sometime between 1245 and 1250 and was buried at the Abbey of Foucarmont. Mathilde married Humphrey de Bohun, second Earl of Hereford and Earl of Essex, and they had seven children together, including four boys. Mathilde died in August 1241 and was buried in Llanthony Secunda Priory, Gloucester. Her husband was buried beside her when he died in September 1275.

In 1139, the Honour of Tickhill in Yorkshire had been granted to Alice's grandfather John, Count of Eu, by King Stephen after John proved his rights as heir to the original owners, the de Busli family, through Beatrice, the sister of Roger de Busli, who died in 1102.[18] However, in 1141, Empress Matilda captured the castle after Count John was taken prisoner at the Battle of Lincoln. The castle was not returned to Count John's son, Henry, and seems to have stayed in royal hands for many years afterwards, with Richard I taking possession on his accession; he then gave it to his brother John, as part of his holdings. As a consequence, the castle was besieged by the bishop of Durham when John rebelled against Richard in 1194; it was surrendered only when the king returned to England following his capture and imprisonment in Germany, three years after Henry of Eu's death.

In 1214 Alice, as Countess of Eu, was restored to the Honour of Tickhill by King John, as part of the conditions of an agreement with her husband's family, the de Lusignans. However, Robert de Vieuxpont, who was in physical possession of the castle, refused to relinquish it, and claimed the castle in his own right. Alice appears in an entry dated 19 May 1221 in the Fine Rolls of Henry III in 1221 concerning Tickhill: 'Order to the sheriff of Nottinghamshire to place in respite the demand that he makes from the men of the countess of Eu of the honour of Tickhill for suits of wapentake, amercements and defaults, until the king's first arrival in those parts. Witness H. etc. By the same.'[19] It took many years and much litigation before Alice finally took possession of Tickhill Castle in 1222.

Her husband, Raoul died on 1 May 1219 and was succeeded as Count of Eu by their son, Raoul II, still only a child. It was left to Alice, now dowager countess, to administer the Eu inheritance. She paid 15,000 silver marks to the French King to receive the county of Eu in her own name and regained control of her English lands, entrusted to her uncle, the earl of Surrey, as her representative, following her husband's death.[20]

Alice was a shrewd political survivor and may well have used the clauses of Magna Carta, which safeguarded the lands of widows, to press her case for the restoration of Tickhill. However, with lands in France and England, two countries often at war, she found herself caught between a rock and a hard place. In 1225 she handed Tickhill Castle to Henry III, until the end of hostilities with France, as a means of safeguarding her lands. Nevertheless, this did not save her when she was ordered to levy troops for the French king, Louis IX, as Countess of Eu, and send her forces to fight for him. As a consequence, Henry III seized Tickhill Castle, although it was only permanently attached to the English crown after Alice's death.

Alice was renowned for her wide patronage, both secular and religious, and has left numerous charters as testament. She was a benefactor of both French and English religious houses, including Battle Abbey and Christ Church, Canterbury in England and Eu and Foucarmont – where her son would be laid to rest – in France. Alice issued a charter in 1219, to Roche Abbey, which was witnessed by her uncle William, Earl de Warenne. She also granted an annual allowance to Loretta de Braose, Countess of Leicester, who was living as a recluse at Hackington. Alice also granted several lands to others, such as Greetwell in the county of Lincoln, which had previously been held by Walter de Tylly in Alice's name and was given to Earl de Warenne in August 1225; the earl was to annually render a sparrowhawk to Philippa de Tylly in payment.[21] In 1232 Alice issued a charter to Malvesin de Hersy, of Osberton in the county of

Nottingham, providing him with all customs due to Tickhill in return for two knights' fees. Malvesin had been constable of Tickhill in 1220–1 and his brother Sir Baldwin de Hersy was constable of Conisbrough Castle, seat of earl de Warenne.

Having spent most of her life fighting for her rights to her lands in England and France, caught between two great nations whose relations were acrimonious to say the least, Alice appears to have conducted herself admirably. Her connections to the powerful de Lusignan and de Warenne families could not have harmed her situation. Having been a widow for almost thirty years, Alice died sometime in May 1246, aged in her sixties, probably between the 13th and 15th, at La Mothe St Héray in Poitou, France, leaving a will. It seems likely that she was buried at her husband's foundation of Fontblanche Priory in Exoudon.[22]

Alice's uncle, William de Warenne, fifth Earl of Surrey, served in the administration of the minority government of Henry III throughout the 1220s. He had been appointed sheriff of Surrey in 1218 and remained in that post until November 1226. In 1220 he took part in the negotiations with both the French and the Scots. In the spring of 1223 Warenne went on pilgrimage to Santiago de Compostela in Spain but was back in England in time to join the campaign against Montgomery, providing the king's army with twenty knights and being a witness to the terms of the truce with the Welsh.[23] The earl was a staunch ally of the justiciar, Hubert de Burgh, who had been married to his cousin Beatrice de Warenne, the daughter and heir of William de Warenne of Wormegay. He supported de Burgh in 1223–4, when the justiciar's position was threatened by rivals at court.

In 1227 Warenne briefly joined the confederation against the king, led by Henry III's brother Richard of Cornwall, after having been replaced as sheriff of Surrey and forced to surrender the castle of Hornby, which he had been granted a couple of years earlier, to its rightful heir. The disaffected barons, including the earls of Pembroke and Chester, met at Warenne's manor of Stamford to confirm their accord. Warenne was forced to surrender custody of Tickhill in the aftermath but was confirmed in his manors of Stamford and Grantham in 1228, his fall from grace having been soon forgiven, if not forgotten.

Warenne continued to be a part of the royal administration throughout the 1230s, serving as cup-bearer at the coronation of Henry III's queen,

Eleanor of Provence, in 1236 and in 1237 he was one of the few surviving barons who had witnessed the original 1215 Magna Carta to witness the charter's reissue. Warenne was also drawn into the downfall of his former patron, Hubert de Burgh, when he was imprisoned in 1232. De Warenne was one of the four earls tasked with keeping de Burgh in custody at Devizes Castle and when de Burgh's enemies themselves fell in 1234, Warenne was the earl to accept the surrender of de Burgh's castles at Bramber and Knepp, which had been taken by the former justiciar's enemies.[24]

William de Warenne was married twice. He was first married to Matilda, daughter of William d'Aubigny, Earl of Arundel, sometime before 1207. The marriage remained childless and Matilda died, possibly on 6 February 1215; she was buried at the Warenne foundation of Lewes Priory in Sussex.[25] Warenne married for a second time, before 13 October 1225, Matilda, widow of Hugh Bigod, Earl of Norfolk, and eldest daughter of the great William Marshal, Earl of Pembroke and regent of England during the minority of Henry III. The marriage appears to have been one of convenience, rather than genuine affection, Warenne being considerably older than his new wife. Warenne died in London on 27 or 28 May 1240, in his early seventies, and was buried before the high altar of Lewes Priory. The king, who referred to Warenne as his 'beloved and faithful Earl Warenne' ordered that a cross should be erected to his memory, on the road between Merton and Carshalton in Surrey.[26] Matilda died in March 1248 and was buried with her mother at Tintern Abbey. The couple had two children together. A son and heir, John, was born in 1231 and was a prominent magnate and military commander in the reigns of Henry III and Edward I. John also had an older sister, Isabel, who was born sometime between 1226 and 1230.

Isabel d'Aubigny

Isabel was a strong character who was not afraid to fight for her rights against the highest in the land. With her impeccable parentage and family connections, it is no surprise that she made a suitably prestigious marriage. At no older than 8 years of age Isabel was married, in 1234, to 20-year-old Hugh d'Aubigny, fifth Earl of Arundel. Hugh's father,

William, third Earl of Arundel, had died in 1221 on his way home from the Fifth Crusade. William had been succeeded as fourth earl by his oldest son and namesake, who died three years after his father, aged just 21, leaving the earldom to his brother Hugh.[27]

On their marriage, Isabel's father granted the couple a manor at Marham in Norfolk, worth £40 a year in rent. The charter for this grant offers the only details available for the marriage. In 1242 Hugh accompanied the king on his expedition to Aquitaine. However, after just nine years of marriage, on 7 May 1243, Hugh died, leaving Isabel, at 17 years of age, a childless widow, with a rather large dower. Within weeks of her husband's death, on 29 May, Isabel's marriage was granted to Pierre de Genevre, a Savoyard favourite of the king, Henry III. However, the Patent Rolls show that provision was made for Isabel to remain unmarried should she so wish, a right guaranteed her by clause 8 of Magna Carta; although she would have to pay Pierre for the privilege. Given that she never remarried, she must have been more than happy to pay.[28]

The Arundel inheritance was divided between Hugh's four sisters: Mabel, Isabel, Nicholaa and Cecily. The earldom itself went to Hugh's nephew, his sister Isabel's son, John FitzAlan. As the earl's widow, Isabel was well provided for, with her dower including the hundred and manor of Bourne in Lincolnshire, the manors of Wymondham and Kenninghall in Norfolk, Stansted in Essex and several properties in Norfolk and Buckinghamshire. Suffice to say, she was a very wealthy widow and would continue to be styled Countess of Arundel until her death.

In 1249, a year after her mother died, Isabel founded the only English convent that was part of the Cistercian order. Established at Marham, two Cistercian abbots had inspected it in its first year. Isabel's brother, John de Warenne, sixth Earl of Surrey, the bishop of Norwich and Henry III himself all issued charters confirming the abbey's foundation. Along with other endowments, Isabel herself made eleven grants to the abbey in its early years, giving it a strong economic foundation. In 1252 Isabel was granted papal permission to visit the Cistercian house at Waverley to consult with the abbot about her convent; Waverley's annals record that she granted 4 marks and a cask of wine to the monks there.

Isabel was very protective of her property rights and went on the offensive when they were threatened, even if that meant going against the king. In 1252 she did just that. One of her tenants, Thomas of Ingoldisthorpe, held a quarter knight's fee from Isabel at Fring and Snettisham; he also had property in the honour of Haughley, as an escheat from the crown. On his death in 1252 Henry III took all of Thomas's lands in wardship until Thomas's heir was of age, including Isabel's quarter knights' fee. In March of 1252 Henry granted the wardship of the lands and marriage of the heir to his former treasurer and keeper of the king's wardrobe, Peter Chaceporc. Had Thomas held his lands in chief from the king, Henry would have been within his rights to take prerogative wardship. However his land at Haughley was held from the honour of Haughley, which was in the king's hands as an escheat and Isabel was treated unjustly in being denied the wardship of his heirs.

Isabel took her grievances direct to the king, in an audience she is said to have berated Henry III for trampling on the rights laid out in Magna Carta. She is said to have asked, 'Where are the liberties of England, so often recorded, so often granted, and so often ransomed?'[29] According to Matthew Paris, the chronicler and a personal friend of Isabel's (though no particular fan of Henry), Henry scorned Isabel's argument, 'derisively and curling his nostrils' and asked if the nobles of the realm had given her permission to speak on their behalf.[30] Isabel argued that the king had given her the right to speak thus in the articles granted in Magna Carta and accused the king of being a 'shameless transgressor' of the liberties laid down in the Great Charter, breaking his sworn oath to uphold its principles. At the end of the audience, Henry refused to be moved. 'After listening to her [civilly] reproachful speech, the king was silent, and the countess, without obtaining or even asking for permission, returned home.'[31]

Isabel was one of the great nobles of England, the daughter of one earl and wife of another, and was obviously undaunted by an audience with the king. Although the king did not react to her reprimand immediately he did, eventually, admit that he may have been in the wrong, issuing a letter to her on 23 May 1253 saying:

Since the king has learnt that Thomas of Ingoldisthorpe, whose son and heir is in the custody of Peter Chaceporc by concession of the king, did not hold from the crown of the king in chief but from the honour of Haughley, which is in the hand of the king as his escheat, and that the same Thomas held from Hugh de Aubigny, once earl of Arundel, a quarter part of the fee of one knight with appurtenances in Fring and Snettisham and the service of which was assigned to Isabella, countess of Arundel, the widow of the foresaid earl, in dower, he has returned to the same countess custody of the foresaid quarter part of a fee with appurtenances; and the foresaid Peter is ordered to give the countess full seizin of the foresaid custody.[32]

Isabel's victory was incomplete, however, as in late 1253, while the king was overseas in Aquitaine, she instigated legal proceedings against Peter Chaceporc 'for custody of Ingoldisthorpe'. Whether Chaceporc had not relinquished the land, or she believed she was entitled to more land than was returned to her, we do not know. Isabel in fact lost the suit and was amerced £20 (30 marks) for a false claim. The writ was witnessed by Henry III's queen, Eleanor of Provence, and his brother Richard, Earl of Cornwall. As persistent as ever, and although he was overseas, Isabel appealed directly to the king, who responded with a pardon, although it seems he still smarted from the upbraiding she had given him earlier in the year:

> 3 April. Meilham. Henry, by the grace of God king of England, lord of Ireland, duke of Normandy and Aquitaine and count of Anjou sends greeting to his beloved consort E, by the same grace queen of England, lady of Ireland, duchess of Normandy and Aquitaine and countess of Anjou and to his beloved and faithful brother, R. earl of Cornwall. Know that we have pardoned our beloved and faithful Isabella countess of Arundel the 30m. at which she was amerced before our justices against our beloved and faithful … Peter Chaceporc, our Treasurer, for custody of Ingoldisthorpe. We, therefore, order you to cause the same countess to be quit of the aforesaid 30m. by our seal of England provided she says nothing opprobrious to us as she did when we were at Westminster and as we have signified to her by letter. Witness myself.[33]

Isabel obviously had an eye for business, given that she could so concern herself with a quarter knight's fee out of the sixty that she held. A wealthy widow with impressive family connections, she was renowned not only for her religious endowment of the Cistercian convent at Marham, but also as a patron of religious texts, having commissioned at least two saints' lives, including the life of St Richard of Wyche by Ralph Bocking. Isabel could count among her friends Richard Wych himself, the bishop of Chichester who was later canonised, and Matthew Paris. Paris translated a life of Saint Edmund of Abingdon into Anglo-Norman verse for Isabel's personal use.

Isabel died shortly before 23 November 1282 and was laid to rest at her own foundation at Marham; her dower properties passed to her husband's great-great nephew, Richard FitzAlan, eighth Earl of Arundel. Having spent almost forty years as a childless widow, Isabel never remarried, her remarkable life was dedicated to the patronage of her convent at Marham and religious writers, such as Paris and Bocking. This incredible woman stands out as the countess who reprimanded and humbled her king for his injustices, using Magna Carta to its greatest effect.

It is notable that not one but two of the granddaughters of Isabel and Hamelin de Warenne used the clauses of Magna Carta to assert their rights, as widows, over their inheritances. The Warenne family had been at the heart of royal administration since the time of Henry II but were not afraid to bring the crown to task when it abused its powers, especially when touching their own rights, and particularly when touching the rights of the Warenne women.

Chapter 9

Isabella of Gloucester

Isabella of Gloucester is a unique individual in the story of Magna Carta. She is a shadow in the pages of history, and yet she held one of the greatest earldoms in England. There are no pictures of her, not even a description of her personality or appearance. At one time, no one even seemed certain of her name; she has been called Isabel, Isabella, Hawise, Avice – but Isabella is how she appears in the Close Rolls.[1] Isabella was the youngest daughter and co-heiress of William, second Earl of Gloucester, who was himself the son of Robert of Gloucester, an illegitimate son of King Henry I. Earl William's wife was Hawise, the daughter of Robert de Beaumont, third Earl of Leicester. Isabella's only brother Robert had died in 1166, making Isabella and her two sisters co-heiresses to the earldom of Gloucester. Although her date of birth has been lost to history, it seems likely she was born in the early 1160s.

We know very little of Isabella's childhood, although, considering her social status, as the daughter of one of England's wealthiest earls, it is likely that she was given the education expected of a high-ranking noblewoman and taught to run a large household, as well as the social graces of singing, dancing and needlework. Her parents' marriage appears to have been a successful one. Isabella's mother, Countess Hawise, was a regular witness to her husband's charters and was mentioned in several of them, especially in the *pro amina* clauses of grants made to religious houses that sought spiritual benefits for those named.[2] Isabella's father had a complicated relationship with King Henry II, especially after the king had taken Bristol Castle from the earl; the castle had been held by William's father before him. Despite remaining loyal to Henry II during the rebellion of the king's sons in 1173–74 and agreeing to the marriage of his youngest daughter to Prince John, Earl William's loyalty remained suspect and he was arrested and imprisoned in 1183. The earl died whilst still a captive, on 23 November 1183.[3]

Isabella was betrothed, in 1176, to Prince John, the youngest son of Henry II and Eleanor of Aquitaine. John was 9 years old at the time of the betrothal, with Isabella probably a few years older. Under the terms of the marriage agreement, Earl William recognised John as heir to the earldom of Gloucester.[4] The marriage was to be a way for Henry II to provide for his youngest son. After the Earl of Gloucester's death in 1183, his entire estate was passed to Isabella, who had been made a ward of the king. Isabella's older sisters were both already married; Mabel was the wife of Amaury of Évreux and Amicia was married to the earl of Hertford. On their father's death they had both been explicitly excluded from the estate to prevent the division of the comital inheritance and they received annuities of £100 each in compensation.[5] Henry II therefore seized all the Gloucester lands, took Isabella into wardship and made the income available for John's use, as her future husband. The king, however, kept his options open and had not finalised John's marriage to Isabella by the time of his death, in case a more suitable alliance came along. King Richard I, on the other hand, thought it expedient to get his brother safely married, on his own accession to the throne in 1189.

The wedding took place at Marlborough Castle in Wiltshire on 29 August 1189; John was 21 and Isabella may have been approaching 30.[6] Baldwin, the archbishop of Canterbury at the time, opposed the marriage as the couple were related within the third degree of consanguinity; they were second cousins, both being great-grandchildren of Henry I. Canon law forbade marriage within seven degrees of consanguinity. When arranging the marriage with Earl William King Henry had agreed that, if the pope opposed the match on these grounds, he would arrange another suitable match for Isabella. The wedding, however, went ahead, despite the archbishop's objections. The archbishop summoned John to appear before him, placing an interdict on John's lands when he ignored the summons.[7] This was removed after the intervention of the papal legate, Giovanni di Anagni, and John promised to seek a papal dispensation to overcome Baldwin's objections, although it appears this was never obtained.

Although Isabella and John were married for ten years, their marriage was neither happy nor successful. They spent some time together in the first years of their marriage as they issued charters together during a visit to Normandy around 1190–91.[8] However, they appear to have spent less and less time together as the years went on. They never had any children and it is during this time in his life that John's illegitimate children were born, a further suggestion that the couple were not close. In 1193, as part of his plotting with Philip Augustus, John promised to marry his half-sister, Alice, who had previously been betrothed to John's own brother, Richard. Nothing eventually came of the marriage proposal, but it was an implicit rejection of Isabella as his wife.

John succeeded to the throne on the death of his older brother Richard the Lionheart, on 6 April 1199. He was crowned, alone, on 27 May 1199; the fact that Isabella was not crowned with him suggests that John was already looking for a way out of the marriage. Isabella would never be styled 'queen' and it was possibly as early as August 1199, but certainly by 1200, that John obtained a divorce on the grounds of consanguinity, the very objection for which he was supposed to have obtained a dispensation when he married Isabella in 1189. The bishops of Lisieux, Bayeux and Avranches, sitting in Normandy, provided the required judgement. One chronicler said of John that 'seized by hope of a more elevated marriage, he acted on wicked counsel and rejected his wife.'[9]

Keen to keep his hold on the substantial Gloucester lands, John took Isabella into wardship, again, holding her in 'honourable confinement' for the next fourteen years. Little is known of her day-to-day life, although she does appear to have remained on civil terms with King John. John met the expenses of Isabella's household and staff and sent her numerous gifts, including wine and cloth. Things may well have been a little awkward at times, however. When John remarried in 1200 to Isabelle d'Angoulême, he appears to have housed his new wife with his ex-wife. Queen Isabelle was still very young, probably no more than 12 years old on her marriage and was placed in Isabella of Gloucester's household at Winchester, until the birth of her first child, Henry, in 1207.[10] Isabella of Gloucester was maintained in her own household at the cost of £80 a year but was moved to Sherborne before the queen gave birth and her allowance was reduced to £50 a year.[11]

The title of earl of Gloucester, and a small portion of the estates, were conferred on Amaury, Count of Évreux, Isabella's nephew by her oldest sister, Mabel, in compensation for John's surrender of Évreux to France in the treaty of Le Goulet in 1200.[12] In 1213, however, Amaury died childless and Isabella was once again heir to the earldom of Gloucester. In anticipation of her death, possibly after succumbing to an illness, Isabella made a will in that same year, disposing of all her movable goods, confirmed by King John at Bristol on 14 March. However, she was still among the living in 1214, when this second wardship ended and Isabella was finally allowed to remarry. This new marriage, arranged for her by John, was to a man who was more than sixteen years her junior. In 1214 she was married to Geoffrey de Mandeville, Earl of Essex, who had paid the considerable sum of 20,000 marks to become her second husband and earl of Gloucester *jure uxoris* (by right of his wife). The new earl was granted all the Gloucester estates, save for the valuable manor of Bristol, which was retained by the crown. King John issued letters patent on 28 January 1214, informing all the knights and tenants of the honour of Gloucester that 'we have given Isabella, countess of Gloucester, our kinswoman' in marriage to Geoffrey de Mandeville, Earl of Essex.[13]

Geoffrey de Mandeville was the son and heir of Geoffrey Fitz Peter, Earl of Essex, a long-serving justiciar to King John and King Richard I before him. Geoffrey's mother was Beatrice, daughter of William de Say and heiress to the Mandeville earls of Essex. Beatrice's children styled themselves 'Mandeville' to emphasise their family's ancestral connections.[14] Geoffrey's first marriage had been to Maud, daughter of Robert Fitzwalter, an important Essex landowner who was one of the leaders of the baronial rebellion against King John. There is a story in the *Histoire des ducs de Normandie* which tells of Fitzwalter jumping to the defence of his son-in-law when Geoffrey de Mandeville was accused of killing a manservant in an argument over lodgings at court. John had threatened to hang de Mandeville. Fitzwalter threatened the king: 'By God's body, you will not hang my son-in-law, you'll see two hundred lanced knights in your land before you hang him!'[15] According to the chronicle, when the case went to trial, Fitzwalter did, indeed, appear in court with 200 knights and de Mandeville escaped execution. Maud later died without issue and was buried at Dunmow Priory in Essex.

Geoffrey's marriage to Isabella was politically motivated and driven by John as a means of raising cash. Indeed, given the age difference, it is possible that Mandeville was a most reluctant groom, but it did not pay to upset one's monarch, especially when it was King John. Mandeville was to pay the 20,000 marks in four instalments of 5,000 marks throughout 1214, the final payment to be made at Michaelmas 1214.[16] The initial payment had been set to be made before John left for Poitou in February 1214. The earl failed to meet even this first deadline and John ordered his sheriffs to initiate the confiscation of the Gloucester estates. By August, Geoffrey de Mandeville had made some headway on the debt and John restored Gloucester, the heartland of Isabella's earldom, to the couple and offered to renegotiate de Mandeville's debt. The marriage appears to have been of little benefit to Geoffrey de Mandeville; now in her late forties or early fifties Isabella was past childbearing age and unable to give de Mandeville an heir. Moreover, although he could enjoy the benefits of the income from her vast Gloucester estates, amounting to 800 marks a year, Isabella's lands and earldom would pass to her heirs, the de Clare earls of Hertford on her death. It seems likely that de Mandeville acquiesced to the marriage having made a bargain with the king, to protect his own lands from rival claimants of the de Say family; indeed, the de Say claims were thrown out of court shortly after King John had set sail for Poitou.[17]

Despite their financial woes, the new earl and countess of Gloucester appear to have had a contented marriage. Isabella regularly issued charters jointly with her husband; she had her own seal which depicted a standing female figure, dressed in a long, flowing gown, girded at the waist. In the seal, the countess is facing forwards, with a bird in her left hand and a flower in the right hand. In the legend on the seal, she is styled as she was when married to John; 'Isabella, countess of Gloucester and Mortain.'[18] The earl and countess of Gloucester's financial burdens, imposed on them by King John, and Geoffrey de Mandeville's connections to one of the leading rebels, Robert Fitzwalter, however, serve to explain why the couple joined the growing baronial rebellion. Another explanation may be gleaned from the rumours mentioned by chroniclers, that his first wife, Robert Fitzwalter's daughter, Maud, had been the victim of the unwanted sexual advances of King John.[19] Whatever the reason, in June 1215, Geoffrey de Mandeville was named among the list of the Twenty-Five, the barons appointed to enforce the terms of Magna Carta (see Appendix B), alongside his former father-in-law. Joining the rebellion, however, had cost de Mandeville his lands, which were declared forfeit and on 20 December 1215. King John granted them to Savary de Mauleon:

> The King to all knights, free men, and all others who held of Geoffrey de Mandeville the lands which came to him from his father and his mother, greetings. Know that we have given to our trusty and well-beloved Savary de Mauleon all the lands and tenements which were the aforesaid Geoffrey de Mandeville's by his patrimony from his father and his mother, excepting the land of William de Mandeville his brother, which he held and which he obtained from the same patrimonies. We therefore command that you do heed and obey the said Savary as your lord in all things. And in testimony hereof we send you etc. ... Witness myself, at Dunstable, the twentieth day of December, in the seventeenth year of our reign. It is also commanded of all the Sheriffs in whose bailiwicks the said Geoffrey had lands and tenements, that they do forthwith cause the said Savary de Mauleon to have full seisin of all those lands, as aforesaid. Given the same.[19]

Unfortunately, the marriage was not to last long. Just two years later, on 23 February 1216, Geoffrey de Mandeville died from wounds he had received at a tournament in London, then occupied by rebels and their French allies. The tournament is described as a 'bohort' by the chronicler known as Anonymous of Béthune, which suggests a non-lethal joust, or mêlée, with weapons. The knights were not dressed in full armour and de Mandeville was wearing merely a padded gambeson to absorb any blows. The chronicler reported:

> At this time there was a notable event in London. The knights began to bouhard to amuse themselves; Geoffrey de Mandeville, who was the earl of Essex, was there with the others, but was not wearing either a gambeson or pourpoint. One of the French knights, called Acroce-Meure, charged towards him with a truncheon. The earl cried out when he saw him coming. "Ha! Crocemeure, don't hit me, I haven't got a pourpoint on." The shouting was futile, for he hit him in the belly and killed him.[20]

Ralph of Coggeshall also recorded the event; 'Geoffrey de Mandeville died at London, from the wound he sustained whilst riding as a knight, in the French fashion, when riders charge each other in turn with spears or lances, on the day before the start of Quadragesima; he was buried at the priory of Holy Trinity in London.'[21] Although the description of events differs slightly, the outcome is the same, Geoffrey de Mandeville died from the encounter and Isabella was now a widow.

For probably the first time in her life, Isabella had some level of independence, and evidence from her charters suggest that she revelled in it. She issued a large number of charters in 1216 and 1217, many confirming gifts by members of her family to religious houses, styling herself as 'countess of Gloucester and Essex in my free widowhood'.[22] As Geoffrey de Mandeville was in rebellion against the king when he died, many of his lands were confiscated by the crown, although her reduced circumstances do not seem to have marred Isabella's new-found sense of freedom.

It was not until the year after King John's death that Isabella's lands were finally returned to her, on 17 September 1217:

> The King to the Sheriff of Oxford, greetings. Know that the Countess of Gloucester has come to our fealty and service. We therefore order that you do forthwith cause her or her accredited messenger bearing these letters to have such seisin of the lands, wardships, and escheats in your Bailiwick, with their appurtenances, as she had before the war that occurred between the lord King John our father and the Barons of England. And since we do not yet have etc. ... Witness the Earl [of Pembroke], at Kingston, the seventeenth day of September. The same is commanded of the Sheriffs of Gloucester, Wiltshire, Worcester, Somerset, Dorset, Bedford, Cornwall and Cambridge.[23]

At about the same time as she recovered her lands, or shortly after, Isabella was married for a third and final time, to Hubert de Burgh. The origins of Hubert De Burgh are quite obscure. His mother's name was Alice, as evidenced by a grant he made to the church of Oulton in about 1230, stating the gift was 'for the soul of my mother Alice who rests in the church at Walsingham.'[24] Hubert de Burgh's father may have been the Walter whose daughter Adelina owed 40 marks in the Pipe Rolls of Henry II, for recognition of a knights' fee at Burgh in Norfolk; although this is little more than a possibility.[25]

De Burgh was the younger brother of William de Burgh who had accompanied the king's youngest son, John, to Ireland in 1185; he eventually became lord of Connacht. Hubert de Burgh also had two younger brothers. Geoffrey became archdeacon of Norwich in 1202 and bishop of Ely in 1225. A third brother, Thomas, was castellan of Norwich Castle in 1215–16.[26] Hubert de Burgh was a self-made man, coming from a family of minor landowners in East Anglia centred on the manor of Burgh in Norfolk. He first appears in official records on 8 February 1198, when he witnessed a charter of John, as count of Mortain, at Tinchebrai in Normandy. In a charter of 12 June in the same year, he was identified as chamberlain of John's household and in 1199, when John succeeded to the throne, he was created chamberlain of the royal household.[27]

Hubert de Burgh's career in royal service developed rapidly. In December 1200 he was made custodian of two important royal castles, Dover and Windsor. In 1201 he was sheriff of Dorset and Somerset and when John departed for France in June 1201, along with the two senior marcher lords, the earl of Pembroke and constable of Chester, de Burgh was created custodian of the Welsh Marches with 100 men-at-arms at his disposal. He was also given the castles of Grosmont, Skenfrith and Whitecastle 'to sustain him in our service.'[28] Further grants followed, making Hubert de Burgh a significant and powerful figure in the royal administration by 1202. In the same year, Hubert de Burgh was one of the ambassadors despatched to Portugal to negotiate a possible marriage between John and a daughter of Portugal's king, but the embassy was abandoned after John married Isabelle d'Angoulême.

Later in 1202 Hubert de Burgh was sent to France and made constable of Falaise Castle in Normandy, where he was entrusted with guarding Arthur of Brittany following the latter's capture at Mirebeau. Hubert was given the order to have Arthur blinded and castrated but refused to carry out the punishment, claiming that the king had given the order in anger and would come to regret it – and lay the blame on the one who carried it out.[29] The fact Hubert de Burgh faced no repercussions on refusing the order suggests that he had read the situation perfectly. Moreover, given the persecution John inflicted on William de Braose, following his complicity in Arthur's murder at Rouen the following year, it is clear that Hubert de Burgh knew John well.

In 1204 Hubert de Burgh was entrusted with the defence of Chinon, against the king of France. He held out for a year, until the summer of 1205, when the walls of the castle had practically been levelled. In a last desperate engagement, de Burgh and his men rushed from the castle to confront the French. A fierce fight followed, in which de Burgh was wounded and captured; he was held for two years. King John helped with his ransom, with writs to the treasurer and chamberlain, in February 1207, ordering them to pay William de Chayv 300 marks 'for the pledge of Hubert de Burgh.'[30] De Burgh returned to England before the end of 1207 and again began to accumulate land and offices. In May 1208 he was given custody of the castle and town of Lafford in Huntingdon and in the following year he married Beatrice de Warenne, a cousin of William de Warenne, Earl of Surrey, who had succeeded her father in the barony of Wormegay; de Burgh became guardian of William, Beatrice's young son by her first husband, Doun Bardolf. Beatrice was the mother of Hubert de Burgh's only son, John, who was probably born before 1212, when de Burgh returned to France in royal service, first as deputy seneschal of Poitou and then as seneschal in association with Philip d'Aubigny and Geoffrey de Neville. After the French defeated the English at Bouvines in 1214, de Burgh was one of the witnesses to the truce with King Philp II of France, which agreed that John should keep all his lands south of the River Loire.[31]

By the time of the Magna Carta crisis in the spring and summer of 1215, Hubert de Burgh was back in England and supporting the king in his attempts to quell the rebellion. He was tasked, alongside the bishop of Coventry, with speaking to the mayor, sheriff and knights of London, who were instructed to listen to what de Burgh and the bishop had to say; despite this, the Londoners opened their gates to the rebels. In the preamble to Magna Carta, Hubert de Burgh is styled seneschal of Poitou and listed eighth among the list of lay barons and by 25 June 1215 he was being styled as justiciar in official documents. Matthew Paris later claimed he had been appointed to the post in the presence of Stephen Langton, Archbishop of Canterbury, and the earls of Surrey and Derby, among other magnates.[32] As justiciar, in the Magna Carta, Hubert de Burgh is mentioned as being the one to hold ultimate responsibility in the realm whenever the king was abroad; this was a considerable change to the role of justiciar in former reigns, when he was primarily responsible as president of the exchequer and chief justice. He was, essentially, the most powerful man in the land after the king himself. De Burgh was also made castellan of Dover Castle, the gateway to England from the Continent, and was besieged there from 22 July 1216 until King John's death in October of the same year, when the Dauphin Louis abandoned the siege.

Hubert de Burgh attended a council of the new king, Henry III, at Bristol on 11 November 1216, when Magna Carta was reissued; he appears as justiciar at the head of the list of lay barons on the witness list. In the spring of 1217, he was back at Dover, having reprovisioned it, and from April he was once again under siege. The Battle of Lincoln on 20 May 1217 saw the allied French and rebel forces defeated by William Marshal, causing Louis to lift the siege at Dover and retire to London and await reinforcements. When the sea battle off Sandwich put the seal on the defeat of the French, a truce was agreed with Louis and he departed for France in September 1217.

Hubert de Burgh's first wife, Beatrice, had died before 18 December 1214. In September 1217 Hubert de Burgh married Isabella of Gloucester, King John's first wife. On 13 October 1217 the sheriffs of nine counties were ordered to relinquish custody of Isabella's lands to de Burgh.[33] This final marriage for Isabella was, sadly, very short-lived and Isabella was dead within a month, possibly only a few weeks, of her wedding day and almost exactly a year after the death of her first husband, King John. Isabella died on 14 October 1217, probably at Keynsham Abbey near Bristol, and was buried at the cathedral of Christ Church, Canterbury.[34] Shortly before her death, Isabella made a grant to the monks of Canterbury, of £10 of land in her manor of Petersfield, Hampshire, which was witnessed by Hubert de Burgh and other members of his household.[35] Hubert de Burgh went on to marry Margaret, princess of Scotland as his third wife; his career continued to rise until he fell from office in 1232, amid charges of financial misconduct and treason. He was imprisoned for a time before being forgiven by the king and retiring to his own lands.

Despite her three marriages, Isabella never had children and the earldom of Gloucester went to her nephew, Gilbert de Clare, Earl of Hertford. We cannot know, of course, whether Isabella would have ever become a mother, nor whether it was through infertility, miscarriages or John's indifference that she did not have a family during their ten years of marriage. Isabella appears to have had very little control over her own life, even less than many women of her time; to the extent that one hopes beyond reason that the year of freedom she experienced, following the death of Geoffrey de Mandeville, was at least a happy one. Isabella endured the whims of John, first as her husband and then as king, through many years, even decades. Her life and future, and her inheritance, were constantly subject to John's desires and political machinations. Although she lived through the Magna Carta crisis, on the rebel side, she did not gain any benefits from its clauses, not even those safeguarding the rights of widows, as her husband, Geoffrey de Mandeville, was considered a traitor when he died. Isabella's lands and income were taken from her on at least three occasions; making it even more remarkable that she managed to pass her earldom of Gloucester, in its entirety, on to her nephew.

Chapter 10

Isabelle d'Angoulême

fter King John, Isabelle d'Angoulême is one of the least sympathetic characters of the Magna Carta crisis. Even in her lifetime she was blamed for much of the nation's ills. Not even a teenager when she was married, it does seem unfair that she was held responsible for the loss of Normandy and the crisis that led to the issuing of Magna Carta. Although her later actions served to add fuel to the fire, it was not Isabelle who caused the problems, but Isabelle's marriage. This marriage has often been depicted as one of lust over common sense, especially in novels, with Isabelle's beauty blinding John to the political implications of stealing his bride from one of his own vassals. However, marrying Isabelle was a politically expedient move at the time, even if it did backfire on King John rather dramatically.

Isabelle d'Angoulême was the only child of Audemar, Count of Angoulême and Alice de Courtenay. Alice had previously been the wife of Guillaume I, Comte de Joigny, but the marriage was annulled in 1184 on the grounds of consanguinity. Alice was the daughter of Peter de Courtenay, Lord of Montargis and Chateaurenard, and a cousin of Philip, the king of France. Through her Courtenay family connections, Isabelle was also related to the royal houses of Jerusalem, Hungary, Aragon and Castile. Her mother Alice is first recorded as the wife of Count Audemar in a document granting land to the abbey of St-Armand-de-Boixe in 1191.[1] This has raised some questions as to Isabelle's age when she married King John in 1200, suggesting that Isabelle may have been as young as 10 at the time of her marriage. The canonical age at which girls were allowed to marry was 12. The chronicler Roger of Howden maintained that Isabelle had not yet reached the age of consent, which was why she was still only betrothed to Hugh de Lusignan, rather than married to him.[2]

Count Audemar was one of the most prominent barons of the duchy of Aquitaine, his province lying between the Plantagenet strongholds of Poitiers and Bordeaux. He had a long-running rivalry with the Lusignan family, who were the lords of neighbouring Lusignan, who had a chequered history with the Plantagenet regime; they had once ambushed Eleanor of Aquitaine in an apparent attempt to abduct the queen of England. However, Hugh de Lusignan had developed a friendship with King Richard I during the Third Crusade and the king showed them favour thereafter, promoting the Lusignans above their Angoulême rivals. In January 1200 John had awarded Hugh IX de Lusignan the county of La Marche.[3] Shortly after Hugh was betrothed to Isabelle; as the heiress to Angoulême marriage between Isabelle and Hugh de Lusignan would make Hugh the most powerful man in the region, having control of two strategically important counties which could, effectively cut Aquitaine into two, jeopardising the stability of the borders of Poitou and Gascony.

John could not help but see the threat posed by the impending marriage. Having divorced his first wife Isabella of Gloucester in 1199, he was free to pursue Isabelle for himself. Count Audemar, it seems, was quite receptive to the suggestion to abandon the Lusignan match so that his daughter might become queen of England. Two chroniclers of the time, Roger of Howden and Ralph of Coggeshall, both reported that King Philip II of France had advised John to marry Isabelle.[4] John had already sent ambassadors to Portugal with a view to marrying the daughter of the Portuguese king, but these plans were hastily abandoned. The speed in which John rushed into marriage did not go unnoticed by the chroniclers:

Lord John, King of England, having in mind to marry a daughter of the king of the Portuguese ... sent from Rouen some great notables to bring her back to him. But he married Isabelle, only daughter and heir of the Count of Angoulême, and he did this while they were on the journey, without having warned them, taking much less care for their safety than was worthy of the Royal majesty.[5]

Isabelle and John were married at Angoulême on 24 August when she was 12 years old at the most while John was 34. The wedding was officiated by the bishop of Bordeaux, with the bishops of Saintes, Périgueux, Angoulême, Limoges and Waterford assisting.[6] Isabelle then accompanied John to Chinon and on to England, where she was crowned queen of England at Westminster Abbey on 8 October 1200:

> with all his enemies pacified and subdued he [King John] returned to England at the time of the feast of St Michael, 29 September. He came with his wife Isabelle, the daughter of the count of Angoulême, whom he had married overseas with the consent of King Philip. He had put aside his first wife in the previous year on the basis of their consanguinity. The next day, John wore the crown at Westminster and his wife, who was about 12 years old, was crowned queen.[7]

John was crowned alongside his bride, in what he described as his 'second coronation'. Unlike Isabelle, however, he was not anointed with holy oil because that was seen as a sacrament he could receive only once, which he did at his first coronation. After the ceremony, John paid those who had assisted in the ritual, ordering: 'Give from our treasure 25 shillings to Eustace the chaplain and Ambrose, our clerks, who sang the Christus Vincit at our second coronation and at the unction and coronation of Queen Isabelle our wife.'[8] A further crown-wearing, or coronation ceremony, was conducted at Canterbury at the beginning of 1201, at which both John and Isabelle were crowned by Hubert Walter, Archbishop of Canterbury.[9]

The marriage humiliated Hugh de Lusignan and John further exacerbated the situation by making no effort to compensate Lusignan for the insult. To make matters worse, in 1201 John confiscated the Lusignan county of La Marche and granted it to his new father-in-law, Audemar of Angoulême. He also confiscated the county of Eu, in Normandy, from Hugh de Lusignan's brother, Raoul d'Exoudun. Ralph of Coggeshall records:

> In the year 1202 peace was made between Philip, king of France and John, king of England. But King John immediately launched a bitter attack on the count of La Marche, namely Hugh known as the Brown and his brother the count of Eu, who had rebelled against him because of his marriage to Isabelle of Angoulême.[10]

The Lusignans appealed to King Philip for justice and John was summoned to the French royal court to answer the charges. The king of England's failure to appear gave Philip the excuse he needed to pronounce the confiscation of all John's French fiefs in April 1202.[11] Philip then accepted the homage of John's rival, Arthur of Brittany, for all the confiscated lands, except Normandy. Over the next three years, the French king pursued a campaign of conquest which drove John from Normandy and the bulk of his Continental domains. Isabelle herself was caught up in the war in 1203, when she was besieged whilst staying at Chinon. She sent frantic messages to John, begging for rescue. The king set out for Chinon but only got as far as Le Mans. Fearful of being captured himself, he sent mercenaries to his wife's aid and the relief of Chinon was achieved.[12]

It was in this light that John's marriage to Isabelle was seen as the start of England's woes, with some of the blame falling unfairly on Isabelle. Contemporary sources report that John spent his mornings in bed with the queen, when he should have been attending to the business of the country, casting the young queen, still only a teenager, as some kind of temptress, irresistible to the king.[13] Isabelle, however, had very little control of her life and actions and John's failures should be laid firmly at his door.

In the early years of their marriage, John appears to have treated Isabelle more like a child than a wife, which she, of course, was and her independence was severely limited by her lack of access to the finances which should have rightfully been hers by right, as queen. Shortly after their marriage in 1200, Isabelle was promised dower lands in Anjou and Poitou, including the lordships of Niort, Saintes and six other towns. Following the death of Eleanor of Aquitaine in 1204, she was also promised the late queen's dower lands in England and Normandy, including the towns of Exeter, Wilton, Ilchester and Malmesbury, the honour of Berkhamsted, the farm of Waltham in Essex and the county of Rutland together with Rockingham.[14] In 1202 Isabelle's father, Count Audemar, died leaving Isabelle as countess of Angoulême in her own right. She had no role in the government of her lands, however, with first her mother and then John's officials governing in her name. In fact, in spite of all the financial provisions made for her, Isabelle appears to have controlled no lands of her own during John's lifetime; with any revenues going into the Exchequer, rather than the queen's hands. Isabelle relied on occasional payments from the king and, possibly, the queen's gold, which was an additional levy charged on fines to the crown; although even this appears to have gone direct to the Exchequer after 1207. When she was not at court with the king, Isabelle spent time at Marlborough or in the household of John's first wife, Isabella of Gloucester, at Winchester. Gloucester's allowance was raised from £50 to £80 a year, to pay for the extra expenses incurred by housing the queen.[15]

One may imagine this was quite awkward for Isabella of Gloucester, the discarded wife being forced to host her ex-husband's young bride. On closer reflection, however, it may also have been a comfort to her. The teenage queen would probably have been lively company for the 40-year-old countess who had never been blessed with children. She may have felt protective and motherly to the girl, especially knowing John as well as she must have done. There is very little mention of Isabelle of Angoulême in the chronicles and not one charter was issued in her own name in the sixteen years she was queen of England, although this may well have been a result of her financial dependence on John and the fact that she did not have money at her disposal to make grants of her own. Furthermore, she is mentioned in only one of John's charters, a grant to Chichester in 1204, and omitted from charters where you would expect to see her included, for example, John's grant to Beaulieu Abbey in 1205, which invokes the souls of his parents and brothers, as well as the well-being of his heirs – but not the queen.[16]

John and Isabelle's relationship does not appear to have been a particularly close one, though he did send her numerous gifts and took care of her safety. In 1207, for example the king sent the queen a gilded saddle and harness, three hoods of varying colours, a hundred yards of fine linen, two tablecloths, four towels, half an otter skin and a belt.[17] Isabelle was rarely in the king's company after 1205, although they still managed to produce five children. The queen was at Winchester in 1207 when she gave birth to her first child, Henry, who would be crowned Henry III in October 1216. Despite what appears to have been a strained personal relationship, John and Isabelle were able to fill the royal nursery with another son and three daughters before John's death in 1216.

After Henry another son, Richard, was born in 1208 and later created earl of Cornwall. Of the daughters, Joan was born in 1210; she was first betrothed to Hugh X de Lusignan, but eventually married Alexander II, King of Scots. Isabella was born in 1214 and married Emperor Frederick II Hohenstaufen. Isabelle and John's youngest daughter was Eleanor, who was around 1 year old when her father died in October 1216. Eleanor was married, firstly, to William (II) Marshal and, secondly, to Simon de Montfort, Earl of Leicester, who was to cause her brother no end of trouble in the 1250s and 1260s. There is little indication of any closeness between Isabelle and her children who were raised in separate households; baby Eleanor was placed in the household of the bishop of Winchester, with her big brother, Henry, shortly after her birth. We cannot, however, say whether this was a choice made by Isabelle, or a decision forced on her by John. Although it has to be said that John was renowned for his great affection for all his children, so the former seems more likely, especially given Isabelle's subsequent abandonment of her English family.

Gossip and rumours of the queen's infidelity spread in Isabelle's lifetime and afterwards. Matthew of Paris recalled a story from Roger of London, sent by John as ambassador to Morocco in 1211, that Isabelle 'has often been found guilty of incest, witchcraft and adultery, so that the king, her husband has ordered those of her lovers who have been apprehended to be strangled with a rope in her own bed.'[18] Another similar account tells of how John had one of Isabelle's lovers strangled and the corpse suspended over his wife's bed. Isabelle has also been accused of incest with her half-brother, Peter de Joigny. In 1233 a man died in Ireland, his name was Piers the Fair and he was known locally as 'the son of the English Queen'; Isabelle is often referred to as Isabelle the Fair. However, these stories seem to have little foundation and belie the fact that John recognised all his children by Isabelle and continued to visit her regularly with their last child being born only a year before the king's death. Such accusations of infidelity can be found to have been levelled against many queens, before and after, including Isabelle's own mother-in-law, Eleanor of Aquitaine

John appears to have remained faithful to Isabelle during the early years of the marriage. No illegitimate children were born and, although there are gifts to women who may have been mistresses in the royal financial accounts, they do not appear until later in the marriage.[19] One of John's mistresses, Hugh de Neville's wife, Joan de Cornhill, is said to have offered to pay the king a fine of 200 chickens, in order to spend a night with her husband, suggesting that she was not too enthusiastic for her role as the king's mistress.[20] After Henry's birth, Isabelle lived for a time at Corfe Castle, the Canterbury Chronicle describing her as being 'in custody', which suggests some kind of house arrest; although it may also mean that she had a strong guard to protect her.[21]

John was not averse to using Isabelle when the situation required it. In 1214, she accompanied him to Poitou, where the king was able to establish his authority over her county of Angoulême. However, once back in England, as civil war loomed in the country in 1214, Isabelle was accompanied by a mercenary, Terric the Teuton, with an armed guard, via Freemantle and Reading to Berkhamsted. On the 30 October King John sent a coded letter to Terric:

> The King sends greeting to Thierry the Teuton. Know that, by God's grace, we are in good health and unharmed and we order you to restore, as soon as you can, the horse that you borrowed from Richard the Fleming. We shall shortly be coming to your part of the country, and we shall be thinking of you, about the hawk, and though it might be ten years since we last saw you, at our coming it shall seem no less than three days. Take good care of the custody that we have entrusted to you, letting us know regularly of the condition of this custody. Witnessed by myself (the King), at the Tower of London, 30 October.[22]

The 'custody' to which John refers is most likely the queen. and given the state of the country, this was more likely for the queen's protection rather than any suggestion that she was under arrest.

During the crisis years of 1215 and 1216, Isabelle stayed mostly in the West Country, where it was relatively safe. When John died on the night of 18/19 October 1216, she was at Bristol, but on hearing the news of her husband's death, immediately set out for Gloucester, where she was reunited with her 9-year-old son Henry. Henry was hastily crowned in Gloucester Cathedral on 28 October, by the papal legate, Guala Bicchieri, fearing that Louis may attempt to hold a coronation for himself in Westminster Abbey on the following Sunday.[23] Henry being too small to bear the weight and size of the crown, a gold chaplet belonging to Isabelle was used.

Isabelle had received no mention in John's will and was not given a place on the regency council, nor the custody of the young king. Excluded from her son's government, Isabelle's unpopularity in England and lack of political experience, led to her isolation. Furthermore, she had had limited contact with her children, given that they lived in separate households, and Isabelle was not responsible for their supervision or education, which probably gave her a sense that they did not need her. She also had difficulty securing her dower lands from the regency council. As a consequence, Isabelle decided to return to Angoulême in 1217.

Back in her homeland, with her first experience of independence in her life, Isabelle quickly established her authority over Angoulême. At first, she appeared to want to work with her son's regency council to secure the region from the king of France and aggressive neighbours. Sometime in 1218 or 1219, she wrote to her son asking for the release of the income from her dower lands so that she may defend her own and her son's interests from aggressors:

To our dearest son, Henry, by the grace of God illustrious king of England, lord of Ireland, duke of Normandy and Aquitaine, count of Anjou, I Y[sable] by that same grace his humble mother, queen of England, greetings and prosperous outcome always to his wishes. Your love will know that we have often implored you to give us and our plans counsel and help, and you have done neither up to now. Thus it is that we implore you diligently again that you give us swift counsel, and do not appease us with words. For you should know that without your help and counsel we can not rule and defend our land. And if the truce of the king of France should be broken, there is much to be feared about the land in this region. And though there may be nothing to be feared from that king, there are however neighbours who should be feared like the aforesaid king of France. Whence it is necessary that you give such fruitful counsel without delay for your land and ours in this region that neither you nor we lose our land for lack of your counsel and help. We also pray you to act on our part so that we may have some part now of what our husband, your father, endowed us with. For you should know as truth that we are much in need and had our husband left us nothing, you should still help us by right with your goods, so we might defend our land, since your advantage and honour is involved. We send you lord Geoffrey of Boteville and lord Waleran, reporting many things to you through them that we cannot set forth in letters; and you may believe what they say on our part about your advantage and ours.[24]

In spite of Isabelle's early protestations that she was seeking to look after Henry's interests in the region as much as her own, her actions in 1220 served to convince the regency council otherwise. Isabelle shocked England, and probably the whole Continent in 1220 in a scandalous about-face, by marrying her daughter's betrothed, Hugh X de Lusignan. Hugh X was the son of Hugh IX, Isabelle's former betrothed, and was of a similar age to Isabelle herself, who was now in her early thirties. And poor 9-year-old Joan's erstwhile betrothed was now her step-father! Moreover, Isabelle's marriage to John in 1200 had been brought about to prevent that which Isabelle had just achieved, the union of the counties of La Marche and Angoulême and thus the creation of one semi-independent power in the middle of Aquitaine. Not ignorant of the way this would appear in England, Isabelle wrote again to Henry, justifying her actions and the reason de Lusignan set aside the daughter in favour of her mother:

To our dearest son Henry, by the grace of God king of England, lord of Ireland, duke of Normandy and Aquitaine, count of Anjou, I[sabel] by that same grace queen of England, lady of Ireland, duchess of Normandy, Aquitaine, countess of Anjou and of Angoulême, greetings and maternal blessings. We make known to you that when the counts of La Marche and Angoulême died, lord Hugh of Lusignan remained alone and without heir in the region of Poitou, and his friends did not permit our daughter to be married to him, because she is so young; but they counselled him to take a wife from whom he might quickly have heirs, and it was suggested that he take a wife in France. If he had done so, all your land in Poitou and Gascony and ours would have been lost. But we, seeing the great danger that might emerge from such a marriage – and your counsellors would give us no counsel in this – took said H[ugh], count of La Marche, as our lord; and God knows that we did this more for your advantage than ours. Whence we ask you as a dear son that this please you, since it is of great utility to you and yours, and we diligently pray you to give him back his right, that is Niort, Exeter and Rockingham, and 3500 marks which your father, once our husband, endowed us with: and so, if it please you, act towards him who is so powerful. For he has good will to serve you faithfully with all his power, and we are certain and take in hand that he will serve you well if you restore his rights to him: and therefore we advise that you take appropriate counsel on the aforesaid. And when it please you, send for our daughter, your sister, since we do not hold her, and by sure messenger and letters patent, fetch her from us.[25]

Instead of sending Joan back to England, however, as Isabelle had promised, Joan went from being Hugh's betrothed – to being his prisoner. She was held hostage to ensure Hugh's continued control of her dower lands, and as a guarantee to the transfer of his new wife's dower. England, on the other hand, was withholding Queen Isabelle's dower against the return of Joan and her dower lands. Little Joan was finally returned to England towards the end of 1220, and in 1221 she was married to Alexander II, King of Scots. The marriage had been negotiated while Joan was still in her mother's custody, with the proviso that her younger sister, Isabella, would be substituted as the bride if Joan was not returned to England in time for the wedding.

The arguments over Isabelle's English lands continued and they were confiscated, for a short time, in 1221. In 1224, however, they were confiscated for good when Hugh de Lusignan allied himself with the French king, Louis VIII. In exchange for a substantial pension, Hugh and Isabelle supported a French invasion of Poitou (the lands in France belonging to the king of England, her son). They were reconciled with Henry in 1226 and Isabelle met her first-born son for the first time in more than twelve years in 1230, when Henry mounted a futile expedition to Brittany and Poitou. Isabelle and Hugh, however, continued to play the kings of France and England against each other, always looking for the advantage. In 1242, for example, when Henry III invaded Poitou, Hugh X initially gave support to his English stepson, only to change sides once more, precipitating the collapse of Henry's campaign.

Isabelle's second marriage proved even more unstable than her first, shaken by Hugh's frequent infidelities and threats of divorce. Despite the rocky relationship, Isabelle and Hugh had nine children together, including Aymer de Lusignan and William de Valence. Many of his Lusignan half-siblings would later cause problems for Henry III, having come to England to seek patronage and advancement from their royal half-brother. Moreover, Isabelle enjoyed greater personal authority within her second marriage; where she had issued no charters whilst married to King John, as Hugh de Lusignan's wife, the couple issued numerous joint charters. Isabelle's relationship with France was rocky. In one instance, she was slighted by the queen of France when she was not offered a chair to sit in the queen's presence, regardless of the fact she herself was a crowned and anointed queen.[26] Following this insult, in 1241, Isabelle castigated Hugh de Lusignan for supporting a French candidate to the county of Poitou, ahead of her son, Henry III. In retaliation, Isabelle stripped Lusignan Castle of its furnishings and refused to allow her husband into her castle at Angoulême for three days. This goes some way to explain Hugh's initial support for the expedition of Henry III of 1242.[27] According to a French writer, William de Nangis, Isabelle was implicated in a plot to poison King Louis IX of France and his brother in 1244 only to be foiled at the last minute; the poisoners claimed to have been sent by Isabelle.[28] There is no evidence of Isabelle denying the accusation, but she never admitted her guilt, either.

In her final years, Isabelle retired to the great Plantagenet abbey at Fontevrault, where she was veiled as a nun before she died on 4 June 1246. She was buried there alongside her first husband's brother, Richard I, and parents, Henry II and Eleanor of Aquitaine. Hugh de Lusignan died in the summer of 1249. Regardless of their rocky relationship since Isabelle's desertion of him in 1217, Henry III celebrated his mother's life, with royal gifts to the canons of Ivychurch in Wiltshire, an endowment of chantry chapels at Malmesbury and Westminster and a feast for the poor scholars of Oxford and Cambridge.[29]

As contemporaries described her as 'more Jezebel than Isabel', accused her of 'sorcery and witchcraft', Isabelle of Angouleme's reputation as a heartless mother and habitual schemer seems set to remain.[30] Married to King John whilst still a child, she was castigated as the cause of the loss of the majority of John's Continental possessions and the subsequent strife and civil war; one could easily sympathise with her lack of love for England.

The accusations of adultery appear to be unfounded; John's jealousy and paranoia meant Isabelle was so well guarded that she was virtually his prisoner, an affair would have been practically impossible. That Isabelle abandoned the children of her first husband within months of his death, and her apparent willingness to betray her son for her own ends goes some way to destroy the compassion one may have felt for her. In the chronicles, when she is mentioned, Isabelle comes across as a harsh, unlovable character, with little to recommend her. She stands out as a woman with an impressive ruthless streak, when protecting her interests, even against her own son. Having said that, however, she was unfairly blamed for the loss of Normandy and the trials in England which led to Magna Carta. Despite her powerlessness in her first marriage, the union made her the scapegoat for England's woes. In her time in England, Isabelle appears to have been very much a pawn, treated as a child for the most part in the early years of her marriage and given little freedom or control in the latter years. One can almost excuse the expressions of independence when she returned to Angoulême, as necessary to the survival of Angoulême itself, even at the expense of her English children.

Chapter 11

Eleanor of Brittany

There was one Plantagenet princess for whom Magna Carta offered no freedom from imprisonment, despite clause 39. She was not a daughter of King John, but his niece, Eleanor of Brittany. Eleanor was the eldest child of Geoffrey, fourth son of Henry II of England, and Constance of Brittany, sole heiress of her father Conan IV, Duke of Brittany. Constance and Geoffrey had married in 1181 and their daughter, Eleanor, was born in 1184. Whilst estranged from his father, Geoffrey had been trampled to death competing in a tournament in Paris in August 1186. His son and heir, and Eleanor's brother, Arthur, was born several months later, in March or April 1187. As a consequence, Eleanor was her father's heir at his death; had Arthur been born a girl, Eleanor would have become duchess after her mother. With a view of her political importance at her father's death King Philip of France claimed Eleanor's wardship.[1]

The birth of Eleanor's brother Arthur in 1187 diminished her value, not only politically but also on the marriage market; she no longer came with Brittany as her dowry, like her mother had done. Described as beautiful, Eleanor has been called the Pearl, the Fair Maid and the Beauty of Brittany.[2] A granddaughter of Henry II and Eleanor of Aquitaine, she was the eldest of her parents' three children; Matilda was born the following year but died young and Arthur was to face a tragic end at the hands of her uncle, King John. Her mother Constance was to marry twice more following Geoffrey's death. In 1188 she married Ranulf de Blundeville, Earl of Chester; it was recorded in *The Chester Chronicles*,

> In the course of the same year Randle [Randulph], earl of Chester, was knighted by Henry, king of England, on the feast of the Circumcision of our Lord [January 1, 1189] at [Caen]. To whom also Henry, king of England, gave as a wife the countess of Brittany,

widow of his son Geoffrey, and daughter of Alan [Conan], count of Brittany, Constance by name, with all the county of Richmond; the said Randle [Randulph], earl of Chester, married her on the feast of S. Werburg the Virgin, that is, February 3.[3]

The marriage appears to have been a miserable one, with Ranulf imprisoning Constance for a time, supposedly for marital reasons but actually to prevent Constance and her duchy from acting against King Richard I. Shortly after she was freed in 1198 Constance obtained an annulment of the marriage. She was married for a third time, in September or October 1199, to Guy of Thouars, with whom she had two daughters, Alix and Catherine, before she died in September 1201, possibly from complications in childbirth.

Initially, Eleanor's life seemed destined to follow the same path as many royal princesses – marriage. Richard I was her legal guardian after his accession to the English throne and the rest of the Plantagenet empire in 1189. It was following his sister Joanna's adamant refusal, that Richard offered Eleanor as a bride to Saladin's brother, Al-Adil, in a failed attempt at a political settlement to the Third Crusade. However, nothing came of the suggestion and, shortly after, at the age of 9, Eleanor was betrothed to Friedrich, the son of Duke Leopold VI of Austria, who had made the betrothal a condition of the ransom for Richard I's release from imprisonment by the duke. Eleanor was travelling to Germany in the care of Baldwin de Béthune when news arrived that Duke Leopold had died suddenly. The duke's s son had 'no great inclination' for the proposed marriage and so Eleanor and her party turned around and returned home.[4]

Further marriage plans were mooted in 1195 and 1198, to Philip II of France's son Louis, the dauphin, and Odo, Duke of Burgundy, respectively; although neither came to fruition. Duchess Constance then pressed for Eleanor to be released from royal custody and by the time of Richard's death, in 1199, Eleanor was living in France with her mother and brother.

Eleanor's fortunes changed drastically when her brother Arthur, supported and encouraged by King Philip II Augustus of France, rebelled against Richard's successor, King John, in the early 1200s. A Plantagenet prince, Arthur of Brittany's story is one of the most tragic of the medieval period. The posthumous son of Geoffrey, fourth son of Henry II of England, he was Duke of Brittany from the moment of his birth. In 1190 the 2-year-old Arthur was named as heir presumptive to his uncle Richard I, King of England, who had succeeded his father Henry II the previous year. As we have seen Richard even arranged a betrothal for young Arthur, to a daughter of Tancred of Sicily. The betrothal was part of a peace deal that would see Richard's sister, Joanna, released by Tancred and Tancred pay Richard 40,000 ounces in gold; half to compensate Joanna for her lack of dower and half in place of the ships and supplies which Tancred's predecessor had promised to provide for Richard's crusade. It was at this moment, probably to boost Arthur's status in the eyes of Tancred, that Richard designated Arthur as his heir, should the king die before fathering a legitimate son of his own. However, the Emperor Henry VI conquered Sicily in 1194 and the betrothal came to nothing. Arthur was a valuable pawn for both the kings of France and England; when Richard tried to take him into his household, in 1196, his mother sent him to the French court, where he spent several months. On his return to Brittany, Constance started involving him in the government of the duchy.

Arthur had been considered as a successor for King Richard I in a meeting between William Marshal and Hubert Walter, the archbishop of Canterbury, within days of Richard's death in 1199. According to *L'Histoire de Guillaume le Maréchale*, Marshal counselled against giving the crown to Arthur, saying, 'Arthur has treacherous advisers about him, and he is haughty and overbearing. If we call him to our side, he will seek to do us harm and damage, for he does not like those in our realm.'[5] Arthur was 12 years old at the time, and firmly under the influence of King Philip of France, two factors that were not in the young duke's favour. Marshal successfully pressed for the succession of John, Richard's brother, a grown man, who it was believed was more aligned with the interests of the Anglo-Norman baronage than the young Breton duke.

It was not cut-and-dried, however, and Arthur and his mother acted quickly after Richard's death, advancing into Angers and receiving the homage of the barons of Anjou, Maine and Touraine. King Philip, in the meantime, advanced on Normandy in support of Arthur, seizing Evreux and advancing on Le Mans, where John was in residence. John stole away from Le Mans as Arthur and Philip advanced on the city which was captured by Arthur a few hours later. When Philip arrived, he recognised Arthur's right to Anjou, Maine and Touraine in return for his homage.[6]

Normandy supported John, however, and he was invested as duke in Rouen Cathedral on 25 April 1199. A month later, on 27 May, John was crowned King of England in Westminster Abbey. It was a flying visit to his new kingdom and by 20 June, John embarked at Shoreham, returning to the Continent with a 'multitude of knights, foot soldiers and ships.'[7] While John was in England, the leading nobles of Poitou, rallied by Eleanor of Aquitaine, had attacked Tours, where Arthur was staying. He escaped, but the attack attracted the attention of King Philip, who sent troops south in support of the young contender, leaving John to land unopposed in Normandy. By late August, hostilities had resumed, but King Philip's heavy handedness in Anjou persuaded a leading Angevin baron, William des Roches, to defect to King John bringing Arthur and his mother with him: 'Arthur, the son of John's brother Count Geoffrey of Brittany, came to the king and obeyed his every wish, but John somewhat incautiously dismissed him. Arthur then went to the king of France who, with an avid eye on his wealth, had him brought up with his own son at Paris.'[8] Arthur, it seems, was warned that John intended to seize him and throw him in prison and so the day after his submission he, his mother and supporters, fled to Angers and then to Tours, where he was received by King Philip. In January 1200, however, John and Philip came to terms, with Philip agreeing to withdraw his support for Arthur's claim; the peace was sealed at Le Goulet on 22 May, with John paying homage to Philip for his Continental possessions, and Arthur performing homage to John for Brittany. Peace was restored, for the moment.

Arthur's claim was revived in the early 1200s when Philip Augustus confiscated John's possessions in northern France for failing to acknowledge the French King as his overlord. As such, Philip recognised Arthur as the rightful heir to Normandy and Anjou. Tensions were again stretched to their limits in 1202, when Philip declared John's Continental lands forfeit as a result of his refusal to deal justly with the Lusignans, who had rebelled following John's marriage to Hugh IX de Lusignan's betrothed, Isabelle d'Angoulême. Eleanor of Brittany's whereabouts in

1200 are unknown, but she did accompany her brother two years later, in 1202, when he next took up arms against King John.

Once more, King Philip sought to promote Arthur's interests against those of King John. Now 15 years old, the young duke was knighted and betrothed to Philip's own infant daughter. The French king then invested Arthur with Anjou, Maine, Touraine and Aquitaine, furnished him with a small army which included 200 knights and sent him south to join forces with the Lusignans. Philip's plan was for Arthur and the Lusignans to pursue the war against John in Aquitaine. When Arthur received intelligence that his grandmother, Eleanor of Aquitaine, had left Fontainebleau and was making her way to Poitiers, Arthur, Eleanor and the Lusignans set a course to intercept. They met up with the dowager queen of England at Mirebeau, where she had sought refuge in the castle and despatched a messenger to John, asking for his assistance.

Having become aware of Arthur's movements and the potential danger to Eleanor, John had already set out and had reached Le Mans by the time his mother's messenger caught up with him on 30 July. Taking a small force he set out at once for Mirebeau and arrived outside the town's walls in the dawn of 1 August, having marched 100 miles in less than two days. Possibly a little over confident in their numbers and abilities, Arthur and his fellow commanders were still at breakfast when John arrived. With surprise on his side, John's forces attacked the one town gate that remained unblocked and stormed the town. After some fierce fighting through the streets, the enemy commanders were all captured, including Arthur, Count Hugh de Lusignan and Geoffrey de Lusignan. In a justifiably jovial mood, John wrote to the English barons announcing the victory, the rescue of his mother as well as the capture of Arthur and over 200 French knights.

As we have seen, it was one of John's most trusted barons, William de Braose, who is credited with capturing Arthur. The young duke was sent to imprisonment at Falaise, which may have been less than comfortable, given John's reputation for the harsh treatment of prisoners. Of the other prisoners captured, the Lusignans were freed after a time, on condition that they 'had surrendered their castles and hostages and given their oath not to rebel against him.'[9] John vainly hoped that they would help stem the tide of disaffection against him. Other prisoners were sent to

England, where twenty-five of them imprisoned at Corfe Castle made an escape attempt and seized the keep; twenty-two of them are said to have chosen to starve to death rather than surrender to John a second time. Eleanor had been with her brother at Mirebeau and was captured at the same time. She was also sent to imprisonment in England, although in more comfortable surroundings than the other Breton captives.

With Arthur imprisoned at Falaise, the Bretons continued to cause trouble. According to Ralph of Coggeshall, the

> counsellors of the king, realising that the Bretons were causing much destruction and sedition everywhere on behalf of their lord Arthur, and that no firm peace could be made while Arthur lived, suggested to the king that he order Arthur to be blinded and castrated, thus rendering him incapable of rule, so that the opposition would cease from their insane programme of destruction and submit themselves to the king.[10]

John gave the order: 'enraged by the ceaseless attacks of his enemies, hurt by their threats and misdeed, at length in a rage and fury, King John ordered three of his servants to go to Falaise and perform this detestable act.'[11] Two of the appointed messengers fled the king's court, to avoid the distasteful duty, while the third carried the order to Falaise where the royal chamberlain, Hubert de Burgh, had custody of Arthur. De Burgh, however, 'having regard for the king's honesty and reputation and expecting his forgiveness, kept the youth unharmed. He thought that the king would immediately repent of such an order and that ever afterwards would hate anyone who presumed to obey such a cruel mandate.'[12]

Despite balking at mutilating a 15-year-old, de Burgh announced that the sentence had been carried out, hoping to put a stop to the Breton revolt. Although it is recorded that, John 'was not displeased for the moment that his order had not been carried out.'[13] The Bretons were so enraged that their revolt rose to a new level of ferocity and the rebels were only pacified when it was announced that Arthur was, in fact, alive and well.

In 1203 Arthur was moved to Rouen. The Bretons and King Philip again called for his release, but John refused. It was in Rouen, at Easter 1203, most likely on 3 April, that Arthur was put to death. A chronicler of the Cistercian monastery of Margam, in Glamorgan, described the murder:

1204. When King John fled to England, Philip, King of the French, occupied Normandy and Anjou. A congregation was sent from Cîteaux, an abbot placed over them, and the abbey of Beaulieu was built. The Cornish first, and then the men of Devon, by pledge of payment, threw off the yoke of forest law. Queen Alienor died. Godfrey, bishop of Winchester, died; Peter des Roches, archdeacon of Poitou, succeeded him and was later consecrated by the lord Pope in Rome. Guido, bishop of Praeneste, once abbot of Cîteaux, was made archbishop of Reims.

The King of the French took the castle of Chinon, and afterwards all the garrisons of Normandy, Anjou, and the city of Poitiers, with other castles, fortified towns and cities, as he so willed it – for this reason; when king John had captured Arthur, he had him kept alive in prison for some time, but finally, in the great tower at Rouen, on the Thursday before Easter, after his dinner and when drunk and possessed by the devil, he killed him by his own hand, and, after a large stone had been tied to the body, threw it in the Seine. It was discovered by a fisherman in his net and recognised when it was brought to the riverbank, and, for fear of the tyrant, secretly buried at the priory of Bec, which is called Notre Dame des Pres.

When the aforesaid king of the French heard the news of this and knew for certain that Arthur had been killed, he had his killer John summoned to the court of France, as was customary with dukes of Normandy, to answer for the murder of such a great man and to defend himself if he could; of such a great man, say I, for he was the legitimate heir of England, the count of Brittany, and the son-in-law of the king of France. John, fully aware of his evil deed, never dared to appear before the court, but fled to England and exercised a most cruel tyranny over his people until he died. When he never came to answer for the death of Arthur or to defend himself, judgement was given against him by the king's court, and he was deprived of all his titles, in all the lands and honours which he held of the French crown; this was an incontrovertible and just sentence.[14]

Although it is believed John was present at Rouen that Easter, it is unknown what role he played in Arthur's death, whether he was the murderer or a mere bystander. Whatever his part, however, it was an act that would be held against John, not only during his lifetime, but for centuries to come. In 1204 Philip, probably suspecting that Arthur was dead, made the young duke of Brittany's release a condition of any peace settlement: 'For if Arthur was now discovered to be dead, Philip hoped to marry his sister and thus to gain all her Continental possessions. King Philip was unwilling to make peace because he was confident that he would soon possess all the lands of the English king.'[15]

Not only was Eleanor Arthur's heir, but with John still having no legitimate children of his own, she was also the heir to England. If the laws of inheritance had been strictly followed, Eleanor would have been sovereign of England after her brother's death. John and his successor, Henry III, could never forget this. In 1203 she was moved to England and would be held a prisoner of successive English kings to her dying day. Although her confinement has been described as 'honourable' and 'comfortable', Eleanor's greater right to the throne meant she would never be freed or allowed to marry and have children, despite repeated attempts over the years by King Philip and the Bretons to negotiate her release.

It seems Eleanor did spend some time with the king and court, particularly in 1214 when she accompanied John to La Rochelle to pursue his war with the French. John planned to use Eleanor to gain Breton support and maybe set her up as his puppet duchess of Brittany, replacing her younger half-sister Alice. Alice was the daughter of Eleanor's mother, Constance, by her third marriage to Guy of Thouars. She was married to Peter of Dreux, a cousin of King Philip of France and duke of Brittany by right of Alice. Using the carrot and stick approach, John offered Peter the earldom of Richmond to draw him to his side, while at the same time dangling the threat of restoring Eleanor to the dukedom, just by having her with him. Peter, however, refused to be threatened or persuaded and chose to face John in the field at Nantes. John's victory and capture of Peter's brother in the fighting persuaded Peter to agree to a truce, and John was content to leave Brittany alone, thereafter, instead advancing on Angers. His plans to restore Eleanor abandoned and forgotten.

As John's prisoner, Eleanor's movements were restricted, and she was closely guarded. Her guards were changed regularly to enhance security, but her captivity was not onerous. She was provided with 'robes', two ladies-in-waiting in 1230, and given money for alms and linen for her 'work'.[16] One order provided her with cloth; however, it was to be 'not of the king's finest.'[17] Eleanor was well-treated and fed an aristocratic diet, as her weekly shopping list attests: 'Saturday: bread, ale, sole, almonds, butter, eggs. Sunday: mutton, pork, chicken and eggs. Monday: beef, pork, honey, vinegar. Tuesday: pork, eggs, egret. Wednesday: herring, conger, sole, eels, almonds and eggs. Thursday: pork, eggs, pepper, honey. Friday: conger, sole, eels, herring and almonds.'[18]

She was granted the manor of Swaffham and a supply of venison from the royal forests. The royal family sent her gifts and she spent some time with the queen and the daughters of the king of Scotland, who were hostages in the king's custody. King John gave her the title of Countess of Richmond on 27 May 1208, but Henry III's regents would take it from her in 1219 and bestow the title elsewhere. From 1219 onwards she was styled the 'king's kinswoman' and 'our cousin'. In her sole surviving letter, written in 1208 with John's consent, she is styled 'Duchess of Brittany and Countess of Richmond.'[19] Throughout her captivity she is said to have remained 'defiant'.[20]

It is difficult to pinpoint exactly where Eleanor was imprisoned at any one time. Over the years, she was held in various strongholds, including the castles of Corfe (Dorset), Burgh (Westmorland), and Bowes (Yorkshire).[21] Corfe Castle is mentioned at various times, and it seems she was moved away from the coast in 1221 after a possible rescue plot was uncovered. She was also held at Marlborough for a time, and was definitely at Gloucester castle in 1236. By 1241 Eleanor was confined in Bristol castle, where she was visited regularly by bailiffs and leading citizens to ensure her continued welfare. Eleanor was also allowed her chaplain and serving ladies to ensure her comfort. She died at Bristol Castle, on 10 August 1241, at the age of about 57, after thirty-nine years of imprisonment, achieving in death, the freedom that had eluded her in life. She was initially buried at St James's Priory church in Bristol but her remains were later removed to the abbey at Amesbury, as instructed in her will; a convent with a long association with the crown.

The freedoms and rights enshrined in Magna Carta in 1215, and reissued in 1216 and 1225 under Henry III, held no relevance for Eleanor. Every other subject of the king was afforded the right to judgement of his peers before imprisonment thanks to clause 39 and guaranteed that justice could not be denied or delayed as a result of clause 40. Eleanor's royal blood and claim to the throne meant that she was awarded no such privilege; justice and freedom were perpetually denied her. Of all the royal family and noblewomen, it is Eleanor who proves that Magna Carta was not always observed and implemented, especially where women were concerned, and particularly where the royal family – and the interests of the succession – were concerned.

Chapter 12

The Royal Family

The legitimate children of King John and Isabelle d'Angoulême were still very young at the time Magna Carta was issued. John's oldest son, Henry, was only 7 years old when the charter was sealed at Runnymede in June 1215. Indeed, he was only nineteen days past his ninth birthday when he was proclaimed king on 19 October 1216, King John having died in the night. John and Isabelle's youngest child, Eleanor, was born the same year as Magna Carta and, although she would play a significant role in the Second Barons' War, as the wife of Simon de Montfort, she and her siblings had nothing to do with the issuing of the charter in 1215. We will look at Eleanor's incredible life and career in the next chapter, but first we will look at the rest of her family.

Joan, Lady of Wales

King John had at least one illegitimate daughter who was already fully grown and married in 1215 and experienced the highs and lows of her father's reign first-hand, and its effects on herself and her family. Joan, or Joanna, also had a legitimate half-sister called Joan, a daughter of King John and his queen, Isabelle d'Angoulême. We know very little of Joan until her appearance on the international stage in 1203, aged around 13 or 14. It was in that year that mention is made of a ship, chartered in Normandy, 'to carry the king's daughter and the king's accoutrements to England.'[1] The daughter in question appears to be Joan, who was probably born in or before 1189 before John's marriage to Isabella of Gloucester and based on the fact she was of marriageable age in 1204. We know practically nothing about Joan's mother, other than that she was possibly a lady by the name of Clemencia or Clementina.[2]

Joan is one of at least twelve illegitimate children fathered by John during the late 1180s and 1190s, who were born to several mistresses, some of whom were noble, but others were of more humble origins.[3] Most of these illegitimate children were born before or during John's first marriage, to Isabella of Gloucester, a marriage that was annulled within months of John attaining the throne. Nothing is known of Joan's childhood, which appears to have been spent with her mother in Normandy, given that the first mention of her in official records is when her father chartered a ship to bring her to England in 1203. However, although she grew up in obscurity, Joan must have received an education suitable to her rank as the daughter of a prince and, later, king; after all, if her father intended for her to make a good marriage, one that benefited him, he would need her to be able to act the part of a noblewoman, at least. The fact she married a prince suggests that she was educated in the role and duties of a princess. Indeed, Joan became one of the most important figures in Anglo-Welsh politics during the reigns of her father, John, and half-brother, Henry III, playing the role of intermediary between her husband and the king of England.

John's loss of Normandy and many of his other Continental territories in 1204 led him to concentrate his interests closer to home, and on his more immediate neighbours, Wales, Scotland and Ireland. As a consequence, by 15 October of that year, Joan was betrothed to the foremost prince in Wales; Llywelyn ap Iorwerth, prince of Gwynedd, later known as Llywelyn Fawr, or Llywelyn the Great. That summer, the Welsh prince had paid homage to King John for his Welsh lands, having recognised the English king as overlord by treaty in July 1201. Llywelyn's subsequent marriage to Joan, albeit John's illegitimate daughter, was a sign of the king's favour although with the unspoken caveat that the Welsh prince was of a lower royal rank than the English king, and therefore subject to England's overlordship. Born around 1173, Llywelyn was almost twenty years older than Joan and by the time of their marriage, Llywelyn was already an accomplished warrior and experienced statesman.[4] He was also the father of at least two children, a son and daughter, Gruffudd ap Llywelyn and Gwenllian, respectively. Their mother was a lady called Tangwystl, but her union with Llywelyn was not recognised by the church and the children were considered illegitimate under canon law, although they still had inheritance rights under Welsh law.

Joan and Llywelyn were probably married in the spring of 1205; part of Joan's dowry, the castle and manor of Ellesmere, were granted to

Llywelyn on 16 April 1205, suggesting the wedding took place around that time.⁵ Joan was 15 or 16 at the time, Llywelyn was 32. Having been uprooted from her home in Normandy, she had probably spent a year at the English court, possibly training for her role as a Welsh princess, before leaving for her new home in Wales. It is not hard to imagine that a large part of the year was spent learning what England and her father expected of her and being reminded of where her loyalties were expected to lie. The language and traditions of her new homeland would have been completely alien to the young woman. Even her name was not the same; in Welsh, she was known as Siwan.

For someone barely out of a childhood lived in obscurity, all these changes must have been daunting. Not only was she expected to become a wife and a princess to a nation that was totally alien to her, but her responsibilities also included the role of peacemaker. It was a prestigious marriage for an illegitimate daughter and one with great responsibilities; Joan was thrown into the heart of Anglo-Welsh relations. She was to become an important diplomatic tool for her husband, father and, later, her half-brother, Henry III; acting as negotiator and peacemaker between the English crown and her husband, almost from the first day of her marriage.

Despite the marriage of Joan and Llywelyn, relations between England and Wales were rarely cordial. A devastating defeat by the English occurred in 1211, in which the king

> led an army into Wales against Llywelyn, but returned very quickly because the Welsh, fearing his advance, withdrew with their property into the mountains, so that the English army was beset with hunger. But after gathering a large quantity of provisions, the king was soon able to make another expedition into Wales, and now with a large force and with plenty of supplies he was able to force hostilities upon the Welsh. After having conducted matters as he wished he emerged with glory.⁶

John had swept into Gwynedd, capturing the bishop of Bangor in his own cathedral, Joan's skills were sorely needed and 'Llywelyn, being unable to suffer the King's rage, sent his wife, the King's daughter, to him by the counsel of his leading men to seek to make peace with the King on whatever terms he could.'[7] Joan managed to negotiate peace, but at a high price, including the loss of the Four Cantrefs (the land between the Conwy and the Dee rivers), a heavy tribute of cattle and horses and the surrender of hostages, including Llywelyn's son, Gruffudd.[8]

In 1212, as the Barnwell annalist tells us, 'The Welsh princes, encouraged by the pope who had absolved them both from the agreement which they had made in the previous year with the English king and from the allegiance and oaths which they had taken upon themselves, attacked the English king in return for the interdict being relaxed throughout their lands.'[9] Following this renewal of hostilities, King John 'stirred up to violent anger, hanged the hostages and gathered an army against them from all parts of the kingdom.'[10] Although Gruffudd was not among them, John hanged twenty-eight Welsh hostages, some of them little older than boys, as a precursor to his invasion. However, the attack was called off when he received word from Joan that his barons were planning treason closer to home, that Robert Fitzwalter and Eustace de Vescy were plotting the king's assassination. Joan's warning was one of two disparate sources (the other being from the king of Scots), which persuaded John to disband his army and head home. From this point on John's paranoia and distrustful nature took hold. He 'would go nowhere without either being armed or accompanied by a great force of armed men.'[11]

The last years of John's reign were taken up with increasingly fraught relations with his barons, leading to the crisis coming to a head in 1215. The barons called for John to agree to reforms, and to confirm the coronation charter of King Henry I. It was said 'that both Alexander, king of the Scots, and Llywellyn, prince of North Wales, were in league with them.'[12] In June 1215, to stave off civil war, John agreed to the terms of Magna Carta, but regretted it almost immediately and sent emissaries to the pope to have the charter annulled. Pope innocent III obliged and excommunicated the leading rebels.

The last thing John needed, if he was to save his kingdom, was to be distracted by discontent in Wales. In 1214 Joan had successfully negotiated with her father for the release of the Welsh hostages still in English hands, including Llywelyn's son, Gruffudd. As with the princesses of Scotland, Gruffudd's release was included as a clause in Magna Carta, clause 58, and the hostages were freed the following year. It cannot have been an easy time for Joan, watching John go through the greatest crisis of his reign, especially when the French advance-guard arrived to try and claim the throne for the dauphin, Louis, at Christmas 1215; Louis himself would join his troops in the spring of 1216. Llywelyn took advantage of the unrest over the border to unite eleven of the Welsh princes and launch a lightning campaign in Wales, capturing seven castles, including the English strongholds of Carmarthen and Cardigan, in just three weeks and establishing himself as *de facto* prince of Wales and therefore Joan as *de facto* princess of Wales.

The tide was turned by King John's death in October 1216 when Joan's half-brother, 9-year-old Henry, was proclaimed king. Almost immediately, Magna Carta was reissued and the Forest Charter, which regulated Forest laws within England, was also issued in December 1217. In 1217 the rebels and their French allies were defeated, first at the battle of Lincoln and then at a sea battle off Sandwich, and forced to negotiate for peace. Prince Louis went home, and the last remaining English rebels were brought into the king's peace.

Following her father's death in October 1216, Joan continued to work towards peace between Wales and England. She visited Henry in person in September 1224, meeting him in Worcester; Joan seems to have had a good relationship with her half-brother, evidenced by his gifts to her of the manor of Rothley in Leicestershire, in 1225, followed by that of Condover in Shropshire, in 1226.[13] An extant letter to Henry III, addressed to her 'most excellent lord and dearest brother' is a plea for him to come to an understanding with Llywelyn. In the letter, Joan uses her relationship with Henry to try to ease the mounting tensions between the two men. She describes her grief 'beyond measure' that discord between her husband and brother had arisen out of the machinations of their enemies and reassures her brother of Llywelyn's affection for him.[14]

In the mid-1220s, Henry acted as a sponsor, with Llywelyn, in Joan's appeal to Pope Honorius III to be declared legitimate; in 1226 her appeal was allowed, thus enhancing her position – and by extension Llywelyn's – as a legitimate member of the royal family. The appeal had been granted on the grounds that neither of Joan's parents had been married to others when she was born, which suggests that she was born either before John married Isabella of Gloucester, or that the pope did not recognise John's marriage to Isabella as ever being lawful.

Joan and Llywelyn's marriage appears to have been, for the most part, a successful one. Joan's high-born status, as the daughter of a king, brought great prestige to Gwynedd. As a consequence, her household was doubled from four to eight staff, including a cook who could prepare Joan's favourite dishes. Llywelyn seems to have valued his wife's opinion; as we have seen, he often made use of her diplomatic skills and relationship with the English court and he often consulted her on other matters. Her influence extended to Welsh legal texts, which, from this period onwards, included French words.

Joan's position was strengthened even further by the arrival of her children. Sometime in the spring of 1212 her son, Dafydd, was born; in 1220 he was recognised as Llywelyn's heir by Henry III, officially supplanting his older, half-brother, Gruffudd, who, despite his illegitimacy, was entitled to his father's lands under Welsh law. The move received papal approval in 1222. As a result, in 1229, Dafydd performed homage to Henry III as his father's heir, his mother Joan was in attendance, thus demonstrating her own important position at the Welsh court. A daughter, Elen, was probably born around 1210, as she was first married in 1222, to John the Scot, Earl of Chester. Her second marriage, in 1237 or 1238, was arranged by Henry III and was to Robert de Quincy, brother of the earl of Winchester; Robert and Elen's great-granddaughter was Margaret Wake, mother of Joan of Kent, and therefore grandmother of King Richard II. Recent research has confirmed that Joan was also the mother to at least two more of Llywelyn's daughters, Gwladus and Margaret, who were previously thought to have been the daughters of a mistress. Gwladus was married to Reginald de Braose. Her stepson, William (V) de Braose, was to play a big part in Joan's scandalous downfall in 1230. Another of Llywelyn's daughters, Susanna, may also have been Joan's.[15]

Joan's life in the first quarter of the thirteenth century had been exemplary; she was the ideal medieval noblewoman, a dutiful daughter and wife, whose marriage helped to broker peace, if an uneasy one, between two countries. She had fulfilled her wifely duties, both by providing a son and heir and being supportive of her husband to the extent that she should not be included in the roll call of scandalous women – however, in 1230, everything changed. William de Braose was a wealthy Norman baron with estates along the Welsh Marches. Hated by the Welsh people, who had given him the nickname Gwilym Ddu, or Black William, he had been taken prisoner by Llywelyn in 1228, near Montgomery. Although he had been released after paying a ransom, de Braose had returned to Llywelyn's court to arrange a marriage between his daughter, Isabella, and Llywelyn's son and heir, Dafydd. During this stay, William de Braose was 'caught in Llywelyn's chamber with the King of England's daughter, Llywelyn's wife'.[16]

William de Braose was publicly hanged, either at Crogan near Bala, or possibly near Garth Celyn, Abergwyngregyn (on the north coast of Gwynedd), on 2 May 1230. Joan, however, escaped with her life and was imprisoned.[17] We cannot say how long the affair had lasted, whether it was a brief fling in 1230, or had started when de Braose was a prisoner of Llywelyn in 1228. Joan's position in the 1220s had appeared unassailable but this scandal rocked Wales, and England, to the core. She was no young girl struggling to come to terms with her position in life; she was about 40 years old, had been Llywelyn's consort for twenty-five years and had borne him at least four children when the affair was discovered. Contemporaries were deeply shocked at Joan's betrayal of her husband; indeed, following this scandal, Welsh law identified the sexual misconduct of the wife of a ruler as 'the greatest disgrace'.[18] However, there was no question over the legitimacy of her children, who had been born at least fifteen years before.

The most surprising thing about the whole affair, moreover, is Llywelyn's response. His initial anger saw William de Braose hanged from the nearest tree, and Joan imprisoned in a tower. This rage, however vicious, was remarkably brief. Under Welsh law, Llywelyn had the right to repudiate Joan and seek a divorce for her betrayal. Maybe it was due to the strength of the previous relationship between Llywelyn and Joan, or maybe it was the high value placed on Joan's diplomatic skills and her links with the English court; but within a year the terms of Joan's imprisonment had been relaxed and just months after that, she was back on the political stage. Llywelyn appears to have forgiven her; the couple were reconciled, and Joan returned to her life and position as Lady of

Wales. Indeed, Joan soon reprised her diplomatic duties. She attended a conference between her husband, son and her brother, Henry III at Shrewsbury, in 1232.

In spite of William de Braose's betrayal with Joan and subsequent execution at his orders, Llywelyn was still anxious that the marriage between his son and de Braose's daughter should go ahead. Isabella de Braose was still in Llywelyn's care and the Welsh prince wrote letters to the girl's mother, William de Braose's widow, Eva Marshal, explaining that he had no choice but to execute her husband, given the nature of his crime, and asking her intentions with regard to the marriage of their children. Llywelyn wrote a second letter to Eva's brother, William Marshal, second earl of Pembroke, again justifying his actions against William de Braose and referring to Braose's deceit and the shame brought down on Llywelyn as a result of his wife's adultery. He also asks William Marshal for his views on the proposed marriage between William's niece and Llywelyn's own son, and whether the earl still wished for the marriage to go ahead.

It seems that Llywelyn's prompt action in writing and his frank words in the letters had the desired effect and healed any possible rift before it escalated. Dafydd and Isabella de Braose were married in 1232. Unfortunately, the marriage would remain childless and Dafydd was succeeded on his death in 1246 by his nephew, Llywelyn, son of Dafydd's half-brother, Gruffudd.

Joan's indiscretion was forgiven by Llywelyn, maybe even forgotten; she was released from her prison within a year and a few months later was back by Llywelyn's side. She was returned to her position as Lady of Wales and continued to work alongside Llywelyn to maintain relations with her brother, Henry III. When she died in February 1237, the Welsh prince was deeply affected by grief. Joan died at Garth Celyn. She was buried close to the shore of Llanfaes, in the Franciscan friary that Llywelyn founded in her memory – a testament to his love for her. The friary was consecrated in 1240, just a few months before Llywelyn's own death in April of that year. The friary was destroyed in 1537, during Henry VIII's dissolution of the monasteries. Joan's remains were lost, but her coffin was eventually believed to have been found, being used as a horse trough in the town of Beaumaris, on Anglesey. The effigy on the large stone coffin depicts a medieval lady wearing a wimple and coronet, with her hands clasped in prayer, and now rests in the porch of Beaumaris church. However, Madaline Grey makes a convincing argument that the effigy is too late to have been Joan, and can be dated to no earlier than the 1260s, given the style of headdress and jewellery featured on it.[19]

It is a testament to Joan's personality, and the strength of her relationship with Llywelyn, not only that her affair with de Braose had few lasting consequences for her, but also that her father, husband and brother all relied on her to help maintain diplomatic connections between England and Wales. She had helped to keep the peace, or re-establish peace when the first could not be achieved, on numerous occasions. As the neighbours of such a powerful nation as England, Joan and Llywelyn had a stake in the good governance of their much bigger neighbour and the implementation of Magna Carta would have been viewed as necessary to curb the excesses of the king and maintain peaceful co-existence – not that it always worked in Wales' favour, however. For a woman who had grown up in obscure surroundings, tarnished somewhat by her illegitimate birth, Joan had proven herself to be a remarkable ally and partner to her Welsh prince, something she deserves to be remembered for, far more than her one indiscretion with William de Braose.

Joan of England

While Joan, the illegitimate daughter of King John, enjoyed a successful marriage to her Welsh prince, her legitimate half-sister and namesake, Joan of England, was to some extent less fortunate. The younger Joan was the oldest daughter of King John and his second wife, Isabelle d'Angoulême. Born 22 July 1210, she was the third of five children; she had two older brothers, and two younger sisters would join the family by 1215. Even before her birth, she was mooted as a possible bride for Alexander of Scotland, son of William I, King of Scots. The humiliating treaty of Norham in 1209 forced on an ill King William, who was threatened with invasion by John, not only obliged William to pay £10,000 and hand over thirteen hostages, but also gave John the authority to arrange the marriages of William's two daughters.[20] The intention was that one of these daughters marry a son of John's, while Alexander would marry one of John's as-yet unborn daughters. Following the death of William I, a further treaty in 1212 agreed to the marriage of the new king of Scots, 14-year-old Alexander II, to 2-year-old Joan. However, the agreement seems to have been made as a way of preventing Alexander from looking to the Continent – in particular, France – for a potential bride, and by extension, allies. Nevertheless, this did not stop John from looking further afield for a more favourable marriage alliance for Joan. Nor did it stop Alexander II from siding with the barons against King John; Alexander was, in fact, one of the signatories of Magna Carta. As mentioned earlier, Clause 59 of the charter specifically refers to the return of the king of Scots' sisters and their fellow Scottish hostages and guarantees him the same privileges and rights as the other barons of England.[21]

John later refused a proposal from his old ally, King Philip II of France, for Joan to marry Philip's son John, and settled instead, in 1214, for a marriage with his old enemies the de Lusignans. In 1214 Joan was betrothed to Hugh X de Lusignan. Hugh was the son of John's rival for the hand of his wife Isabelle in 1200; Isabelle's engagement to Hugh IX was broken off in order for her to marry John. Following the betrothal Hugh, Lord of Lusignan and Count of La Marche, was given custody of the towns of Saintes, Saintonge and the Isle of Oleron as pledges for Joan's dowry.

Left in the custody of her future husband's family when John returned to England, Joan was kept well away from the intrigues and crisis caused by her father's increasing tyranny in 1215. Her father's death in October 1216, however, did not dissolve the agreement with the Lusignans. In 1218, when Isabelle d'Angoulême left England, it was not only with the intention of going home to Angoulême where she was countess in her own right, but also to supervise the arrangements for Joan's marriage to Hugh de Lusignan; abandoning her four other children, who would remain in England.

In 1220, in a scandalous *volte-face*, Hugh repudiated Joan and married her mother, his father's former betrothed – so poor 9-year-old Joan's erstwhile future husband was now her step-father. Isabelle d'Angoulême wrote to her 12-year-old son, King Henry III, excusing her actions and saying Sir Hugh de Lusignan could not yet marry Joan, on account of her tender years, but was in desperate need of an heir. Isabelle claimed she married him herself to prevent him looking to France for a suitable bride, and to safeguard the Plantagenet lands of Poitou and Gascony. The letter read:

> We do to wit that the Counts of La Marche and Eu being both dead, Sir Hugh de Lusignan was left, as it were, alone and without an heir, and his friends would not allow him to marry our daughter on account of her tender age, but counselled him to make such a marriage that he might speedily have an heir; and it was proposed that he should take a wife in France; which if he should do, all your land in Poitou and Gascony, and ours too, would be lost. We therefore, seeing the great danger that might arise if such a marriage should take place, and getting no support from your counsellors, have taken the said Hugh Count La Marche to be our lord and husband.[22]

However, instead of sending little Joan back to England, as you might expect, the now 10-year-old princess went from being Hugh's betrothed to his prisoner. She was held hostage to ensure not only Hugh's continued control of her dower lands, but also the transfer of his new wife's dower as queen. At the same time, England was withholding Queen Isabelle's dower against the return of Joan and her dower lands. Negotiations to resolve the situation went on for several months. In the meantime, despite her captivity, Joan's older brother, Henry III, and his advisers were already looking to arrange a new marriage for her. On 15 June 1220, in York, a conference between Alexander II and Henry III saw the Scots king agree to marry Joan, with a provision that he would marry Joan's younger sister, Isabella, if Joan was not returned to England in time. Negotiations for Joan's return were long and difficult and not helped by the fact Hugh was threatening war in Poitou. Eventually, after papal intervention, agreement was reached in October 1220 and Joan was surrendered to the English. Joan and Alexander II were married on 19 June 1221, at York Minster. Joan was just weeks from her eleventh birthday, while Alexander was 22. The archbishop of York performed the ceremony, which was witnessed by Henry III and the great magnates of both realms. Henry III's Pipe Rolls suggest the wedding was followed by three days of celebrations, costing £100.[23] Talking of her wedding day, the Chronicle of Lanercost had described Joan as 'a girl still of a young age, but when she was an adult of comely beauty'.[24]

According to the Chronicle of Melrose 'having celebrated the nuptials most splendidly, as was befitting, with all the natives of either realm rejoicing, [Alexander] conducted [Joan] to Scotland.'[25] The day before the wedding Alexander had assigned dower estates to Joan, worth an annual income of £1,000, including Jedburgh, Crail and Kinghorn. However, part of the dower was still held by Alexander's mother, the dowager queen Ermengarde, and Joan was not entitled to the income until after her mother-in-law's death in 1233. This left Joan financially dependent on Alexander from the beginning, a situation which mirrored that of her mother's marriage to King John and severely curbed Joan's independence, as it had her mother.

There is a suggestion that Joan was not enamoured with Scotland and its society, and that she found it difficult to settle into the Scottish court. She was hampered by her youth, her domineering mother-in-law and, eventually, by the fact she failed to produce the desired heir. Joan's position was further hindered from time to time by tensions between her husband and brother. In this, though, she seems to have found her purpose. Joan regularly acted as intermediary between the two kings.

Alexander often used Joan's personal letters to her brother as a way of communicating with Henry, bypassing the formality of official correspondence between kings. One such letter is a warning, possibly on behalf of Alexander's constable, Alan of Galloway, of intelligence that Haakon IV of Norway was intending to aid Hugh de Lacy in Ireland. In the same letter, she assured Henry that no one from Scotland would be going to Ireland to fight against Henry's interests.[26] Another letter, this time from Henry, was of a more personal nature; written in February 1235, it informed Joan of the marriage of their 'beloved sister' Isabella to the Holy Roman Emperor Frederick II, news at which he knew Joan 'would greatly rejoice'.[27]

In December 1235 Alexander and Joan were summoned to London, possibly for the coronation of Henry's new queen, Eleanor of Provence. This would have been a long and arduous journey for the Scottish monarchs, especially in the deepest part of winter. Henry's use of Joan as an intermediary suggests she did have some influence over her husband; this theory is supported by the fact that Joan accompanied Alexander to negotiations with the English king at Newcastle in September 1236 and again at York in September 1237. In 1234, Henry had granted Joan the manor of Fenstanton in Huntingdonshire, and during the 1236 negotiations she was granted that of Driffield in Yorkshire, thus giving Joan an income independent of Scotland. Many have seen this as an indication that Joan was intending to spend more time in England, especially seeing as the chronicler Matthew Paris hints at an estrangement, although we cannot be certain.[28] The 1236 and 1237 councils were attempts at resolving the ongoing claims by Alexander that King John had agreed to gift Northumberland to him as part of the marriage contract between Alexander and Joan. Henry, of course, denied this. With the mediation of a papal legate, agreement was eventually reached in York at the 1237 council, with both queens, Joan and Eleanor of Provence, present. Alexander gave up the claim to Northumberland in return for lands in the northern counties with an annual income of £200.[29]

Following the 1237 council, Joan and her sister-in-law, Eleanor of Provence, departed on pilgrimage to the shrine of Saint Thomas Becket at Canterbury. Given that Joan was now 27 and Eleanor already married for two years, it is possible both women were praying for children, and an heir to their respective husbands' thrones. Joan stayed in England for the rest of the year; much of the stay seems to have been informal and pleasurable. She spent Christmas at Henry's court and was given new robes for herself, her clerks and servants, in addition to gifts of deer and wine. Her sister Eleanor, Countess of Pembroke, widow of William II Marshal and future wife of Simon de Montfort, was present, with their niece the countess of Chester and Joan's cousin, the captive Eleanor of Brittany.

In late January arrangements were made for Joan's return to Scotland, but she fell ill before she could travel north. Only 27 years of age, Joan died on 4 March 1238 at Havering-atte-Bower in Essex. Her brothers, King Henry III and Richard, Earl of Cornwall, were at her side. Before her death, she had had time to get her affairs in order, as testified by the rolls of Henry III:

1238. 18 March. Sandleford. The king has granted to J. queen of Scots while she lives that if she happens to die, her executors may hold in their hands the manors of Driffield and Fenstanton for two years from Michaelmas in the twenty-second year, in order to make execution of [the testament] of the aforesaid queen as would seem best for the king, so that they would hold those manors in their hand, as has been agreed between the king and the aforesaid executors, by a certain price. Order to Robert of Crepping to take the manor of Driffield into the king's hand and keep it safely until the king orders otherwise, saving to the aforesaid executors the corn in the land, rent of assise and all stock found in the same manor up to Michaelmas in the twenty-second year.[30]

According to Matthew Paris 'her death was grievous, however she merited less mourning, because she refused to return [to Scotland] although often summoned back by her husband.'[31] Even in death Joan chose to stay in England. Her will requested that she be buried at the Cistercian nunnery of Tarrant in Dorset. The convent benefited greatly from Henry III's almsgiving for the soul of his sister; in 1252, more than thirteen years after her death, the king ordered a marble effigy to be made for her tomb (which unfortunately has not survived). Alexander II married again just over a year after Joan's death, to Marie de Coucy, and their son and longed-for heir, Alexander III, was born in 1241. Alexander II died of a fever in 1249.

The debacle of Joan's betrothal and imprisonment by Hugh de Lusignan, and her unhappy marriage to Alexander II, are prime examples of the lot of a Plantagenet princess. She was too young to have any influence when Magna Carta was issued, but her husband had been a part of its creation, although it seems to have had little relevance to her as an English princess and Scottish queen. However, Joan rose above her marriages and found a purpose in her pursuit of peace between England and Scotland. She was a conduit to maintaining communications, even when relations were tense. Joan was also lucky to enjoy a happy, close relationship with her siblings, especially her brothers, Henry III and Richard, Earl of Cornwall, although once she married, she seems to have had little contact with her mother, Isabelle d'Angoulême, hundreds of miles away in France and with her new Lusignan family to concentrate on.

Isabella of England

Joan's younger sister, Isabella, also had very little to do with Magna Carta and its aftermath, but it seems unfair to leave her out of the story, after including all her sisters. Nearly everyone knows that Henry I's daughter Matilda, Lady of the English, was Empress as the wife of German Emperor Henry V. What is less well-known is that, almost seventy years after Matilda's death, her great-granddaughter followed in her footsteps. Isabella of England was born in 1214; she was the fourth of five children born to King John and Isabelle d'Angoulême. Born at a time when her father's strife with his barons was at its height, her early childhood was turbulent, to say the least. John died just two years later, in October 1216, leaving 9-year-old Henry as king of a country in the midst of civil war and fighting off an occupying French army. As with many medieval princesses, we know very little about her childhood. Her nurse was a lady named Margaret Biset, who was given an allowance of 1*d.* a day from the royal treasury in 1219 and would accompany the young princess to Germany when she married in 1235.[32]

Just over a year after her father's death, Isabella's mother left England, ostensibly to finalise the wedding arrangements of Isabella's older sister, Joan, to Hugh de Lusignan. Isabella was left in England, with her siblings, as her mother supplanted Joan as Hugh de Lusignan's bride. Whilst Joan was still in the hands of the Lusignans, her marriage to Alexander II of Scotland was negotiated, with an added clause that Isabella could be substituted for her older sister, should Joan not make it back to England in time for the wedding. In the event Joan was released by Lusignan and returned in time, allowing Henry III to look elsewhere for a husband for Isabella.

The young princess was to become part of Henry's policy of Continental diplomacy. The king looked at several possible husbands for his sister, such as Henry VII, king of the Romans and Louis IX of France. After some prompting by Pope Gregory IX, German Emperor Frederick II sent a Sicilian embassy to England in 1234 to pursue his own suit for the English princess to become his third wife. Frederick Hohenstaufen was born near Ancona in 1194, the son of Henry VI, King of Germany and Holy Roman Emperor, and Constance, heiress to the Norman kingdom of Sicily. Orphaned at the age of 4, Frederick was raised under the guardianship of Pope Innocent III. During his childhood, the empire was contested between Otto IV, nephew of King John, and Philip of Swabia. However, Philip of Swabia died in 1208 and Otto was defeated at the Battle of Bouvines in 1214, fighting against Philip II Augustus of France, and thereafter was forced to abdicate in 1215. In the same year, 20-year-old Frederick was crowned King of Germany at Aachen, seated on Charlemagne's marble throne. He was then crowned Holy Roman Emperor by Pope Honorious III in 1220. In spite of his disputes with the papacy over his sceptical attitude to Christianity, and despite being excommunicated by Pope Gregory IX, Frederick went on crusade and captured Jerusalem in 1229, where he was crowned in the Holy Sepulchre. The excommunication was lifted after Frederick crushed a papal army which was threatening Sicily. In August 1230, 'Pope Gregory IX and Emperor Frederick II came to an agreement. The emperor went to Rome and was absolved, all sentences touching on his imperial rights being fully revoked.'[33]

In November 1234, Pope Gregory encouraged Frederick to consider Isabella for his third wife. Frederick despatched the Sicilian embassy, under his close adviser, Piero della Vigna, which arrived in England in February 1235. According to Roger of Wendover 'The king of England was extremely interested in this idea and discussed it for three days on end with the nobles and bishops of the kingdom.'[34] Henry was agreeable to the match, which complimented his keen interest in the Holy Roman Empire and 'declared unanimously that Isabella should be given to the emperor.'[35] When the envoys asked to see Isabella Henry had her brought from the Tower of London, where she was residing, to Westminster to 'show her to the messengers of the emperor, a beautiful girl in her twenty-first year, distinguished by her maidenhood, and properly bedecked with the accustomed trappings of royalty. The ambassadors were pleased with the girl and judged her fitting in every way to be an imperial bride'[36] The ambassadors were so impressed with Isabella that they 'offered her a betrothal ring on the emperor's behalf, and when they had placed it on her finger, they shouted together: "Long live the empress!"'[37]

The marriage contract was signed on 22 February 1235, with Henry giving Isabella a dowry of 30,000 marks. Although Isabella already had her own fine chapel silver, Henry gave her a magnificent trousseau, which included a service of gold and silver plate.[38] The English people were irritated by Henry's demand for a substantial marriage aid, but

Henry saw the marriage as adding to his personal prestige, and a possible alliance against Louis IX of France. Roger of Wendover described the arrangements:

> The preparations for that wedding were so lavish that they seemed to exceed all the riches of the kingdom. For the sake of the empress's dignity, her crown was most skilfully crafted from the purest gold and studded with precious stones. On it were sculpted the four kings of England who were confessors and martyrs, and to whom King Henry had especially commended the care of his sister's soul. In her festal robes, which were made of silk and wool, and also of linen of different hues, decked out in all the dignity that befits an empress, Isabella shone out so that it was impossible to tell which of all her many adornments would most induce love in the emperor's heart. In addition to all this, her bed, with its silk covers and gaily coloured mattresses, different hangings and draperies sewn from the most delicate muslin, stood so splendidly that its softness actively invited those seeking repose to sweet sleep. All the vessels sent, whether for wine or for food, were cast in completely unalloyed silver and gold and, what seemed almost superfluous to everyone, even the cooking pots, large and small, were of the finest silver.[39]

Emperor Frederick then sent the archbishop of Cologne and duke of Louvain to England with an escort of high-ranking nobles to escort his bride to her new homeland. On 11 May 1235 Isabella set sail from Sandwich, entrusted to her imperial escort and 'to the charge of William, Bishop of Exeter, Ralph, the king's steward, and to other aristocratic nobles of her household, aristocratic ladies-in-waiting and high-born pages who were all versed in courtly manners and suitable to serve and escort an empress.'[40] She arrived at Antwerp four days later. Proceeding with a substantial bodyguard, to protect against kidnap threats from Frederick II's enemies, Isabella arrived in Cologne on 24 May. She made a processional entry into the city, to the cheers of a 10,000 strong crowd, endearing herself to the noble ladies by throwing her veil back. She was to spend six weeks in Cologne waiting for Frederick, who was dealing with a rebellion by his oldest son, Henry VII, to send for her.

By July 1235 they were together in Worms where, with the archbishop of Mainz officiating, 'on Sunday, 30 July, Frederick II solemnly wed Isabella, the sister of the king of England.'[41] Isabella was crowned Holy Roman Empress at the same time. Roger of Wendover continued in his commentary with a more personal observation of Isabella, saying, 'Much as she had pleased him in outward appearance, she pleased him even more in the marriage bed, when he found the signs of her virginal purity.'[42] Four days of wedding festivities followed, with guests including – according to Matthew Paris – four kings, eleven dukes and thirty counts and marquesses.[43]

Frederick, it seems, put great store by astrology; in 1228 Michael Scot had completed his encyclopaedia of astrology while at Frederick's court. And it was on the advice of the emperor's court astrologers that the marriage was not consummated until the second night.[44] Isabella was the emperor's third wife; his first, Constance of Aragon, had died of malaria in 1222 and his second wife, Queen Isabella-Yolanda of Jerusalem had died in childbirth in 1228. Frederick was twenty years Isabella's senior and expended all his energy on war, travelling and ceremonials in order to maintain his authority throughout his vast empire. Frederick was delighted with his bride; she was beautiful and popular. He sent three leopards to Henry III in England as a sign of his appreciation. However, following the wedding celebrations he also dismissed the majority of Isabella's English attendants; she was allowed to retain only her nurse, Margaret Biset – who had been with her since her early childhood – and a maid, called Kathrein. Isabella travelled with Frederick's slaves to his palace at Hagenau, where Frederick spent the winter with his new empress. Their first child was probably born around 1237/8, although there does seem to be some confusion over how many children there were, and when they were born. What is certain is two children survived childhood; Henry, King of Jerusalem, died unmarried in his teens in 1254 and Margaret married Albert I, Margrave of Meissen and Langrave of Thuringia and Misnes, in 1256.[45]

Isabella travelled extensively through her husband's lands, residing in Apulia, Lombardy, and Noventa between 1238 and 1239. Frederick was always close by, despite his battles with the papacy, and arrived in southern Italy shortly after his wife's arrival in February 1240. Isabella was expected to live in some magnificence, but Henry III was irritated that she was only rarely allowed to appear in public. There were rumours that Frederick kept his wives in a harem, although these were probably unfounded and arose from the seclusion that firstly Isabella–Yolanda and then Isabella lived in. When Richard, Earl of Cornwall visited the Emperor in 1241, he did not immediately see his sister. However, this was probably down to court protocol, as the empress was pregnant at the time. When they did meet the brother and sister were treated to a lavish court entertainment, being delighted by a magnificent display of jugglers and Muslim dancers. Although there is no apparent record of it, Isabella may also have been reunited for a time with her younger sister, Eleanor, wife of Simon de Montfort, who stayed in one of Frederick's palaces, in Brindisi, while her husband Simon de Montfort, Earl of Leicester, was on crusade to the Holy Land in 1240.[46]

Following Richard's visit, Frederick II returned to war. Before his departure on campaign, Isabella had urged Frederick to stay on good terms with her brother who was leaning more and more towards the papacy. Frederick was besieging Faenza in northern Italy when his wife died in childbirth on 1 December 1241; tragically, the baby died with her. Frederick wrote to Henry III of Isabella's death; 'And though the loss of the Augusta our consort and your sister cannot be named without disturbance, nor can anxiety be banished from our inmost breast, yet in her two children the memory of their parent still survives.'[47] She was buried at Andria, Sicily, alongside the emperor's second wife, Isabella–Yolanda. Isabella had been married for just over six years and was only 27 years of age. Through her daughter Margaret, Isabella is the ancestor of Queen Victoria's beloved husband, Prince Albert.

As the daughter of King John, the illegitimate Joan, Lady of Wales, through her husband, was involved in the birth of Magna Carta and the struggles of the last years of her father's reign. For Joan, Queen of Scots, and Isabella, Empress of Germany, Magna Carta had little relevance in their lives; particularly Isabella who, once she was living on the Continent, was far removed from the political struggles of the thirteenth century. There was one daughter of King John and Queen Isabelle, however, for whom Magna Carta was particularly significant and acted as the starting point of the long years of struggle for herself, her husband and her family. It was left to John's youngest daughter, Eleanor, born in the same year as the Great Charter, to make the most of the implications of Magna Carta, and the rights enshrined therein.

Chapter 13

Eleanor, Countess of Pembroke and Leicester

T here was one daughter of King John for whom Magna Carta and the struggle for political reform held particular significance. The life of Eleanor of England, and her husband Simon de Montfort, stands as the epilogue of the Magna Carta story. Although democratic government was still many centuries in the future, Magna Carta was the first step. The political movement led by Simon de Montfort was the second step ...

Eleanor of England was the youngest child of John and Isabelle d'Angoulême; she is said to have inherited her mother's beauty and feisty temperament.[1] She was most likely born at the height of her father's troubles, in the midst of the Magna Carta crisis in 1215. Named for her grandmother, Eleanor of Aquitaine, she was placed in the household of the bishop of Winchester, where her eldest brother, Henry, had been living since 1212.[2] In 1224 she was married to William (II) Marshal, Earl of Pembroke. The younger Marshal was the son of the first earl of Pembroke who had been regent in the early years of Henry III's reign, and who had driven the French out of England following his victory at the Battle of Lincoln in May 1217. The first earl had a reputation for integrity and loyalty, having remained unwavering in his loyalty to King John during the Magna Carta crisis. The second earl, Eleanor's husband, had been a hostage of the king between 1207 and 1213, as a guarantee of his father's good behaviour. He later joined the baronial rebellion and was appointed marshal of the forces of the invader, Prince Louis. However, he returned to the Royalists when Louis refused him possession of Marlborough Castle, which had previously belonged to the younger Marshal's grandfather.[3] He fought alongside his father at the Battle of Lincoln.

On his father's death in 1219, William (II) Marshal had succeeded him as earl of Pembroke and marshal of England; when his mother died in 1220, he succeeded to her lordships of Leinster and Netherwent. His younger brother, Richard Marshal, succeeded to the Clare lands in Ireland. In 1214 Marshal married Alice, the daughter of Baldwin de Béthune, Count of Aumâle, to whom he had been betrothed in 1203. The marriage was short-lived, however, as poor Alice died in 1216. On 23 April 1224, William (II) Marshal was married to Eleanor; born in the 1290s, he was some twenty-or-so years older than his bride, who was no more than 9 years old on her wedding day.[4] The marriage was agreed at the behest of the justiciar, Hubert de Burgh, and the papal legate, Pandulf, as a way of guaranteeing Marshal remained firmly in the justiciar's camp, and to prevent the marshal making a foreign marriage. The match put an end to three years of indecision, as to whether Eleanor should marry a foreign prince or an English magnate. The king settled ten manors, confiscated from a French nobleman and already administered by Marshal, on his sister as her marriage portion.[5]

For the first five years of her marriage Eleanor continued to live at court, under the guardianship of Cecily of Sandford.[6] In 1229, when she was 14, she went to live with her husband, travelling with him in England, France and Ireland. In May 1230, Marshal had taken twenty knights with him, on Henry III's expedition to Poitou. He also took his wife, probably at the behest of the king. Eleanor became seasick during the voyage to France and Henry had his ship drop anchor at the nearest landfall to give her time to recover, ordering the fleet to continue without them.[7] Henry was probably hoping that Eleanor's presence would help to secure the support of his mother and her second husband, Hugh de Lusignan, to his expedition against the French. Mother and daughter had not seen each other since Eleanor was 2 or 3. Isabelle's maternal affection for the children of her first husband, however, was practically non-existent, and Eleanor's presence failed to persuade her mother and stepfather to remain loyal to Henry III. As we have seen, Isabelle d'Angoulême had a penchant for putting her own interests ahead of those of her English family.

Marshal and Eleanor returned from France in the spring of 1231, with William handing over command of the English forces to Ranulf, Earl of Chester, for the wedding of his widowed sister, Isabel, to the king's brother, Richard, Earl of Cornwall. William (II) Marshal died suddenly in London a week later, on 6 April and was buried beside his father at the Temple Church on 15 April 1231. At the tender age of 15 or 16, Eleanor was a childless widow. The earldom of Pembroke passed to William's younger brother, Richard, and Eleanor would spend many years fighting unsuccessfully to get the entirety of her dowry from the Marshal family, which amounted to one third of the Marshal estates, according to the guarantees established by Magna Carta. The Great Charter stipulated a widow should receive the allocation of a dower within forty days of her husband's death. A year after William's death Richard Marshal offered Eleanor £400 a year as her settlement. Henry III persuaded his sister to take it, wanting to be done with the business and probably well aware that it was as much as Eleanor was likely to get, despite the Marshal holdings amounting to an income of £3,000 a year.[8] Henry stood as guarantor for the settlement but the payments would always be sporadic and unreliable, not helped by the fact that the earldom passed through four successive Marshal brothers between 1231 and 1245, each with differing priorities and more Marshal widows to assign their dowers.

In the midst of her grief, and influenced by her former governess, Eleanor took a vow of chastity in the presence of Edmund of Abingdon, archbishop of Canterbury in 1234. Although she did not become a nun, the archbishop put a ring on her finger, to signify that she was a bride of Christ; she was, therefore, expected to remain chaste and virtuous for the rest of her life. As a result, the king seized her estates and Richard Marshal, as her husband's heir, took many of her valuable chattels. Knowing how teenagers see lost love as the end of the world, even today, one can understand Eleanor's decision to take a vow of chastity, even if we cannot comprehend anyone giving such advice to a grieving 16-year-old. Eleanor may also have seen taking such a vow as a way of staving off her brother, the king, forcing her to remarry in the interests of the crown. It put Eleanor's life in her own hands and also served to appease the Marshal family, who would have seen their own lands, which made up Eleanor's dower, controlled by another magnate or foreign prince had she remarried.

The widowed Eleanor retired to the castle of Inkberrow in Worcestershire. Henry continued to watch over his sister throughout the 1230s; he sent her gifts of venison and timber for her manors. Throughout her life, Eleanor was known for her extravagant spending, which led to substantial debts; Henry lent her money and made sporadic payments to reduce the debts. In 1237 her brother granted her Odiham Castle in Hampshire, which would become her principal residence.[9]

In 1238, Eleanor met Simon de Montfort, Earl of Leicester. Simon was the third son of Simon de Montfort, Lord of Montfort l'Amaury and Alice, daughter of Bouchard de Montmorency. As a third son, Simon's prospects would have appeared bleak during his younger years. An opportunity arose for him through his father's claim to the earldom of Leicester, through the elder Simon's mother, Amicia, coheiress of Robert de Breteuil, Earl of Leicester. The earldom had been divided between the elder Simon and his mother's sister, Margaret, wife of Saher de Quincy, Earl of Winchester. The continuing hostilities between England and France in the early years of the thirteenth century meant that Simon de Montfort was never able to take possession of this inheritance. The senior Simon de Montfort had died in 1218 and was succeeded by his eldest son Amaury de Montfort. By 1230, Amaury had transferred all or some of his claims to the earldom of Leicester to his younger brother, Simon, who then departed for England to claim his inheritance.[10]

Simon de Montfort was able to gain control of his family's portion of the Leicester lands, which had been in the custody of Ranulf, Earl of Chester, since 1215, rather quickly. Although he was not able to obtain the earldom that went with them. In 1231, he did homage to Henry III for his lands and he continued to rise through the ranks of the court throughout the 1230s. From 1234 he attended meetings of the great council, pursued diplomacy with Scotland and Wales and acted as steward – a post traditionally held by the earls of Leicester – at Henry III's wedding to Eleanor of Provence in 1234, although the earldom had still not been conferred on him.[11] Simon did make enemies, however; his closeness to Henry and the fact he was a foreigner, did not endear Simon to his fellow nobles.

At some point after the mid-1230s, possibly at the wedding of Henry and Eleanor of Provence, Simon met the king's youngest sister, Eleanor, and the couple fell in love.[12] With the king's permission, they married in January 1238, in a secret ceremony in Henry's private chapel; Matthew Paris called it a '*matrimonium clandestinum*', a clandestine marriage.[13] Simon was probably about 30 years old while Eleanor was 22 or 23. Due to Eleanor's vow of chastity, and the fact Simon was a foreigner and a minor noble, and Eleanor was a princess, secrecy was essential. The secret got out, nevertheless, with Richard, Earl of Cornwall, Eleanor's other brother, and several other councillors being greatly angered by the news. It probably did not help matters that Simon had quite a reputation for chasing after wealthy widows; he had previously been refused marriage by at least two of them.

Archbishop Edmund of Canterbury appealed to the pope on the grounds that Eleanor had broken her vows of chastity.[14] In March 1238 Simon departed for Rome to obtain a dispensation for the marriage from the pope. The king gave him a glowing reference and an unknown amount of money. On the journey south, Simon also visited his new brother-in-law, Emperor Frederick II, who gave him additional letters of support. The dispensation was granted in May 1238 and Simon was back home in England in time for the birth of his first child. Eleanor entered her confinement at Kenilworth Castle in October and Henry, named after his uncle the king, was born on 26 November 1238, ten months after his parent's wedding.[15] The following spring, Simon was confirmed as earl of Leicester by the king, who ordered that Eleanor's dowry should be paid to him.

In August 1239, however, at the churching of Eleanor of Provence, following the birth of Lord Edward, the king's eldest son and heir, Henry turned on his brother-in-law. He accused Simon of seducing his sister and defiling her before their marriage, of bribing the pope and using the crown as surety for his debts without the king's permission.[16] Apparently, Simon had borrowed a large amount of money, for his trip to Rome, from the queen's uncle, Thomas of Savoy, Count of Flanders, giving the king's name as security. The king only discovered this when Thomas asked for his money. Matthew Paris recounted Henry's charges against Simon:

You seduced my sister before marriage, and when I found it out, I gave her to you in marriage, although against my will, in order to avoid scandal; and, that her vow might not impede the marriage, you went to Rome, and by costly presents and great promises you bribed the Roman court to grant you permission to do what was unlawful. The Archbishop of Canterbury here present knows this, and intimated the truth of the matter to the pope, but truth was overcome by bribes; and on your failing to pay the money you promised, you were excommunicated; and to increase the mass of your wickedness, you, by false evidence named me as your security, without consulting me, and when I know nothing at all of the matter.[17]

The debt arose from the £200 Simon had borrowed in order to pay Earl Ranulf of Chester for the earldom of Leicester. The papal curia had arranged for the debt to be passed from Peter of Dreux, Duke of Brittany, to Thomas, Count of Flanders, accumulating interest as it went and probably with the cost of the papal dispensation added to it for good measure. It was now £1,400. Over twenty years later, Simon gave his own account of the incident to the French court, saying:

The King of England honoured me by giving me his sister; but shortly afterwards he was incensed by a debt which my lord Thomas, Count of Flanders, was claiming from me and for which he sued me at the court of Rome. The king wished me to pay; to which I replied that I was ready to do so, if I was legally the debtor; but I asked that justice should be done to me, as to the poorest man in the kingdom. He refused, with ugly and shameful words which it would be painful to recall.[18]

Henry was renowned for his mercurial moods and temper tantrums (much like his grandfather, Henry II). He forbade Simon and a pregnant Eleanor from attending the queen's churching ceremony and the stunned couple had to flee London, taking ship to France; so hasty was their departure that they were forced to leave their son behind, with his wet nurse. As Simon related his story to the French court, he continued:

Then, the same day that he had invited us to the queen's churching, he ordered the men of the commune of London to arrest me at the inn where I was lodging and to take me off to the Tower; but Richard, who was there, would not allow that to happen at that moment. Seeing his great wrath and that he would not listen to reason, I left the country.[19]

Simon de Montfort had a strong friendship with Robert Grosseteste, Bishop of Lincoln, who agreed to intervene with the king on Simon's behalf. Simon was able to return to England in April 1240, ostensibly to raise funds for his crusade. He also collected his young son, Henry, so that he could be reunited with his mother. While in France, Eleanor gave birth to a second son, Simon. She was pregnant again when she and their two sons accompanied Simon eastwards as he set out to join the crusade of his brother-in-law Richard, Earl of Cornwall. Taking an overland route, Simon and his family travelled through Italy as a guest of Emperor Frederick II. Eleanor set up her household at Brindisi, in a palace lent to them by the emperor, where she would await Simon's return from the Holy Land. Although there is no record of it, it is entirely possible that Eleanor was reunited with her sister, Isabella, Emperor Frederick's wife, who also spent time in Italy. There was only a year's difference in the young women's ages, which may mean that the sisters were close, although the chronicles of the time made very little mention of affection where women were concerned.

In 1242, following Simon's return from crusade, the couple were restored to Henry's favour. Eleanor accompanied Simon as he went on campaign to Poitou. The campaign was a financial disaster for Simon, exacerbating his already-dire financial situation. Simon's earldom of Leicester brought in an income of £500 a year, while Eleanor had £400 a year, albeit sporadically, from her inadequate Marshal dower. King Henry now settled a further £500 on Simon as Eleanor's dower for her second marriage, something which should have been done at the time of the marriage but was not. Simon's financial position was, therefore, precarious and made worse by the knowledge that Eleanor's Marshal dower would revert to the Marshals on her death, leaving Simon with less resources to provision his own growing family with lands and income.

After the births of Henry and Simon, two more sons, Amaury and Guy, followed in quick succession, born in 1242/3 and 1244 respectively. A fifth son, Richard, was born before 1252 and a daughter, Eleanor, probably born in 1258. In 1242, Henry formally granted Kenilworth Castle to his sister, and Eleanor made this her principal residence, the family home.[20] The older boys were educated in the household of Bishop Grosseteste and the Franciscan theologian, Adam Marsh, was Eleanor's confessor.

Marsh was a great confidant of Eleanor's, and regularly wrote her with advice and encouragement. He was also not shy in calling attention to her weaknesses; in one letter, her confessor reprimanded Eleanor for her contentiousness and extravagance. In another he wrote of her devotion to God and motherhood:

> To the illustrious lady A., countess of Leicester, Brother Adam [sends] greetings in the Lord. The blessed glory of the Lord which did not spurn your devotion and was mindful of your prayer from its place, granting you both freedom from very troubling dangers and the exultation of very pleasing progeny. What then? In so far as he would be worthy to be consulted, that we continually give back to heavenly clemency praise of the divine name and praiseworthy participation in a more perfect life, progressing with most eager heart from day to day. May your serenity be well. May the children be well. May your friends be well. May your ministers in Christ and the blessed Virgin always be well.[21]

Between 1248 and 1252 Simon was in Gascony, acting as Henry's seneschal. In the four years that Simon was abroad, Eleanor visited him in 1249–50, 1251 and 1253. When Simon was in Gascony, Adam Marsh wrote to Eleanor to advise her husband on avoiding taking the wrong course of action in the region:

> To the excellent lady A., countess of Leicester, Brother Adam [sends] greetings and the glory of rewards after the grace of merits. So the renowned count, your husband, for the honour of God and the salvation of the church, for the faith of the lord king and advantage of the peoples, entrusted with magnificent power from the Saviour, magnificently took on the desperate business of very great danger, to save the land of Gascony for the said king, your brother, and his heirs, about which I hope without doubt that he is led to praiseworthy success from careful counsel of discreet discussions of your serenity, with divine help, and with all those joined to said count with faithful love, should gloriously rise in happy praise of the Divinity. So that if by human thoughtlessness, even with praiseworthy intention, he

entered into either pacts or treaties or contracts, less than should have been assured, with immoderate expending of money, yet as seemed impelled by necessity, it will be up to you to direct him through most pious diligence of benign circumspection, having completely removed the struggles of irritating quarrels, in the spirit of gentleness to negotiating cautiously about the rest through tranquillity of counsels. About what you ordered, on brother Gregory, I shall speak, the Lord willing, in brief, when opportunity is granted me. The blessed son of God, the lord of Lincoln is well. May your illustrious children be well progressing from good to better. The lady queen granted me that she would act with master Hugh of Mortuo Mari so that in time he would discharge master Ralph of Canterbury and lord William de la Hose in peace. I do not know what will come of that. May the most worthy integrity of your nobility be always well in Christ and the most blessed Virgin. Lord John de la Haye will be better able to reveal the state of the lord king, the lady queen, prelates and magnates, clergy and people in the kingdom of England, to your lordship. Again, be well forever.[22]

In 1252 Henry III called Simon to Westminster to answer charges of brutal high-handedness in Gascony. Henry was thwarted by the baronial support for Simon, who countered with arguments that Henry had contravened the terms of his commission and failed to support Simon financially.[23] Eleanor accompanied Simon on his visits to Paris, during the negotiations with Louis IX over Gascony. The arguments concerning Eleanor's Marshal dower found their way into the discussions as the treaty included Henry's sisters renouncing their claims to the former Plantagenet lands in France. Eleanor initially refused to do so until her dower was formally settled, and the French king and queen offered to act as mediators. In the end, a payment of 15,000 marks, due to Henry through the treaty, was set aside to act as a pledge for the future settlement of Eleanor's dower.[24] The treaty had been delayed for two years by the time Henry agreed to give Eleanor an annual pension so that she would sign it.[25]

As relations between the king and the barons caused tensions, Simon became involved in the baronial opposition to Henry III's unpopular policies. Magna Carta had set out guidelines whereby the king should be guided by his barons, and the barons expected to be consulted on his policies and actions. Henry was increasingly acting on his own initiative, going against the various interests of the barons. In 1258 the Provisions of Oxford set up a new form of government, with a fifteen-man privy council established to advise the king and oversee the government's administration. The Provisions were confirmed and extended in 1259, in the Provisions of Westminster, but were overthrown by Henry, with the help of a papal bull, in 1261. As attempts to control the king failed, Simon became the baronial leader as they rose up in revolt and the Second Barons' War broke out.

Simon's forces defeated and captured the king and his son and heir, Lord Edward, at the Battle of Lewes in 1264. Edward was held under guard, first residing with Eleanor and later with her son, Henry. With the king's defeat, Simon de Montfort was now the effective ruler of England. He established a government based on the Provisions of Oxford and in 1265 called the Great Parliament, at which towns were asked to send their own representatives for the first time, in addition to the usual attendance of the barons and knights of the shires. This act earned for Simon recognition as the founder of the House of Commons.

Simon's victory was short-lived. Within months Edward had escaped his captors and mounted a new Royalist opposition to his uncle. He faced Simon de Montfort at the Battle of Evesham on 4 August 1265. Simon and his oldest son, Henry, were killed in the fighting. Eleanor had been staying at Odiham but had left for Dover as the tide turned against her family. It was at Dover Castle that Eleanor heard the news of her husband's death and defeat. She withdrew into seclusion for ten days, to mourn her husband and son, but when she reappeared she was ready to take charge again. Rather than running for the Continent, she settled down to defend the castle. Her son, Simon, was holding Eleanor's brother, Richard, at Kenilworth and only released him on condition that he would protect Eleanor's interests; Henry, however, was in no mood to be compassionate towards his sister. He wanted to disinherit and banish Eleanor. The younger Simon then fled north, continuing the insurgence in the Isle of Axeholme in Lincolnshire, which had been a hotbed for rebellion during the First Barons' War against King John. Edward took

Dover in October 1265, allowing Eleanor a dignified retreat into exile, taking her daughter, Eleanor, with her.

Eleanor retired to the Dominican convent of Montargis, founded by her sister-in-law, Amicia de Montfort. In 1267 she was granted an annual payment of £500 from the English Exchequer, providing she remained in exile, thanks to the intervention of Louis IX, King of France. Edward I confirmed this soon after his accession; he had met his aunt on his way home from crusade in 1273 and loaning her £200, he wrote to his chancellor, saying that he had admitted her to his 'grace and peace.'[26] Edward and Eleanor were eventually reconciled, with the help of Marguerite, Queen of France and sister of Edward's mother, Eleanor of Provence, who wrote to the new English king:

> To the very high and very noble prince, our very dear nephew, Edward, by the grace of God king of England, Marguerite, by the same grace queen of France, greetings and true love. Dear nephew, the countess of Leicester entreated us and asks that we entreat you to have pity on her and her will, and asked us also that we entreat for Amaury, her son the cleric, that you have pity on him and do right by him and render him your favour. And since we promised her that we would do it, we entreat for ... things, and we entreat you also that you would act and command that the need that involves the will of said lady ... and delivered as right, usage and custom of the country might give. And ... as to the cleric, that there be honour and good, so much that God, and I, may be grateful to you, and that you cannot be blamed. And of these things ... your will ..., if it please you, the Monday before the feast of St Denis.[27]

Eleanor had been a strong-willed, independent woman. Her seal depicted her as countess on one side and sister of the king on the other.[28] She was involved in the governance of her estates and in disputes with lords over customs and property. She held wardships in her English manors and issued charters in her own name. She was a benevolent mistress, procuring grants and pardons for the men and women in her service. She supported Simon in his rebellion and was entrusted with the custody of her nephews, Edward and Henry (the son of Richard of Cornwall) after the Battle of Lewes. After Simon de Montfort's defeat and death at Evesham, Eleanor continued to support her surviving sons, providing money for them to pay their soldiers and sending two of them to France with 11,000 marks in their possession. She negotiated the surrender of Dover Castle to Lord Edward, her safe passage to France and the safety of her people left behind in England.[29]

In her French exile, Eleanor had the company of her only daughter, Eleanor de Montfort, who was probably born in 1258, at Kenilworth Castle. Eleanor de Montfort was the only daughter and sixth child of Eleanor of England and Simon de Montfort, Earl of Leicester. On her father's death, Eleanor had fled into exile in France with her mother and brothers. Her brothers continued to Italy, where Guy and Simon went to seek knightly employment, while Amaury studied medicine and theology at the university in Padua. The two Eleanors remained settled at the abbey at Montargis, until the elder Eleanor's death there before 3 June 1275, with her daughter Eleanor and her son Amaury by her side. Eleanor, Countess of Pembroke and Leicester and a princess of England, was buried at the abbey which had been her home for the last ten years of her life.[30]

In 1265, in return for Welsh support, Simon de Montfort had agreed to the marriage of his daughter, Eleanor, to Llewelyn ap Gruffudd, Prince of Wales. Simon's downfall had postponed the marriage but, in 1275, in a move guaranteed to rile Edward I, King of England, Llewelyn reprised his marriage plans and the couple were married by proxy while Eleanor was still in France.

Shortly afterwards, Eleanor set sail for Wales, accompanied by her brother, Amaury, a papal chaplain and canon of York. Believing the marriage would 'scatter the seeds which had grown from the malice her father had sown', Edward arranged for Eleanor to be captured at sea.[31] When Eleanor's ship was intercepted in the Bristol Channel, the de Montfort arms and banner were found beneath the ship's boards. Eleanor was escorted to Windsor Castle, where she was held in comfortable confinement, while her brother Amaury was imprisoned at Corfe Castle for six years. In 1276, with his bride in Edward I's custody, Llewelyn refused to pay homage to the English king, and was declared a rebel. Faced with Edward's overwhelming forces, and support slipping away, within a year Llewelyn was forced to submit. The Treaty of Aberconwy reduced his lands to Gwynedd, but paved the way for his marriage to Eleanor, at last; it is possible that the marriage was one of the conditions of Llewelyn's submission.[32] The wedding of Eleanor de Montfort and Llewelyn ap Gruffudd was an extravagant affair, celebrated at Worcester Cathedral on the Feast of St Edward, 13 October 1278. The illustrious guests included both the English king, Edward I, and Alexander III, King of Scots. Edward and also, possibly his brother, Edmund of Lancaster, gave the bride away at the church door, and Edward paid for the lavish wedding feast.

While the marriage did not prevent further struggles between the Welsh and the English king, there was relative peace for a short time and Eleanor may have encouraged her husband to seek political solutions. She is known to have visited the English court as the Princess of Wales and was at Windsor on such a visit in January 1281. Eleanor herself wrote to Edward on 8 July, probably in 1279, to assure him of her 'sincere affection' and loyalty and warn him against listening to reports unfavourable to Wales from his advisers:

> Although as we have heard, the contrary hereto hath been reported of us to your excellency by some; and we believe, notwithstanding, that you in no wise give credit to any who report unfavourably concerning our lord and ourself until you learn from ourselves if such speeches contain truth: because you showed, of your grace, so much honour and so much friendliness to our lord and yourself, when you were at the last time at Worcester.[33]

As a testament to her diplomatic skills, Eleanor uses words of affection and flattery whilst clearly getting her point across, a technique her predecessor Joan, Lady of Wales, had used to good effect with Henry III. As it had been with Joan, Eleanor, too, was not beyond humbling herself to King Edward in order to achieve her objectives and wrote to him again in October 1280, this time regarding her brother, Amaury, who was still in the king's custody. She wrote to the king,

> with clasped hands, and with bended knees and tearful groanings, we supplicate your highness that, reverencing from your inmost

soul the Divine mercy (which holds out the hand of pity to all, especially those who seek Him with their whole heart), you would deign mercifully to take again to your grace and favour our aforesaid brother and your kinsman, who humbly craves, as we understand, your kindness. For if your excellency, as we have often known, mercifully condescends to strangers, with much reason, as we think, ought you to hold out the hand of pity to one so near to you by the ties of nature.[34]

Amaury was released shortly afterwards.

On 22 March 1282, Llewelyn's younger brother, Dafydd, attacked the Clifford stronghold of Hawarden Castle and Llewelyn found himself in rebellion against Edward I yet again. At the same time, Eleanor was in the final few months of her pregnancy and Llewelyn held off taking the field until the birth of his much hoped for heir.[35] Eleanor and Llewelyn's only child, a daughter, Gwenllian, was born on or around 19 June 1282; Eleanor died two days later. Eleanor de Montfort was the first woman known to have used the title Princess of Wales. She was buried alongside her aunt Joan, illegitimate daughter of King John and wife of Llywelyn the Great, at Llanfaes on the Isle of Anglesey.

Llewelyn himself was killed in an ambush on 11 December of the same year, at Builth, earning himself the name of Llewelyn the Last – the last native Prince of Wales. Gwenllian, a descendant of both Welsh and English royalty, was an orphan just six months after her birth. Her uncle Dafydd, Llewelyn's younger brother, became the little princess's legal guardian. After his brother's death, Dafydd continued the fight for Welsh independence but was betrayed to the English in June 1283. Dafydd, his wife, children and little Gwenllian were captured at Bera Mountain in Snowdonia, where they had been in hiding.

At just 1 year old, Gwenllian was taken, by sea, probably to thwart any attempt at rescue, from the land of her birth, Wales to English captivity. She would never see her homeland again. The baby girl was placed behind the high walls of the Gilbertine priory of Sempringham, in Lincolnshire, just south of the great city of Lincoln. Her female cousins, the seven daughters of Dafydd, were also placed in various nunneries, so it is possible some of her cousins were with her. Dafydd's legitimate daughter, Gwladus, who was a similar age to Gwenllian, was placed in Sixhills, another Gilbertine priory, in the Lincolnshire Wolds. Dafydd's two sons, Llywelyn and Owain, were imprisoned in Bristol Castle; Llywelyn died there in 1287, just four years after his capture, Owain was still living in 1325, spending every night securely incarcerated in a specially constructed timber cage within Bristol Castle. Dafydd himself suffered the horrendous 'traitor's death'; he was hanged, drawn and quartered at Shrewsbury.

The Gilbertines were the only wholly-English monastic community. Their founder, St Gilbert, had some form of physical deformity, which prevented him from pursuing a career as a knight. He trained as a clerk in France, studying under Master Anselm at Laon. He eventually entered the household of the bishop of Lincoln and, in 1129, was appointed vicar of Sempringham and West Torrington. He established the first priory there in 1131, with seven local women vowing to live a life of chastity, poverty and obedience. Sempringham Priory was a double-house, housing both men and women in segregated quarters. At its height, the priory housed 200 nuns and 40 canons. The order followed strict rules, based on those of the Augustinian and Premonstratensian monasteries. By the time of Gilbert's death in 1189 there were thirteen priories in England; this number had risen to twenty-five at the time of the Reformation.[36]

Gwenllian was a prisoner at the Gilbertine Priory of St Mary, at Sempringham, for the rest of her life. A prisoner of three English kings, Edward I, Edward II and Edward III, she could be a rallying figure for the subjugated Welsh and was therefore too valuable to ever be freed. Edward I wrote to the prior and prioress of Sempringham of his decision to place Gwenllian in their custody, on 11 November 1283: 'Having the Lord before our eyes, pitying also her sex and her age, that the innocent may not seem to atone for the iniquity and ill-doing of the wicked and contemplating especially the life in your Order.'[37] Although Edward wanted Gwenllian to be forgotten, he could not afford to forget her, and four years after she was placed in the convent, Edward ordered Thomas Normanvill to 'go to the places where the daughters of Llewellyn and of David his brother, who have taken the veil in the Order of Sempringham, are dwelling, and to report upon their state and custody by next Parliament.'[38] Gwenllian is said not to have spoken a word of Welsh and may not have even known how to spell her name; she is referred to as 'Wencillian', in a document sent to Edward III at the time of her death.

Gwenllian was probably well-cared for, Edward III endowed her with a pension of £20 a year, which was paid to the priory for her food and clothing. Whether Gwenllian was treated according to her rank at the priory is unknown; however, it is highly likely that she was aware of some of her history and her family connections, she does in fact call herself Princess of Wales, daughter of Llywelyn ap Gruffudd in a petition inside the volume of petitions from Wales edited by William Rees. She is said to have received gifts from her cousin the king, and may have spent time in Edward III's company, when he visited the priory at Easter-time in 1328; the young king issued a charter from Sempringham on 2 April of that year.[39]

Gwenllian only found release in death, hers occurred on 7 June 1337, the same month as her fifty-fifth birthday. She was buried at the priory where she had spent all but eighteen months of her life. Her grave was lost at the time of the dissolution of the monasteries, in the sixteenth century. A memorial plaque was placed near St Andrew's church in Sempringham in 1993: 'In memory of Gwenllian, daughter of the last Prince of Wales. Born at Abergwyngregyn 12.06.1282. Died at Sempringham 7.6.1337. Having been held prisoner for 54 years.'[40]

The death of Gwenllian, in a convent in her English exile, was a sad mirror of that of her grandmother, Eleanor of England. Eleanor and her family had continued the struggle that had started with the First Baron's War and the Magna Carta crisis. Eleanor had proved the most capable and strongest of King John's children, and the one most willing to embrace the ideals of Magna Carta and its promises for the future government of the realm. She also serves to highlight the limitations of Magna Carta, however, in that the barons appear to have seen them as restrictions on the king but only guidelines for themselves, and easy to set aside if they did not work in their favour, as evidenced by Eleanor's on-going battle with the Marshal family to have a fair and reasonable dower paid to her on a regular basis.

Nevertheless, Eleanor's life and experiences, her challenges and struggles, stand out as the legacy of Magna Carta. She is evidence that women saw their own rights enshrined in Magna Carta, just as her male counterparts did. Eleanor also stands out as demonstrating that the 1215 Magna Carta was the beginning of a struggle that would go on for many years, centuries, even.

Epilogue

The Enduring Legacy of Magna Carta

'Magna carta, the single most important legal document in
history. The foundation for global constitutions, commerce and
communities. The anchor for the Rule of Law.'

The Rt. Hon. Fiona Woolf, C.B.E.[1]

Although a failure in the short term, in the long term, Magna
Carta was to be the first step in the process of establishing
defined limitations to royal rights, creating a standard that would
be observed by both the crown and its agents. By the late 1200s Magna
Carta was regarded as a fundamental statement of English liberties. It
set the precedent for future reform programmes, such as the Provisions
of Oxford of 1258, the Ordinances of 1311, the Petition of Right of 1628
and the Grand Remonstrance of 1641. It is the closest thing England has
to a constitution. Moreover, the influence of Magna Carta has spread far
beyond England's shores. It can be seen in the United States' 1791 Bill of
Rights, in the 1948 Universal Declaration of Human Rights and the 1950
European Convention on Human Rights.

The provisions of the 1215 Magna Carta give us an insight into the
situation in England at the time, giving us some sense of the abuses of
which the barons had been the victims for years. The crown was forbidden
to interfere in church placements, in the dispersal of a deceased's property
and to wrongfully dispossess people of their land and goods, without the
proper writs being prepared by a sheriff and read in a court of assize. In
short, the king was no longer able to inflict arbitrary judgement on his
people without following the rule of law. Magna Carta meant the king
was no longer above the law; it put the king firmly within it, subject to
checks and balances through his barons.

What is remarkable about Magna Carta is that in a world dominated
by men, so many incredible women played a part in the life of this great

charter, in its instigation, implementation and endurance. Although most of the sixty-three clauses of Magna Carta are now defunct, three still remain on the statute books, two of which refer to the church and London's rights, respectively. The third surviving clause promises 'to no one will we sell, to no one will we deny or delay right or justice.' That no person could be imprisoned, outlawed or deprived of his lands except by judgement of his peers and the law of the land has remained the cornerstone of the English legal system ever since. That this clause was brought into existence through the tragedy and suffering of Matilda de Braose, and her family, is a stark reminder of the influence that women, often seen as powerless chattels, could exert on their own life and times.

No individual woman is identified in Magna Carta; the princesses of Scotland are mentioned but not named. The queen is mentioned in the security clause, but not by name, while the names of thirty-nine men are given, including King John. The words 'man' or 'men' appear nineteen times, while 'woman' appears just once and 'widow' and 'wife' each appear twice.[2] This imbalance is indicative of the male-dominated times. Women had a very limited public role; they did not sit on juries and only rarely held public office; two exceptions highlighted in this book being Nicholaa de la Haye and Ela of Salisbury, who each took on the role of sheriff of their respective shires following the deaths of their husbands.

Although it was initially a political failure, torn asunder within weeks of its creation, Magna Carta started England on the road to democratic government and, more importantly, universal suffrage, culminating in votes for women in 1918. Magna Carta was the first step. Within a generation of the charter's first issue, women such as Eleanor de Montfort were helping to fight for political reform and others, such as Isabel d'Aubigny, were using its clauses to their advantage. Women had been a part of the fight for and against King John in the lead up to the first issuing of Magna Carta. They had influenced its creation and continued to use its clauses to fight for their rights and those of their families. There was still a long way to go, especially for women. Magna Carta was not the start of the women's rights movement, but it serves as a benchmark for how far society has come in the last eight centuries.

The 1215 Magna Carta

John, by the grace of God, King of England, lord of Ireland, duke of Normandy and Aquitaine, count of Anjou, to the archbishops, bishops, abbots, earls, barons, justiciars, foresters, sheriffs, stewards, servants and all his officials and faithful subjects, greeting. Know that we, from reverence for God and for the salvation of our soul and those of all our ancestors and heirs, for the honour of God and the exaltation of Holy Church and the reform of our realm, on the advice of our reverend fathers, Stephen, archbishop of Canterbury, primate of all England and cardinal of the Holy Roman Church, Henry, archbishop of Dublin, William of London, Peter of Winchester, Jocelin of Bath and Glastonbury, Hugh of Lincoln, Walter of Worcester, William of Coventry and Benedict of Rochester, bishops, Master Pandulf, subdeacon and member of the household of the lord pope, Brother Aimeric, master of the knighthood of the Temple in England, and the noble men, William Marshal, earl of Pembroke, William, earl of Salisbury, William, earl of Warenne, William, earl of Arundel, Alan of Galloway, constable of Scotland, Warin fitz Gerold, Peter fitz Herbert, Hubert de Burgh, seneschal of Poitou, Hugh de Neville, Matthew fitz Herbert, Thomas Basset, Alan Basset, Philip d'Aubigny, Robert of Ropsley, John Marshal, John fitz Hugh and others, our faithful subjects:

Clause 1

In the first place have granted to God and by this our present charter have confirmed, for us and our heirs in perpetuity, that the English church shall be free, and shall have its rights undiminished and its liberties unimpaired: and we wish it thus observed, which is evident from the fact that of our own free will before the quarrel between us and our barons began, we conceded and confirmed by our charter freedom of elections, which is thought to be of the greatest necessity and importance to the

English church, and obtained confirmation of this from the lord pope Innocent III, which we shall observe in good faith in perpetuity. We have also granted to all the free men of our realm for ourselves and our heirs for ever, all the liberties written below, to have and hold, them and their heirs from us and our heirs.

Clause 2

If any of our earls or barons, or others holding of us in chief by knight service shall die, and at his death his heir be of full age and owe relief, he shall have his inheritance on payment of the ancient relief, namely the heir or heirs of an earl £100 for a whole earl's barony, the heir or heirs of a baron £100 for a whole barony, the heir or heirs of a knight 100s. at most for a whole knight's fee; and anyone who owes less shall give less according to the ancient usage of fiefs.

Clause 3

If, however, the heir of any such person has been under age and in wardship, when he comes of age he shall have his inheritance without relief or fine.

Clause 4

The guardian of the land of such an heir who is under age shall not take from the land more than the reasonable revenues, customary dues and services, and that without destruction and waste of men or goods. And if we entrust the wardship of the land of such a one to a sheriff, or to any other who is answerable to us for its revenues, and he destroys or wastes the land in his charge, we will take amends of him, and the land shall be entrusted to two lawful and prudent men of that fief who will be answerable to us for the revenues or to him to whom we have assigned them. And if we give or sell to anyone the wardship of any such land and he causes destruction or waste, he shall lose the wardship and it shall be transferred to two lawful and prudent men of the fief who shall be answerable to us as aforesaid.

Clause 5

Moreover so long as the guardian has the wardship of the land, he shall maintain the houses, parks, preserves, fishponds, mills and the other things pertaining to the land from its revenues; and he shall restore to the heir when he comes of age all his land stocked with ploughs and wainage such as the agricultural season demands and the revenues of the estate can easily bear.

Clause 6

Heirs shall be given in marriage without disparagement, yet so that before a marriage is contracted it shall be made known to the heir's next of kin.

Clause 7

After her husband's death, a widow shall have her marriage portion and her inheritance at once and without any hindrance; nor shall she pay anything for her dower, her marriage portion, or her inheritance which she and her husband held on the day of her husband's death; and she may stay in her husband's house for 40 days after his death, within which period her dower shall be assigned to her.

Clause 8

No widow shall be compelled to marry so long as she wishes to live without a husband, provided that she gives security that she will not marry without our consent if she holds of us, or without the consent of the lord of whom she holds, if she holds of another.

Clause 9

Neither we nor our bailiffs will seize any land or rent in payment of a debt so long as the chattels of the debtor are sufficient to repay the debt; nor shall the sureties of the debtor be distrained so long as the debtor himself is capable of paying the debt; and if the principal debtor defaults in the payment of the debt, having nothing wherewith to pay it, the sureties shall be answerable for the debt; and if they wish, they may have the lands and revenues of the debtor until they have received satisfaction for the debt they paid on his behalf, unless the principal debtor shows that he has discharged his obligations to the sureties.

Clause 10

If anyone who has borrowed from the Jews any amount, great or small, dies before the debt is repaid, it shall not carry interest unless the heir is under age, of whomsoever he holds; and if that debt falls into our hands, we will take nothing except the principal sum specified in the bond.

Clause 11

And if a man dies owing a debt to the Jews, his wife may have her dower and pay nothing of that debt; and if he leaves children under age, their needs shall be met in a manner in keeping with the holding of the deceased; and the debts shall be paid out of the residue, saving the service due to the lords. Debts owing to others than Jews shall be dealt with likewise.

Clause 12

No scutage or aid shall be levied in our realm except by the common counsel of our realm, unless it is for the ransom of our person, the knighting of our eldest son or the first marriage of our eldest daughter; and for these only a reasonable aid is to be levied. Aids from the city of London are to be treated likewise.

Clause 13

And the city of London is to have all its ancient liberties and free customs both by land and water. Furthermore, we will and grant that all other cities, boroughs, towns and ports shall have all their liberties and free customs.

Clause 14

And to obtain the common council of the realm for the assessment of an aid (except in the three cases aforesaid) or a scutage, we will have archbishops, bishops, abbots, earls and greater barons summoned individually by our letters, and we shall also have summoned generally through our sheriffs and bailiffs all those who hold of us in chief, for a fixed date, with at least forty days' notice, and at a fixed place; and in all letters of the summons we will state the reason for the summons. And when the summons has thus been made, the business shall go forward in the day arranged according to the council of those present, even if not all those summoned have come.

Clause 15

Henceforth we will not grant anyone that he may take an aid from his free men except to ransom his person, to make his eldest son a knight and to marry his eldest daughter once; and for these purposes only a reasonable aid is to be levied.

Clause 16

No man shall be compelled to perform more service for a knight's fee or for any other free tenement that is due therefrom.

Clause 17

Common pleas shall not follow our court but shall be held in some fixed place.

Clause 18

Recognizances of novel disseisin, mort d'ancestor, and darrein presentment shall not be held elsewhere than in the court of the county in which they occur, and in this manner: we, or if we are out of the realm our chief justiciar, shall send two justices through each county chosen by the county, shall hold the said assizes in the county court on the day and in the place of meeting of the county court.

Clause 19

And if the said assizes cannot be held on the day of the county court, so many knights and freeholders of those present in the county court on that day shall remain behind as will suffice to make judgements, according to the amount of business to be done.

Clause 20

A free man shall not be amerced for a trivial offence, except in accordance with the degree of the offence; and for a serious offence he shall be amerced according to its gravity, saving his livelihood; and a merchant likewise saving his merchandise; in the same way a villein shall be amerced saving his wainage; if they fall into our mercy. And none of the aforesaid amercements shall be imposed except by testimony of reputable men of the neighbourhood.

Clause 21

Earls and barons shall not be amerced except by their peers and only in accordance with the nature of the offence.

Clause 22

No clerk shall be amerced on his lay tenement except in the manner of the others aforesaid and without reference to the size of his ecclesiastical benefice.

Clause 23

No vill or man shall be forced to build bridges at river banks, except those who ought to do so by custom and law.

Clause 24

No sheriff, constable, coroners or others of our bailiffs may hold pleas of our Crown.

Clause 25

All shires, hundreds, wapentakes and ridings shall be at the ancient farm, without any increment, except our demesne manors.

Clause 26

If anyone holding a lay fief of us dies and our sheriff or bailiff shows our letters patent of summons for a debt which the deceased owed us, it shall be lawful for the sheriff or our bailiff to attach and list the chattels of the deceased found in lay fee to the value of that debt, by the view of lawful men, so that nothing is removed until the evident debt is paid to us, and the residue shall be relinquished to the executors to carry out the will of the deceased. And if he owes us nothing, all the chattels shall be accounted as the deceased's saving their reasonable shares to his wife and children.

Clause 27

If any free man dies intestate, his chattels are to be distributed by his nearest relations and friends, under supervision of the Church, saving to everyone the debts which the deceased owed him.

Clause 28

No constable or any other of our bailiffs shall take any man's corn or other chattels unless he pays cash for them at once or can delay payment with the agreement of the seller.

Clause 29

No constable is to compel any knight to give money for castle guard, if he is willing to perform that guard in his own person or by another reliable man, if for some good reason he is unable to do it himself; and if we take or send him on military service, he shall be excused the guard in proportion to the period of his service.

Clause 30

No sheriff or bailiff of ours or anyone else is to take horses or carts of any free man for carting without his agreement.

Clause 31

Neither we nor our bailiffs shall take other men's timber for castles or other work of ours, without the agreement of the owner.

Clause 32

We will not hold the lands of convicted felons for more than a year and a day, when the lands shall be returned to the lords of the fiefs.

Clause 33

Henceforth all fish-weirs shall be completely removed from the Thames and the Medway and throughout all England, except on the sea coast.

Clause 34

The writ called *praecipe* shall not, in future, be issued to anyone in respect of any holding whereby a free man may lose his court.

Clause 35

Let there be one measure of wine throughout our kingdom and one measure of ale and one measure of corn, namely the London quarter, and one width of cloth whether dyed, russet or halberjet, namely two ells within the selvedges. Let it be the same with weights as with measures.

Clause 36
Henceforth nothing shall be given or taken for the writ of inquisition of life or limb, but it shall be given freely and not refused.

Clause 37
If anyone holds of us by fee-farm, by socage or by burgage, and holds land of someone else by knight service, we will not, by virtue of that fee-farm or socage or burgage have wardship of his heir or of land of his that belongs to the fief of another; nor will we have custody of that fee-farm or socage or burgage unless such fee-farm owes knight service. We will not have custody of the heir or land of anyone who holds of another by knight service, by virtue of any petty sergeanty which he holds of us by the service of rendering to us knives or arrows or the like.

Clause 38
Henceforth no bailiff shall put anyone on trial by his own unsupported allegation, without bringing credible witnesses to the charge.

Clause 39
No free man shall be taken or imprisoned or disseised or outlawed or exiled or in any way ruined, nor will we go or send against him, except by the lawful judgement of his peers or by the law of the land.

Clause 40
To no one will we sell, to no one will we deny or delay right or justice.

Clause 41
All merchants are to be safe and secure in leaving and entering England, and in staying and travelling in England, both by land and by water, to buy and sell free from all maletotes by the ancient and rightful customs, except, in time of war, such as come from an enemy country. And if such are found in our land at the outbreak of war they shall be detained without damage to their persons or goods, until we or our chief justiciar know how the merchants of our land are treated in the enemy country; and if ours are safe there, the others shall be safe in our land.

Clause 42

Henceforth anyone, saving his allegiance due to us, may leave our realm and return safe and secure by land and water, save for a short period in time of war on account of the general interest of the realm and excepting those imprisoned and outlawed according to the law of the land, and natives of an enemy country, and merchants, who shall be treated as aforesaid.

Clause 43

If anyone dies who holds of some escheat such as the honours of Wallingford, Nottingham, Boulogne or Lancaster, or of other escheats which are in our hands and are baronies, his heir shall not give any relief or do any service to us other than what he would have done to the baron if that barony had been in the baron's hands; and we shall hold it in the same manner as the baron held it.

Clause 44

Henceforth men who live outside the forest shall not come before our justices of the forest upon a general summons unless they are impleaded or are sureties for any person or persons who are attached for forest offences.

Clause 45

We will not appoint justices, constables, sheriffs or bailiffs who do not know the law of the land and are willing to keep it well.

Clause 46

All barons who have founded abbeys of which they have charters of the kings of England, or ancient tenure, are to have custody of them when they are vacant, as they ought to have.

Clause 47

All forests which have been afforested in our time shall be disafforested at once; and river banks which we have enclosed in our time shall be treated similarly.

Clause 48

All evil customs of forests and warrens, foresters and warreners, sheriffs and their servants, river banks and their wardens are to be investigated at once in every county by twelve sworn knights of the same county who are to be chosen by worthy men of the county, and within forty days of the inquiry they are to be abolished by them beyond recall, provided that we, or our justiciar, if we are not in England, first know of it.

Clause 49

We will restore at once all hostages and charters delivered to us by Englishmen as securities for peace or faithful service.

Clause 50

We will dismiss completely from their offices the relations of Gerard d'Athée that henceforth they shall have no office in England, Engelard de Cigogné, Peter and Guy and Andrew de Chanceaux, Guy de Cigogné, Geoffrey de Martigny with his brothers, Philip Marc with his brothers and his nephew, Geoffrey, and all their followers.

Clause 51

Immediately after concluding peace. We will remove from the kingdom all alien knights, crossbowmen, sergeants and mercenary soldiers who have come with horses and arms to the hurt of the realm.

Clause 52

If anyone has been disseised or deprived by us without lawful judgement of his peers of lands, castles, liberties or his rights we will restore them to him at once; and if any disagreement arises on this, then let it be settled by the judgement of the Twenty-Five barons referred to below in the security clause. But for all those things for which anyone was disseised or deprived without lawful judgement of his peers by King Henry our father, or by King Richard our brother, which we hold in our hand or which are held by others under our warranty, we shall have respite for the usual crusader's term; excepting those cases in which a plea was begun or inquest made on our order before we took the cross; when, however, we return from our pilgrimage, or if perhaps we do not undertake it, we will at once do full justice in these matters.

Clause 53

We shall have the same respite, and in the same manner, in doing justice or disafforesting or retaining those forests which Henry our father or Richard our brother afforested, and concerning custody of lands which are of the fee of another, the which wardships we have hitherto by virtue of a fee held of us by knight's service, and concerning abbeys founded on fees other than our own, in which the lord of the fee claims to have a right. And as soon as we return, or if we do not undertake our pilgrimage, we will at once do full justice to complainants in these matters.

Clause 54

No one shall be taken or imprisoned upon the appeal of a woman for the death of anyone except her husband.

Clause 55

All fines which were made with us unjustly and contrary to the law of the land, and all amercements imposed unjustly and contrary to the law of the land, shall be completely remitted or else they shall be settled by the judgement of the Twenty-Five barons mentioned below in the security clause, or by the judgement of the majority of the same, along with the aforesaid Stephen, archbishop of Canterbury, if he can be present, and others whom he wishes to summon with him for this purpose. And if he cannot be present the business shall nevertheless proceed without him, provided that if any one of more of the aforesaid Twenty-Five barons are in such a suit they shall stand down in this particular judgement, and shall be replaced by others chosen and sworn in by the rest of the same Twenty-Five, for this case only.

Clause 56

If we have disseised or deprived Welshmen of lands, liberties, or other things without lawful judgement of their peers, in England or in Wales, they are to be returned to them at once; and if a dispute arises over this it shall be settled in the March by judgement of their peers; for tenements in England according to the law in England, for tenements in Wales according to the law in Wales, for tenements in the March according to the law of the March. The Welsh are to do the same to us and ours.

Clause 57

For all those things, however, of which any Welshman had been disseised or deprived without lawful judgement of his peers by King Henry our father, or King Richard our brother, which we have in our possession or which others hold under our legal warranty, we shall have respite for the usual crusader's term; excepting those cases in which a plea was begun or inquest made on our order before we took the cross. However, when we return, or if perhaps we do not go on our pilgrimage, we will at once give them full justice in accordance with the laws of the Welsh and the aforesaid regions.

Clause 58

We will restore at once the son of Llywelyn and all the hostages from Wales and the charters delivered to us as security for peace.

Clause 59

We will treat Alexander, king of Scots, concerning the return of his sisters and hostages and his liberties and rights in the same manner in which we will act towards our other barons of England, unless it ought to be otherwise because of the charters which we have from William his father, formerly king of Scots; and this shall be determined by the judgement of his peers in our court.

Clause 60

All these aforesaid customs and liberties which we have granted to be held in our realm as far as it pertains to us towards our men, shall be observed by all men of our realm, both clerk and lay, as far as it pertains to them, towards their own men.

Clause 61

Since, moreover, we have granted the aforesaid things for God, for the reform of our realm and the better settling of the quarrel which has arisen between us and our barons, wishing these things to be enjoyed fully and undisturbed in perpetuity, we give and grant them the following security: namely, that the barons shall choose any twenty-five barons of the realm they wish, who with all their might are to observe, maintain and cause to be observed the peace and liberties which we have granted and confirmed to them by this our present charter; so that if we and our justiciar or our bailiffs or any of our servants offend against anyone in any way, or transgress any of the articles of peace or security, and the offence is indicated to four of the aforesaid twenty-five barons, those four barons shall come to us or our justiciar, if we are out of the kingdom, and shall bring it to our notice and ask that we have it redressed without delay. And if we or our justiciar, should we be out of the kingdom, do not redress the offence within forty days from the time it was brought to the notice of us or our justiciar, should we be out of the kingdom, the aforesaid four barons shall refer the case to the rest of the twenty-five barons and those twenty-five barons with the commune of all the land shall distrain and distress us in every way they can, namely by seizing castles, lands and possessions, and in such other ways as they can, saving our person and those of our queen and our children, until, in their judgement, amends have been made; and when it has been redressed they are to obey us as they did before. Anyone in the land who wishes may take an oath to obey the orders of the said twenty-five barons in the execution of the aforesaid matters, and to join with them in distressing us to the best of his ability, and we publicly and freely permit anyone who wishes to take the oath, and we will never forbid anyone to take it. Moreover we shall compel and order all those in the land who of themselves and of their own free will are unwilling to take an oath to the twenty-five barons to distrain and distress us with them, to take the oath aforesaid. And if any of the twenty-five barons dies or leaves the country or is otherwise prevented from discharging these aforesaid duties, the rest of the aforesaid barons shall on their own decision choose another in his place, who shall take the oath in the same way as the others. In all matters the execution of which is committed to these twenty-five barons, if it should happen that the twenty-five are present and disagree among themselves or anything, or if any of them who has been summoned will not or cannot come, whatever the majority of those present shall provide or order is to be taken as fixed and settled as if the whole twenty-five had agreed to it; and the aforesaid twenty-five are to swear that they will faithfully observe all the aforesaid and will do all they can to secure its observance. And we will procure nothing from anyone, either personally or through another, by which any of these concessions and liberties shall be revoked or diminished; and if only such thing is procured, it shall be null and void, and we will never use it either ourselves or through another.

Clause 62

And we have completely remitted and pardoned to all any ill will, grudge and rancour that have arisen between us and our subjects, clerk and lay, from the time of the quarrel. Moreover we have fully forgiven and completely condoned to all, clerk and lay, as far as pertains to us, all offences occasioned by the said quarrel from Easter in the sixteenth year of our reign to the conclusion of peace. And moreover we have caused letters patent of the Lord Stephen, archbishop of Canterbury, the Lord Henry, archbishop of Dublin, the aforesaid bishops and Master Pandulf to be made for them on this security and the aforesaid concessions.

Clause 63

Wherefore we wish and firmly command that the English church shall be free, and the men in our realm shall have and hold all the aforesaid liberties, rights and concessions well and peacefully, freely and quietly, fully and completely for them and their heirs in all things and places forever, as is aforesaid. Moreover an oath has been sworn, both on our part and on the part of the barons that all these things aforesaid shall be observed in good faith and without evil intent. Witness the above-mentioned and many others. Given under our hand in the meadow which is called Runnymede between Windsor and Staines on the fifteenth day of June in the seventeenth year of our reign.

Appendix B

Enforcers of Magna Carta – The Twenty-Five

A committee of twenty-five barons, all in the forefront of the opposition to King John, were appointed to oversee the enforcement of the terms of Magna Carta, as directed by clause 61 of the charter, the security clause, which authorised the barons to:

> choose any twenty-five barons of the realm they wish … so that if we transgress any of the articles … then those twenty-five with the commune of all the land shall distress and distrain us in every way they can, namely by seizing our lands, castles and possessions.[1]

In no particular order, the Twenty-Five were:

Richard de Clare, Earl of Hertford
Gilbert de Clare
Geoffrey de Say
Geoffrey de Mandeville, Earl of Essex and Gloucester
Robert Fitzwalter
Roger (II) Bigod, Earl of Norfolk
Hugh Bigod
Robert de Vere, Earl of Oxford
Richard de Montfichet
William of Huntingfield
William de Lanvallei, Lord of Walken in Hertfordshire
Henry de Bohun, Earl of Hereford
William Mallet, Lord of Shepton Mallet
William Marshal the younger
Saher de Quincy, Earl of Winchester
William d'Aubigné, Lord of Belvoir
John de Lacy, Lord of Pontefract, later Earl of Lincoln

John fitz Robert, Lord of Warkworth
Robert de Ros, Lord of Wark-on-Tweed
William de Forz, Count of Aumale
Eustace de Vescy
William de Mowbray
Richard de Percy
Roger de Montbegon, Lord of Hornby
Serlo the Mercer, Mayor of London[2]

The Charter of the Forest 1217

Henry, by the grace of God, king of England, lord of Ireland, duke of Normandy, Aquitaine, and count of Anjou, to the archbishops, bishops, abbots, priors, earls, barons, justiciars, foresters, sheriffs, governors, officers, and all his bailiffs and faithful subjects. Greeting.

Know that we, for the honour of God and for the salvation of our own soul and the souls of our ancestors and successors, for the exaltation of Holy Church and the reform of our realm, have granted and by this present charter have confirmed for us and our heirs for ever, by the counsel of our venerable father, the lord Guala, cardinal priest of St Martin and legate of the apostolic see, of the lord Walter archbishop of York, William bishop of London and the other bishops of England and of William Marshal earl of Pembroke, guardian of us and of our kingdom, and of others our faithful earls and barons of England, these underwritten liberties to be held in our kingdom of England for ever.

1. In the first place, all the forests made by our grandfather king Henry [II], shall be viewed by good and lawful men, and if he made any other than his own proper woods into forests to the damage of him whose wood it was, it shall forthwith be disafforested. And if he made his own proper woods forest, it shall remain forest, saving the common right of pasturage, and of other things in the same forest, to those who were formerly accustomed to have them.

2. Men who live outside the forest, from henceforth shall not come before our justiciars of the forest, upon a common summons, unless they are impleaded there or are sureties for any other persons who were attached for something concerning the forest.

3. Also all woods which were afforested by King Richard our uncle, or by King John our father, until our own first Coronation, shall forthwith be disafforested, unless they shall be our demesne.

4. Archbishops, bishops, abbots, priors, earls, barons, knights and freeholders who have woods within forests shall have them the same as they held them at the time of the first coronation of our grandfather king Henry [Sunday 19 December 1154], so that they shall be discharged forever of all purprestures [trespass and the erection of illegal dwellings], wastes [wasteland], and assarts [land cleared for cultivation] made in their woods after that time until the beginning of the second year of our coronation. And those who in future shall without our licence make wastes, purprestures or assarts within them, shall answer for such wastes, purprestures or assarts.

5. Our regarders shall go through the forests to make a view as it was used to be made at the time of the first coronation of our grandfather, king Henry, and not otherwise.

6. The inquisition or view for declawing dogs [cutting off the claws of a dog to hinder its chasing of deer] living within the forest, for the future shall be when the view ought to be made, namely, the third year in three years; and then it shall be done by the view and testimony of lawful men, and not otherwise. And he whose dogs shall be found then still clawed shall give three shillings for mercy, and for the future no one's ox shall be taken for failure to declaw. Such declawing also shall be done by the assize commonly used; which is, that three claws shall be cut off outside the ball of the fore-foot. Nor shall dogs be declawed from henceforth, excepting in places where it hath been customary to expedite them from the time of the first coronation of king Henry our grandfather.

7. No forester nor beadle shall for the future make any scotale [keeping of an ale-house within a forest by an officer of the forest], nor collect sheaves of corn or oats, or any grain, or lambs, nor shall make any gathering but the view and oath of twelve regarders; and when they shall make their view: as many foresters shall be appointed to keep the forests, as they shall think reasonably sufficient for the purpose.

8. No swainmote [court held by the foresters as judges, with freemen of the forest as jury] for the future shall be held in our kingdom, excepting thrice a year; namely, in the beginning of fifteen days before the feast of Saint Michael when the agistators meet for the agisting of our (royal) demesne woods; and about the feast of Saint

Martin, when our agistators ought to receive our pannage-dues: and in those two swainmotes the foresters, verderers, and agistators shall meet, and no others by distraint; and the third swainmote shall be held in the beginning of the fifteen days before the Feast of Saint John the Baptist concerning the fawning of our does; and at that swainmote the tenants shall meet the foresters and verderers, and no others shall be distrained to be there. Moreover every forty days through the whole year, the foresters and verderers shall meet for seeing to attachments of the forests, as well of vert [green forest vegetation supporting deer] as of venison, by the presentment of the foresters themselves and before those who are attached. And the aforesaid swainmotes shall not be holden, except in those counties where they were accustomed to be held.

9. Every free man shall agist [to pasture livestock] his own wood in the forest as he wishes and have his pannage [the right to allow pigs to forage in woodland]. We grant also that every free-man may drive his swine through our demesne wood freely and without impediment to agist them in his own woods or anywhere else he wishes. And if the swine of any free-man shall remain one night in our forest, he shall not on that account lose anything of his for it.

10. No man henceforth shall lose life or limb for taking our venison, but if he shall be seized and convicted of taking venison he shall be fined heavily if he has the means to pay; but if he has not the means, he shall lie in our prison for a year and a day; and if after a year and a day he can find sureties, he shall leave prison; but if not, he shall abjure the kingdom of England.

11. Whatever archbishop, bishop, earl or baron shall be passing through our forest, it shall be lawful for them to take one or two deer under the view of the forester, if he shall be present; but if not, he shall cause a horn to be blown, lest it should seem like theft.

12. Every free-man for the future, may, without being prosecuted, erect a mill in his own wood or upon his own land which he has in the forest; or make a warren, or pond, or marl-pit, or ditch, or turn it into arable land, so that it be not to the detriment of any of the neighbours.

13. Every free-man shall have the eyries of hawks, sparrowhawks, falcons, eagles and herons in his own woods, and he shall likewise have the honey found in his woods.

14. No forester from henceforth, who is not a forester in fee-farm, giving to us rent for his bailiwick, shall take any cheminage [toll on transport in the forest], within his bailiwick; but a forester in fee, paying to us rent for his bailiwick, shall take cheminage; that is to say, for every cart two-pence for the one half year, and two-pence for the other half year; and for a horse that carries burdens, one half-penny for the one half year, and one half-penny for the other half year: and not that excepting of those who come out of their bailiwick by licence of their bailiff as dealers, to buy underwood, timber, bark, or charcoal; to carry it to sell in other places where they will: and of no other carts nor burdens shall any cheminage be taken; and cheminage shall not be taken excepting in those places where anciently it used to be and ought to be taken. Also those who carry wood, bark, or coal, upon their backs to sell, although they get their livelihood by it, shall not for the future pay cheminage. Also cheminage shall not be taken by our foresters, for any besides our demesne woods.

15. All persons outlawed for forest offences from the time of king Henry our grandfather up to our first coronation, shall be released from their outlawry without legal proceedings; and they shall find sureties that for the future they will not trespass unto us in our forests.

16. No castellan or other person shall hold forest pleas whether concerning vert or venison but every forester-in-fee shall attach forest pleas as well concerning both vert and venison and shall present them to the verderers of the provinces; and when they have been enrolled and put under the seals of the verderers they shall be presented to our chief forester, when he comes into those parts to hold forest pleas and before him they shall be determined.

And these liberties concerning the forests we have granted to all men, saving to the archbishops, bishops, abbots, priors, earls, barons, knights, and others, ecclesiastical as well as secular; Templars and Hospitallers, their liberties and free customs, in forests and outside, in warrens and other places, which they had previously. All these aforesaid customs and liberties which we have granted to be observed in our kingdom for as much as it belongs to us; all our kingdom shall observe, clergy as well as laity, for as much as belongs to them. Because we have at present no seal, we have caused the present charter to be sealed with the seals of our venerable father the lord Guala, cardinal-priest of St Martin, legate of the apostolic see, and of William Marshal earl of Pembroke, guardian of us and of our kingdom. Witness the before-named and many others. Given by the hands of the aforesaid lord, the legate, and of William Marshal at St Paul's, London, on the sixth day of November in the second year of our reign.

Notes

Introduction

1. Winston Churchill quoted in 'Magna Carta Quotations', magnacarta800th. com.
2. Danny Danziger and John Gillingham, *1215: The Year of Magna Carta*.
3. Ibid.
4. Ibid.
5. Marc Morris, *King John: Treachery, Tyranny and the Road to Magna Carta*.
6. Nicholas Vincent, 'Tournaments, Ladies and Bears', and 'King John's Diary and Itinerary', The Magna Carta Project, magnacartaresearch.org, accessed 27 November 2018.

Chapter 1: King John – The Path to the Throne

1. Alison Weir, *Britain's Royal Families: The Complete Genealogy*.
2. Morris, *King John*.
3. Gillingham, John, 'John (1167–1216)', Oxforddnb.com.
4. Ibid.
5. Ibid.
6. Giraldus Cambrensis, *The Conquest of Ireland*, translated by Thomas Forester.
7. Ibid.
8. Ibid.
9. Ibid.
10. Ibid.
11. Ibid.
12. Ibid.
13. Benedict of Peterborough, *Gesta Regis Henrici Secundi, Benedicti Abbatis, The Chronicle of the Reigns of Henry II and Richard I A.D. 1169–1192*: Known Commonly Under the Name of Benedict of Peterborough, edited by W. Stubbs.
14. Giraldus Cambrensis, *The Conquest of Ireland*.
15. Ibid.
16. Joyce Marlow, *Kings and Queens of Britain*.
17. Ibid.
18. Gillingham, 'John'.
19. William of Newburgh, quoted in Morris, *King John*.

20. Ibid.
21. Richard of Devizes in *Chronicles of the Reigns of Stephen, Henry II and Richard I.*
22. Morris, *King John.*
23. Elizabeth Hallam (editor), *The Plantagenet Chronicles.*
24. Richard of Devizes in *Chronicles of the Reigns of Stephen, Henry II and Richard I.*
25. Morris, *King John.*
26. Ibid.
27. Ibid.
28. Ibid.
29. Gillingham, 'John'.
30. Morris, *King John.*
31. Ibid.
32. Ibid.
33. Ibid.
34. Roger of Hoveden, *The Annals of Roger de Hoveden: Comprising the History of England and of other Countries of Europe from A.D. 732 to A.D. 1201*, translated by Henry T. Riley.
35. Ibid.
36. *L'Histoire de Guillaume le Maréchale* quoted in Morris, *King John.*
37. Ibid.

Chapter 2: The Road to Magna Carta

1. Morris, *King John.*
2. Ibid.
3. David Crouch, *William Marshal.*
4. Danziger and Gillingham, *1215.*
5. Ibid.
6. Ralph of Coggeshall quoted in Morris, *King John.*
7. Gervase of Canterbury quoted in Morris, *King John.*
8. Hallam, *The Plantagenet Chronicles.*
9. Ralph of Coggeshall quoted in Morris, *King John.*
10. Ralph of Coggeshall quoted in Hallam, *The Plantagenet Chronicles.*
11. Ibid.
12. Ibid.
13. Ibid.
14. Sharon Bennett Connolly, *Heroines of the Medieval World.*
15. Ralph of Coggeshall quoted in Hallam, *The Plantagenet Chronicles.*
16. Ibid.
17. Morris, *King John.*
18. Ralph of Coggeshall quoted in Hallam, *The Plantagenet Chronicles.*
19. Ibid.

20. Ibid.
21. Gillingham, 'John'.
22. Ibid.
23. Ibid.
24. Ibid.
25. Gervase of Canterbury quoted in Hallam, *The Plantagenet Chronicles*.
26. Ibid.
27. Gillingham, 'John'.
28. The Barnwell annalist quoted in Hallam, *The Plantagenet Chronicles*.
29. Ibid.
30. S. Mac Airt, *Annals of Innisfallen*, quoted in Gillingham, 'John'.
31. *Memoriale fratis Walteri de Coventria* quoted in Gillingham, 'John'.
32. David Hillman, *Kings, Queens, Bones and Bastards*.
33. The Barnwell annalist quoted in Hallam, *The Plantagenet Chronicles*.
34. Ibid.
35. Ibid.
36. Ibid.
37. Ibid.
38. Gillingham, 'John'.
39. Morris, *King John*.
40. The Barnwell annalist quoted in Hallam, *The Plantagenet Chronicles*.
41. Gillingham, 'John'.
42. *L'Histoire de Guillaume le Maréchale* quoted in Gillingham, 'John'.
43. Coronation Charter of Henry I in bl.uk.
44. *Select Charters* quoted in Morris, *King John*.
45. The Barnwell annalist quoted in Hallam, *The Plantagenet Chronicles*.
46. Danziger and Gillingham, *1215*.
47. Letter from Pope Innocent III, quoted in Danziger and Gillingham, *1215*.
48. Gillingham, 'John'.
49. Ralph of Coggeshall quoted in Hallam, *The Plantagenet Chronicles*.
50. Matthew Paris's *Chronicon* quoted in Gillingham, 'John'.
51. Ralph of Coggeshall quoted in Hallam, *The Plantagenet Chronicles*.

Chapter 3: The Fall of the Braose Family
1. Ralph V. Turner, 'William de Briouze [Braose] (d. 1211)', Oxforddnb.com.
2. Ibid.
3. Ibid.
4. Anonymous of Béthune paraphrased in Morris, *King John*.
5. Turner, 'William de Briouze'.
6. Ibid.
7. David Nash Ford, 'Matilda de St Valery, Lady Bergavenny (c. 1153–1210)', berkshirehistory.com, 2003.
8. Ralph of Diceto quoted in Hallam, *The Plantagenet Chronicles*.

9. Gerald of Wales quoted in Louise J. Wilkinson, *Women in Thirteenth-Century Lincolnshire*.

10. Thomas Asbridge, *The Greatest Knight: The Remarkable Life of William Marshal, The Power Behind Five English Thrones*.

11. *Rotuli de oblatis et finibus*, quoted in Turner, 'William de Briouze'.

12. Ibid.

13. Ralph of Coggeshall quoted in Hallam, *The Plantagenet Chronicles*.

14. *L'Histoire de Guillaume le Maréchale* quoted by Gillingham, 'John'.

15. Ralph of Coggeshall quoted in Hallam, *The Plantagenet Chronicles*.

16. *The Annals of Margam, Annales Monastici*, translated by Rich Price.

17. Roger of Wendover, *Roger of Wendover's Flowers of History: Comprising the History of England from the Descent of the Saxons to A.D. 1235*, vol. II, edited and translated by J.A. Giles.

18. Roger of Wendover quoted in Morris, *King John*.

19. Morris, *King John*.

20. Ibid.

21. King John quoted in Morris, *King John*.

22. Ibid.

23. Anonymous of Béthune quoted in Morris, *King John*.

24. Magna Carta, British Library, transcript from bl.uk.

25. Nicholas Vincent, 'From the Tower: John Sends a Coded Message to his Queen', magnacartaresearch.org.

26. Morris, *King John*.

27. David Crouch, 'Robert de Breteuil, fourth Earl of Leicester (d. 1204)', Oxforddnb.com.

28. Ibid.

29. Susan M. Johns, 'Loretta de Briouze, Countess of Leicester (d. in or after 1266)', Oxforddnb.com.

30. Crouch, 'Robert de Breteuil (d. 1204)'.

31. Ibid.

32. Johns, 'Loretta de Briouze'.

33. Nicholas Vincent, 'John Deals with Loretta de Braose and Isaac of Norwich', The Magna Carta Project, magnacarta.cmp.uea.ac.uk.

34. Morris, *King John*.

35. Ibid.

36. Johns, 'Loretta de Briouze'.

37. Janina Ramirez, *Julian of Norwich: A Very Brief History*.

38. Johns, 'Loretta de Briouze'.

39. *Ancrene Wisse: Guide for Anchoresses*, translated by Hugh White.

40. Johns, 'Loretta de Briouze'.

41. Paraphrased from *De adventu Fratrum monirum* in Johns, 'Loretta de Briouze'.

42. Ibid.

43. Doug Thompson, 'Annora de Braose Married to Hugh de Mortimer', douglyn.co.uk/Braose, accessed 06/05/2019.
44. Ibid.

Chapter 4: Nicholaa de la Haye

1. Wilkinson, *Women in Thirteenth-Century Lincolnshire*.
2. Ibid.
3. Brian Golding, 'Gerard de Canville (d. 1214)', Oxforddnb.com.
4. Nicholas Vincent, 'Richard de Canville (d. 1191)', Oxforddnb.com.
5. Wilkinson, *Women in Thirteenth-Century Lincolnshire*.
6. In Latin: '*cum custodia et constabularia ca[ste] Ui Lincolnie*'. Wilkinson, *Women in Thirteenth-Century Lincolnshire*.
7. In Latin: '*pro vicecomitatu Loncolnie et castello civitatis habendis*'. Wilkinson, *Women in Thirteenth-Century Lincolnshire*.
8. Richard of Devizes quoted in Wilkinson, *Women in Thirteenth-Century Lincolnshire*.
9. William of Newburgh quoted in Golding, 'Gerard de Canville'.
10. In Latin: '*uxor eius Nicholaa nichil femineum cogitans, castellum viriliter custodiebat*'. Richard of Devizes quoted in Wilkinson, *Women in Thirteenth-Century Lincolnshire*.
11. Ibid.
12. Morris, *King John*.
13. Richard of Devizes in *The Chronicles of the Reigns of Stephen, Henry II and Richard I*.
14. Morris, *King John*.
15. Susan M. Johns, 'Nicola de la Haie (d. 1230), landowner', Oxforddnb.com.
16. Golding, 'Gerard de Canville'.
17. Wilkinson, *Women in Thirteenth-Century Lincolnshire*.
18. Ibid.
19. Letter of 5 April 1216. Price, Rich, *King John's Letters*, Facebook Study Group, 5 April 2019.
20. Letter of 16 April 1216. Price, *King John's Letters*.
21. Ibid.
22. Dan Jones, *The Plantagenets: The Kings Who Made England*.
23. Letter of 4 February 1216. Price, *King John's Letters*.
24. Letter of 22 February 1216. Price, *King John's Letters*.
25. Hallam, *The Plantagenet Chronicles*.
26. Letter of 4 September 1216. Price, *King John's Letters*.
27. Hallam, *The Plantagenet Chronicles*.
28. *Rotuli hundredonum*, 1.315 quoted in Johns, 'Nicola de la Haie'; and Irene Gladwin, *The Sheriff: The Man and his Office*.
29. Golding, 'Gerard de Canville'.
30. Wilkinson, *Women in Thirteenth-Century Lincolnshire*.

31. Letter of 12 February 1217. Price, *King John's Letters*.
32. Letter of 12 February 1217. Price, *King John's Letters*.
33. *Historical Collections of Walter of Coventry*, edited by W. Stubbs.
34. Thomas Asbridge, *The Greatest Knight*.
35. William Marshal quoted in Asbridge, *The Greatest Knight*.
36. David Crouch and Anthony J., *History of William Marshal: Text and Translation*.
37. William Marshal quoted in Asbridge, *The Greatest Knight*.
38. Ibid.
39. Elizabeth Hallam, *Chronicles of the Age of Chivalry*.
40. Anonymous de Béthuune quoted in Wilkinson, *Women in Thirteenth-Century Lincolnshire*.
41. *Annales Monastici: Annales prioratus de Dunstaplia (A.D. 1–1297), Annales monasterii de Bermundesia (A.D. 1042–1432)*, edited by Henry Richards Luard.
42. catherinehanley.co.uk/historical-background/nicola-de-la-haye.
43. www.finerollshenry3.org.uk/content/calendar/roll_030.html#it072_008a. Membrane 8.
44. Wilkinson, *Women in Thirteenth-Century Lincolnshire*.
45. *Histoire de Guillaume le Maréchal*, quoted in Wilkinson, *Women in Thirteenth-Century Lincolnshire*.

Chapter 5: Ela of Salisbury

1. 'Ela, Countess of Salisbury', medievalwomen.org.
2. Emilie Amt, 'Patrick Salisbury, first Earl of Salisbury [Earl of Wiltshire] (d. 1168)', Oxforddnb.com.
3. 'Ela, Countess of Salisbury', medievalwomen.org.
4. W.L. Bowles and J.G. Nicholls, *Annals and Antiquities of Lacock Abbey*, quoted in Ally McConnell, 'The Life of Ela, Countess of Salisbury', Wiltshire and Swindon History Centre, wshc.eu, 15 September 2015.
5. 'Ela, Countess of Salisbury', medievalwomen.org.
6. Matthew Strickland, 'William Longespée [Lungespée], third earl of Salisbury (b. in or before 1167, d. 1226)', Oxforddnb.com.
7. Ibid.
8. Ibid.
9. Ibid.
10. Ibid.
11. Ibid.
12. Ibid.
13. David Crouch, *William Marshal*, third edition.
14. Strickland, 'William Longespée'.
15. Ibid.
16. David Crouch and Anthony J. Holden, *History of William Marshal: Text and Translation*

17. Strickland, 'William Longespée'.
18. With thanks to Rich Price for clarification of events. Rich is currently translating King John's letters.
19. Strickland, 'William Longespée'.
20. Crouch, *William Marshal*.
21. Roger of Wendover, *Flowers of History*, vol. II, translated by J.A. Giles.
22. B.R. Kemp, 'Nicholas Longespée (d. 1297)', Oxforddnb.com.
23. Letter of 22 February 1216. Price, *King John's Letters*.
24. William Farrer and Charles Travis Clay, editors, *Early Yorkshire Charters, Volume 8: The Honour of Warenne*.
25. Magna Carta, British Library, transcript from bl.uk.
26. Bowles and Nicholls, *Annals and Antiquities of Lacock Abbey*, quoted in McConnell, *The Life of Ela*.
27. 'Ela, Countess of Salisbury', medievalwomen.org.
28. Wilkinson, *Women in Thirteenth-Century Lincolnshire*.
29. 'Ela, Countess of Salisbury', medievalwomen.org.
30. finerollshenry3.org.uk content/calendar/roll_027.html#it003_009, 29 Oct. 1227.
31. The National Archives, Ref: WARD 2/27/94B/137.
32. Ibid., WARD 2/27/94B/28.
33. 'Ela, Countess of Salisbury', medievalwomen.org.
34. The National Archives, Ref: WARD 2/27/94B/146.
35. Jennifer C. Ward, 'Ela, suo jure Countess of Salisbury (b. in or after 1190, d. 1261)', Oxforddnb.com, October 2009.
36. 'Ela of Salisbury', stanfordmagnacarta.worpress.com.
37. 'Ela, Countess of Salisbury', medievalwomen.org.

Chapter 6: The Marshal Sisters
1. Crouch and Holden, *History of William Marshal*.
2. Crouch, David, *William Marshal*.
3. Ibid.
4. Ibid.
5. Ibid.
6. Ibid.
7. David Crouch, 'William Marshal [called the Marshal], fourth earl of Pembroke (*c.* 1146–1219)', Oxforddnb.com.
8. Crouch, *William Marshal*.
9. Crouch, 'William Marshal'.
10. Crouch and Holden, *History of William Marshal*.
11. Crouch, 'William Marshal'.
12. Roger of Hovedon, *Annales*.
13. Crouch, 'William Marshal'.
14. Ibid.

15. Ibid.
16. Crouch and Holden, *History of William Marshal.*
17. M.T. Flanagan, 'Isabel de Clare, suo jure countess of Pembroke (1171x6–1220)', Oxforddnb.com.
18. Crouch, 'William Marshal'.
19. Asbridge, *The Greatest Knight.*
20. Crouch, 'William Marshal'.
21. Crouch and Holden, *History of William Marshal.*
22. *L'Histoire de Guillaume le Maréchale* quoted in Morris, *King John.*
23. Ibid.
24. Crouch, 'William Marshal'.
25. Ibid.
26. Crouch and Holden, *History of William Marshal.*
27. Crouch, 'William Marshal'.
28. Ibid.
29. Ibid.
30. Asbridge, *The Greatest Knight.*
31. Crouch, 'William Marshal'.
32. Ibid.
33. Crouch and Holden, *History of William Marshal.*
34. Flanagan, 'Isabel de Clare'.
35. Crouch and Holden, *History of William Marshal.*
36. Ibid.
37. Flanagan, 'Isabel de Clare'.
38. Ibid.
39. Elizabeth Chadwick, 'Clothing the Bones: Finding Mahelt Marshal', livingthehistoryelizabethchadwick.blogspot.com, 7 September 2008.
40. Crouch and Holden, *History of William Marshal.*
41. Ibid.
42. Ibid.
43. Letter of 13 March 1216. Price, *King John's Letters.*
44. Ibid.
45. Crouch and Holden, *History of William Marshal.*
46. Ibid.
47. Robert C. Stacey, 'Roger Bigod, fourth earl of Norfolk (*c.* 1212-1270)', Oxforddnb.com.
48. finerollshenry3.org.uk/content/calendar/roll_024.html#it353_002, 27 Oct. 1226
49. Ibid.
50. Nicholas Vincent, 'William de Warenne, fifth earl of Surrey [Earl Warenne] (d. 1240)', Oxforddnb.com.
51. Ibid.
52. Ibid.

53. Chadwick, *Clothing the Bones*.
54. Vincent, 'William de Warenne'.
55. Ibid.
56. Chadwick, 'Clothing the Bones'.
57. David Crouch quoted in Chadwick, 'Clothing the Bones'.
58. T.A. Archer, revised by Michael Altschul, 'Gilbert de Clare, fifth earl of Gloucester and fourth earl of Hertford (*c.* 1180–1230)', Oxforddnb.com.
59. Ibid.
60. *Annals of Tewkesbury* quoted in Archer and Altschul, 'Gilbert de Clare'.
61. Ibid.
62. Michael Altschul, 'Richard de Clare, sixth earl of Gloucester and fifth earl of Hertford (1222–1262)', Oxforddnb.com.
63. Darren Baker, *With All For All: The Life of Simon de Montfort*.
64. Nicholas Vincent, 'Richard, first earl of Cornwall and king of Germany (1209–1272)', Oxforddnb.com.
65. Baker, *With All For All*.
66. *The Annals of Margam*, translated by Rich Price.
67. Ralph of Coggeshall quoted in Hallam, *The Plantagenet Chronicles*.
68. 'Eva Marshal', Revolvy.com, accessed 13 March 2019.
69. finerollshenry3.org.uk/content/calendar/roll032.html#it319_003, 13 August 1233.
70. Ibid.
71. Ibid.
72. 'Eva Marshal', Revolvy.com.
73. Ibid.
74. Chadwick, 'Clothing the Bones'.
75. H.W. Ridgeway, 'Warin de Munchensi (1195–1255)', Oxforddnb.com.
76. Ibid.

Chapter 7: The Princesses of Scotland
1. Morris, *King John*.
2. W.W. Scott, 'William I [known as William the Lion] (*c.* 1142–1214)', Oxforddnb.com.
3. Ibid.
4. Ibid.
5. Ibid.
6. David Ross, *Scotland: History of a Nation*.
7. E.L.G. Stones, quoted in Scott, 'William I'.
8. Scott, 'William I'.
9. Ibid.
10. Ross, *Scotland: History of a Nation*.
11. Ibid.
12. W.W. Scott, 'Ermengarde de Beaumont (1233)', Oxforddnb.com.

13. Ibid.
14. Ibid.
15. Anderson quoted in Scott, 'Ermengarde'.
16. Scott, 'William I'.
17. Ibid.
18. Ibid.
19. Ibid.
20. Scott, 'Ermengarde'.
21. Bower quoted in Scott, 'Ermengarde'.
22. Scott, 'William I'.
23. Ross, *Scotland: History of a Nation*.
24. Keith Stringer, 'Alexander II (1198–1249)', Oxforddnb.com.
25. Ibid.
26. Louise J. Wilkinson, 'Margaret, Princess of Scotland', magnacarta800th.com.
27. Bower paraphrased in Wilkinson, 'Margaret, Princess of Scotland'.
28. W.W. Scott, 'Margaret, countess of Kent (b. 1187x1195, d. 1259)', Oxforddnb.com.
29. Wilkinson, 'Margaret, Princess of Scotland'.
30. Scott, 'Margaret, countess of Kent'.
31. F.J. West, 'Hubert de Burgh, earl of Kent (*c.* 1170–1243)', Oxforddnb.com.
32. Ibid.
33. Wilkinson, 'Margaret, Princess of Scotland'.
34. Jessica Nelson, 'Isabella [Isabella Bigod], countess of Norfolk (b. 1195/1196, d. 1270)', Oxforddnb.com.
35. Nelson, Jessica A., 'Isabella, Countess of Norfolk', magnacarta800th.com.
36. Nelson, 'Isabella Bigod'.
37. finerollshenry3.org.uk /content/calendar/roll_022.html#it204_001, 20 May 1225.
38. Nelson, 'Isabella Bigod'.
39. *Calendar of Patent Rolls* quoted in Nelson, 'Isabella Bigod'.
40. Matthew Paris, Robert de Reading and others, *Flores Historiarum*, volume III.
41. Nelson, 'Isabella Bigod'.

Chapter 8: The House of Warenne

1. Vincent, 'William de Warenne'.
2. William Farrer and Charles Travis Clay, editors, *Early Yorkshire Charters, Volume 8: The Honour of Warenne*, p. 13. Through his mother, Isabel de Vermandois, granddaughter of Henry I of France, William de Warenne was a second cousin of Louis VII.
3. Ibid, pp. 16–17.
4. Ibid, p. 14. Richard Brito struck his blow with the words '*Hoc habeas pro amore domini mei Willelmi fratris regis.*' Quoted from *Vita S. Thomas* (*Becket Materials*, Rolls Ser., vol. iii).

5. Susan M. Johns, 'Isabel de Warenne, suo jure Countess of Surrey (d. 1203)', Oxforddnb.com.
6. Farrer and Clay, *The Honour of Warenne*, p. 19.
7. Ibid, p. 127.
8. Vincent, 'William de Warenne'.
9. Ibid.
10. Farrer and Clay, *The Honour of Warenne*.
11. Ibid., p. 21.
12. Ibid.
13. Ibid., p. 22.
14. Ibid.
15. *Annales Cestrienses: Chronicle of the Abbey of S. Werburg, at Chester*, edited by Richard Copley Christie, pp. 36–49. *British History Online* http://www.british-history.ac.uk/lancs-ches-record-soc/vol14/pp36-49, accessed 1 May 2019.
16. Farrer and Clay, *The Honour of Warenne*.
17. Susan M. Johns, 'Alice de Lusignan, suo jure countess of Eu', Oxforddnb.com.
18. Tickhill Castle Guide Leaflet, *Lords of the Honour of Tickhill*, author unknown, 2017.
19. finerollshenry3.org.uk content/calendar/roll_015.html#it158_006, 19 May 1221.
20. Johns, 'Alice de Lusignan'.
21. Farrer and Clay, *The Honour of Warenne*.
22. Johns, 'Alice de Lusignan'.
23. Vincent, 'William de Warenne'.
24. Ibid.
25. Ibid.
26. Ibid.
27. Ralph V. Turner, 'William d'Aubigny, third earl of Arundel', Oxforddnb.com.
28. John A. Nichols, 'Isabel de Warenne [married name Isabel d'Aubigny], countess of Arundel', Oxforddnb.com.
29. Waugh quoted in Nichols, 'Isabel de Warenne'.
30. Matthew Paris quoted in Nichols, 'Isabel de Warenne'.
31. Quoted by Susan Annesley in finerollshenry3.org.uk content/month/fm-08-2009.html, August 2009.
32. Ibid.
33. Ibid.

Chapter 9: Isabella of Gloucester

1. Price, *King John's Letters*.
2. Louise Wilkinson, 'Isabel of Gloucester, wife of King John', magnacarta800th.com.

3. Ibid.

4. Ibid.

5. Morris, *King John*, p. 61.

6. Robert B. Patterson, 'Isabella, suo jure Countess of Gloucester (c. 1160–1217)', Oxforddnb.com.

7. Wilkinson, 'Isabel of Gloucester'.

8. Ibid.

9. Ralph of Diceto, *Images of History*, pp. 166-75.

10. Lisa Hilton, *Queens Consort: England's Medieval Queens*.

11. Ibid.

12. Patterson, 'Isabella of Gloucester'.

13. Wilkinson, 'Isabel of Gloucester'.

14. Nigel Saul, 'Geoffrey de Mandeville', magnacarta800th.com.

15. *Histoire des ducs de Normandie* quoted in Saul, 'Geoffrey de Mandeville'.

16. Saul, 'Geoffrey de Mandeville'.

17. Ibid.

18. Wilkinson, 'Isabel of Gloucester'.

19. Morris, *King John*, p. 242.

20. Letters patent, 20 December 1215. Price, *King John's Letters*.

21. Anonymous de Béthune, *Histoires des ducs de Normandie et rois d'Angleterre*, quoted by Price, *King John's Letters*, accessed 23 February 2019.

22. Ralph of Coggeshall, *Chronicon Anglicanum*, quoted by Price, *King John's Letters*, accessed 23 February 2019.

23. Patterson, 'Isabella of Gloucester'.

24. *The Calendar of Close Rolls*, 17 September 1217, translated and edited by Price, *King John's Letters*, accessed 23 February 2019.

25. BL Cotton MS Nero E, vii, fol. 91, quoted in West, 'Hubert de Burgh'.

26. Henry II (1179/80) quoted in West, 'Hubert de Burgh'.

27. West, 'Hubert de Burgh'.

28. Ibid.

29. Ralph of Coggeshall quoted in Hallam, *The Plantagenet Chronicles*.

30. Ibid.

31. West, 'Hubert de Burgh'.

32. Ibid.

33. Ibid.

34. Ibid.

35. Wilkinson, 'Isabel of Gloucester'.

36. Lambeth Palace Library ms.20 quoted in Nicholas Vincent, 'Feature of the Month: May 2015 – A Glimpse of London, May 1216', magnacarta800th. com, May 2015.

Chapter 10: Isabelle d'Angoulême

1. Hilton, *Queens Consort*.

2. Ibid.

3. Vincent, 'Isabella of Angoulême'.
4. Gillingham, 'John'.
5. Ralph of Diceto, quoted in Hilton, *Queens Consort*.
6. Church, *King John*.
7. Ralph of Coggeshall, quoted in Hallam, *The Plantagenet Chronicles*.
8. Church, *King John*.
9. Ibid.
10. Ralph of Coggeshall quoted in Hallam, *The Plantagenet Chronicles*.
11. Hallam, *The Plantagenet Chronicles*.
12. Elizabeth Norton, *She Wolves: The Notorious Queens of England*.
13. Ibid.
14. Vincent, 'Isabella of Angoulême'.
15. Hilton, *Queens Consort*.
16. Ibid.
17. Morris, *King John*.
18. Matthew Paris quoted in Hilton, *Queens Consort*.
19. Morris, *King John*.
20. Hilton, *Queens Consort*.
21. Ibid.
22. Vincent, 'From the Tower'.
23. Church, *King John*.
24. Letter to Henry III, translated by Joan M. Ferrante, 'Isabel of Angoulême', *Epistolae*, epistolae.ctl.columbia.edu/women.
25. Ibid.
26. Norton, *She Wolves*.
27. Ibid.
28. Louise Wilkinson, 'Isabella of Angoulême, wife of King John', magnacarta800th.com.
29. Vincent, 'Isabella of Angoulême'.
30. Matthew Paris described Isabelle as 'more Jezebel than Isabel, while Roger of Wendover attributed John's failure in Normandy to Isabelle's skills in 'sorcery and witchcraft. Wilkinson, 'Isabella of Angoulême'.

Chapter 11: Eleanor of Brittany

1. Michael Jones, 'Eleanor suo jure duchess of Brittany (1182x4–1241)', Oxforddnb.com.
2. Connolly, *Heroines of the Medieval World*.
3. 'The Chronicle: 1187–1214', in *Annales Cestrienses: Chronicle of the Abbey of S. Werburg at Chester*, ed. Richard Copley Christie (London, 1887), pp. 36–49. *British History Online* http://www.british-history.ac.uk/lancs-ches-record-soc/vol14/pp36-49, accessed 1 May 2019.
4. Douglas Boyd, *Eleanor: April Queen of Aquitaine*.
5. *L'Histoire de Guillaume le Maréchale* quoted by Morris, *King John*.

6. Morris, *King John.*
7. Ralph of Diceto quoted in Hallam, *The Plantagenet Chronicles.*
8. Ibid.
9. Ralph of Coggeshall quoted in Hallam, *The Plantagenet Chronicles.*
10. Ibid.
11. Ibid.
12. Ibid.
13. Ibid
14. *The Annals of Margam*, translated by Rich Price.
15. Ralph of Coggeshall quoted in Hallam, *The Plantagenet Chronicles.*
16. David Williamson, 'Eleanor, Princess (1184–1241)', Brewer's British Royalty.
17. *Rotuli litterarum clausarum* quoted in Jones, 'Eleanor, duchess of Brittany'.
18. Danziger and Gillingham, *1215.*
19. *Rotuli litterarum patentum* quoted in Jones, 'Eleanor, duchess of Brittany'.
20. Williamson, 'Eleanor, Princess'.
21. Jones, 'Eleanor, duchess of Brittany'.

Chapter 12: The Daughters of King John

1. *Magna rotuli, 2-569*, quoted in Kate Norgate and revised by A.D. Carr, 'Joan, d. 1237', Oxfroddnb.com.
2. Louise Wilkinson, 'Joan, Daughter of King John', magnacarta800th.com, 2016.
3. David Hillman, *Kings, Queens, Bones and Bastards.*
4. Norgate and Carr, 'Joan'.
5. Ibid.
6. The Barnwell annalist quoted in Hallam, *The Plantagenet Chronicles.*
7. *Brut y Tywysogyn* or *The Chronicle of the Princes: Peniarth MS 20 Version*, editor T.
8. Carr, A.D., 'Llywelyn ab Iorwerth (*c.* 1173–1240)', Oxfroddnb.com.
9. The Barnwell annalist quoted in Hallam, *The Plantagenet Chronicles.*
10. Ibid.
11. Ibid.
12. Ibid.
13. finerollshenry3.org.uk /content/calendar/roll_027.html#it119_007 12/119 (27 March 1228), *27 March. Reading. Concerning lands to be taken into the king's hand. Order to the sheriff of Leicestershire to take the manor of Rothley with appurtenances into the king's hand, which the king has committed to Joan, wife of L. prince of North Wales, for as long as it pleases the king, and to keep it safely until the king orders otherwise*; and https://finerollshenry3.org.uk/content/calendar/roll_027.html#it279_002 (21 September 1228). *Concerning the corn of Condover. Order to the sheriff of Staffordshire and Shropshire to take into the king's hand without delay the corn of this autumn that Joan, wife of L. prince of*

North Wales, caused to be sown in the manor of Condover, which she had by bail of the king for as long as it pleases him, notwithstanding the king's command to him to demise that corn to her in peace.

14. *Letters of Medieval Women*, edited and translated by Anne Crawford.
15. D.R. Messer, 'Joan (Siwan) (died 1237), princess and diplomat', *Dictionary of Welsh Biography*, from https://biography.wales/article/s12-JOAN-TYW-1237, 19 Aug 2019.
16. *Brut y Tywysogyn.*
17. 'Joan, Lady of Wales (c.1191–1237)', englishmonarch.co.uk, 2004.
18. Robin Chapman Stacey, 'Divorce, Medieval Welsh Style', *Speculum*, Volume 77, issue 4 (October 2002), pp. 1107-1127.
19. Madeleine Grey, 'Four Weddings, Three Funerals and a Historic Detective Puzzle: A Cautionary Tale', 2014, https://biography.wales/article/s12-JOAN-TYW-1237?&query=prince&lang[]=en&sort=sort_name&order=asc&rows=12&page=8.
20. Danziger and Gillingham, *1215.*
21. Ibid.
22. Matthew Lewis, *Henry III: The Son of Magna Carta*, p. 68.
23. finerollshenry3.co.uk/ content/calendar/roll_015.html#it192_005, 19 June 1221.
24. *The Chronicle of Lanercost*, 1272–1346.
25. A.O. Anderson and M.M.O Anderson, editors, *Chronicle of Melrose*, 1936.
26. Keith Stringer, 'Joan (1210–1237)', Oxforddnb.com.
27. Ibid.
28. Matthaei Parisiensis, Chronica majora, edited by H.R. Luard.
29. finerollshenry3.co.uk/content/calendar/roll_005E.html#it019_004, 5 May 1238.
30. Ibid.
31. Matthaei Parisiensis, *Chronica majora.*
32. D.S.H. Abulafia, 'Isabella [Elizabeth, Isabella of England] (1214–1241)', Oxforddnb.com.
33. Roger of Wendover, *Flowers of History*, volume II.
34. Ibid.
35. Ibid.
36. Ibid.
37. Ibid.
38. Abulafia, 'Isabella'.
39. Roger of Wendover, *Flowers of History*, volume II.
40. Roger of Wendover quoted in Hallam, *The Plantagenet Chronicles.*
41. Ibid.
42. Ibid.
43. Matthew Paris, Robert de Reading and others, *Flores Historiarum*, vol. III, edited by Henry Richards Luard.

44. Abulafia, 'Isabella'.
45. Ibid.
46. Baker, *With All For All*.
47. Mary Anne Everett Green, *Lives of the Princesses of England from the Norman Conquest*, Volume 2, Longman, Brown, Green, Longman, & Roberts, London, 1857.

Chapter 13: De Montfort
 1. Carol, 'Eleanor of Leicester: A Broken Vow of Chastity', historyofroyalwomen. com, 28 February 2017.
 2. Norton, *She Wolves*.
 3. R.F. Walker, 'William Marshal, fifth earl of Pembroke (*c.* 1190–1231)', oxforddnb.com.
 4. Ibid.
 5. Baker, *With All For All*.
 6. Elizabeth Hallam, 'Eleanor, Countess of Pembroke and Leicester (1215?–1275)', Oxforddnb.com.
 7. Baker, *With All For All*.
 8. Ibid.
 9. Hallam, 'Eleanor, Countess of Pembroke'.
10. J.R. Maddicott, 'Montfort, Simon de, eighth Earl of Leicester (1208–1265)', oxforddnb.com.
11. Ibid.
12. Baker, *The Two Eleanors*.
13. 'Eleanor of England', *Epistolae*, epistolae.ctl.columbia.edu/women.
14. Hallam, 'Eleanor, Countess of Pembroke'.
15. Baker, *With All For All*.
16. Hallam, 'Eleanor, Countess of Pembroke'.
17. Matthew Paris quoted in Baker, *With All For All*.
18. Simon de Montfort quoted in quoted in Ibid.
19. Ibid.
20. Hallam, 'Eleanor, Countess of Pembroke'.
21. Letter from Adam Marsh to Eleanor, Countess of Leicester, 1252, *Epistolae*, 'Eleanor of England'.
22. Letter from Adam Marsh to Eleanor, Countess of Leicester, 1252, *Epistolae*, 'Eleanor of England'.
23. Maddicott, 'Simon de Montfort'.
24. Hallam, 'Eleanor, Countess of Pembroke'.
25. *Epistolae*, 'Eleanor of England'.
26. Baker, *With All For All*.
27. Royal Letters, Tower Collection #1125, quoted in *Epistolae*, 'Eleanor of England'.
28. *Epistolae*, 'Eleanor of England'.

29. Ibid.
30. Hallam, 'Eleanor, Countess of Pembroke'.
31. 'Eleanor de Montfort', englishmonarchs.co.uk, 2004.
32. Ibid.
33. Crawford, *Letters of Medieval Women*.
34. Ibid.
35. 'Eleanor de Montfort', englishmonarchs.co.uk, 2004.
36. Connolly, *Heroines of the Medieval World*.
37. 'Eleanor de Montfort', englishmonarchs.co.uk.
38. Ibid.
39. *Calendar of the Charter Rolls*, 1–14, Edward III.
40. The Princess Gwenllian Society, princessgwenllian.co.uk.

Epilogue
1. The Rt. Hon. Fiona Woolf, quoted in *Magna Carta Quotations*, magnacarta800th.com.
2. David Carpenter, *Magna Carta* (translated with a new commentary).

Appendix A: 1215 Magna Carta
Danziger and Gillingham, *1215*
Morris, *King John*
David Starkey, *Magna Carta: The True Story Behind the Charter* (Hodder, London, 2015)
H. Summerson et al, translator, *Magna Carta*, The Magna Carta Project, http://magnacarta.cmp.uea.ac.uk/read/magna_carta_1215, accessed 13 March 2019

Appendix B: Enforcers of Magna Carta – The Twenty-Five
Danziger and Gillingham, *1215*
Matthew Strickland, '*Enforcers of Magna Carta (act, 1215–1216)*', oxforddnb.com

Appendix C: The Charter of the Forest 1217
Dan Jones, *Realm Divided: A Year in the Life of Plantagenet England* (Head of Zeus, London, 2015)
National Archives, nationalarchives.gov.uk/education/resources/magna-carta/charter-forest-1225-westminster

Bibliography

Primary Sources

Annales Monastici: Annales prioratus de Dunstaplia (A.D. 1–1297) Annales monasterii de Bermundesia (A.D. 1042–1432), edited by Henry Richards Luard, Longmans, London, 1866

Annales Monastici: Annales prioratus de Dunstaplia (A.D. 1–1297), translated by Rich Price, *King John's Letters*, Facebook Study Group, 20 June 2016 onwards

The Annals of Roger de Hoveden: Comprising the History of England and of other Countries of Europe from A.D. 732 to A.D. 1201, edited and translated by Henry T. Riley, H.G. Bohn, London, 1853

The Autobiography of Giraldus Cambrensis, edited and translated by H.E. Butler, 1937, archive.org

The 'Barnwell' Annals (anon.), edited by W. Stubbs, in *The Historical Collections of Walter of Coventry*, Rolls Series, 1873

Carlin, Martha and David Crouch (eds and trans), *Lost Letters of Medieval Life: English Society, 1200–1250*, University of Pennsylvania Press, Pennsylvania, 2013

Carpenter, David, *Magna Carta* (translated with a new commentary), Penguin Random House, London, 2015

'The Chronicle: 1187–1214', in *Annales Cestrienses Chronicle of the Abbey of S. Werburg, at Chester*, edited by Richard Copley Christie, London, 1887, pp. 36–49; *British History Online* http://www.british-history.ac.uk/lancs-ches-record-soc/vol14/pp36–49 [accessed 1 May 2019]

Anderson, A.O. and M.M.O Anderson (eds), *Chronicle of Melrose 731–1270*, 1936

Chronicles of the Reigns of Stephen, Henry II and Richard I, Nabu Press, 2012

Crawford, Anne (ed. and trans.), *Letters of Medieval Women*, Sutton Publishing, Stroud, 2002

Crouch, David and Anthony J. Holden (eds), *History of William Marshal: Text & Translation (II. 10032–end)*, Anglo-Norman Text Society from Birkbeck College, 2002

Dronke, Peter, *Abelard and Heloise in Medieval Testimonies*, Glasgow, University of Glasgow Press, 1976

Florentii Wigorniensis monachi chronicon ex chronicis, edited by B. Thorpe, 2, English Historical Society, 10 (1849)

Fine Rolls of Henry III Project, Finerollshenry3.co.uk

Gervase of Canterbury, *The Deeds of Kings*, edited by W. Stubbs, in *The Historical Works of Gervase of Canterbury*, Rolls Series, 1880

Gesta Regis Henrici Secundi Benedicti Abbatis: The Chronicle of the Reigns of Henry II and Richard I A. D. 1169–1192:Known Commonly Under the Name of Benedict of Peterborough, edited by William Stubbs, Longmans, 1867

Giraldus Cambrensis, *The Conquest of Ireland*, translated by Thomas Forester, Medieval Latin Series, Ontario, 2001

John of Salisbury, *The Letters of John of Salisbury*, edited by W.J. Miller, S.J. Butler, H.E. Butler and revised by C.N.L. Brooke, Thomas Nelson and Sons, London, 1955

Mackay, A.J.G. (ed.), *The Historie and Chronicles of Scotland ... by Robert Lindesay of Pitscottie,* 3 vols, Scottish Text Society, 42–3, 60 (1899–1911)

Magna Carta, British Library, transcript from bl.uk

National Archives; nationalarchives.gov.uk/education/resources/magna-carta/charter-forest-1225-westminster/

Ordericus Vitalis, *The Ecclesiastical History of England and Normandy*, edited by H.G. Bohn, London, 1853

Paris, Matthew, Robert de Reading and others, *Flores Historiarum*, volume III, edited by Henry Richards Luard, H.M. Stationary Office, 1890

Ralph of Coggeshall, *The English Chronicle*, edited by J. Stevenson, in *Chronicon Anglicanum,* Rolls Series, 1875

Richard of Devizes, *Chronicle,* Objective Systems Pty Ltd., ebook, 2008

Richard of Devizes, *The Chronicle of Richard of Devizes: Concerning the Deeds of Richard the First King of England also Richard of Cirencester's Description of Britain*, edited and translated by J.A. Giles, London, 1841

Ralph of Diceto, *Images of History*, edited by W. Stubbs, in *The Historical Works of Master Ralph of Diceto*, Rolls Series, 1876

Roger of Wendover, *Roger of Wendover's Flowers of History: Comprising the History of England from the Descent of the Saxons to A.D. 1235*, volume II, edited by J.A. Giles, H.G. Bohn, London, 1849

Rymer, T. (ed.), *Foedera, conventions, literae*, Record Commission, edition li, 144, London, 1816–69

Sawyer, P.H., *Anglo-Saxon Charters: An Annotated List and Bibliography*, Royal Historical Society Guides and Handbooks (1968)

Sharpe, J. (trans.), *The History of the Kings of England and of his Own Times by William Malmesbury*, Seeleys, 1854

Shirley, W.W. (ed.), *Royal and other Historical Letters*, Rolls Series, Chronicles and Memorials, London, 1862–6

Stow, John, *The Annales of England: The Race of the Kings of Brytaine after the received Opinion since Brute, &c*, G. Bishop and T. Adams, London, 1605

Strachey, J. (ed.), *Rotuli parliamentorum ut et petitiones, et placita in parliamento*, 6 vols (1767–77)

Summerson, H. et al (trans), *Magna Carta*, The Magna Carta Project, http://magnacarta.cmp.uea.ac.uk/read/magna_carta_1215, accessed 13 March 2019

Thomas of Walsingham, *Thomae Walsingham Historia Anglicana*, edited by H.T. Riley, in part one of *Chronica Monasterii Sancti Albani*, vol. 4, Rolls Series, 1863–4

Thompson, Doug (trans.), *Royal Letter 763a*, douglyn.co.uk/Braose

Thomson, Doug (trans.), *Royal Letter 763b*, douglyn.co.uk/Braose

Trivet, Nicholas, *Annales Sex Regum Angliae*, edited by T. Hog, 1845

Van Houts, Elisabeth M.C. and Rosalind C. Love (eds and trans), *The Warenne (Hyde) Chronicle*, Clarendon Press, Oxford, 2013

White, Hugh (trans.), *Ancrene Wisse: Guide for Anchoresses*, Penguin, Harmondsworth, 1993

William of Malmesbury, *Chronicles of the Kings of England, From the Earliest Period to the Reign of King Stephen, c. 1090–1143*, Perennial Press, ebook, 2016

William of Malmesbury, *Chronicles of the Kings of England, From the Earliest Period to the Reign of King Stephen, c. 1090–1143*, edited by John Sharpe and J.A. Giles, H.G. Bohn, London, 1847

Yonge, C.D. (trans.), *Medieval Sourcebook: Matthew of Westminster: Simon de Montfort's Rebellion 1265*, excerpt from Matthew Paris, *The Flowers of History*, sourcebooks.fordham.edu

Secondary Sources

6 Facts about Magna Carta (article), historyextra.com, 22 August 2018

A History of the County of Rutland: Volume 2, Victoria County History, London, 1935

Abulafia, D.S.H., *Isabella [Elizabeth, Isabella of England] (1214–1241)* (article), *Oxford Dictionary of National Biography*, Oxford University Press, online edition, 23 September 2004

Adams, George Burton, *The History of England from the Norman Conquest to the Death of John*, public domain, ebook

Altschul, Michael, *Clare, Richard de, sixth earl of Gloucester and fifth earl of Hertford* (article), *Oxford Dictionary of National Biography*, Oxford University Press, online edition, 23 September 2004

Ambler, Sophie, *Advisers of King John* (article), *Oxford Dictionary of National Biography*, Oxford University Press, online edition, 28 May 2015

Ambler, Sophie, *Henry III's Confirmation of Magna Carta in 1265* (article), magna carta research.org, March 2014

Ambler, Sophie, *Simon de Montfort's 1265 Parliament and Magna Carta* (article), thehistoryofperliament.wordpress.com, 20 January 2015

Amt, Emilie, *Salisbury, Patrick, first Earl of Salisbury [Earl of Wiltshire]* (article), *Oxford Dictionary of National Biography*, Oxford University Press, online edition, 23 September 2004

Archer, T.A., revised by Michael Altschul, *Clare, Gilbert de, fifth earl of Gloucester and fourth earl of Hertford* (article), *Oxford Dictionary of National Biography*, Oxford University Press, online edition, 23 September 2005

Asbridge, Thomas, *The Greatest Knight: The Remarkable Life of William Marshal, the Power behind Five English Thrones*, Simon & Schuster, London, 2015

Ashley, Maurice, *The Life and Times of King John*, George Weidenfield and Nicolson, London, 1972

Ashley, Mike, *A Brief History of British Kings and Queens*, Constable & Robinson Ltd., London, 2014

Ashley, Mike, *The Mammoth Book of British Kings & Queens*, Robinson, London, 1998

Baker, Darren, *The Two Eleanors of Henry III: The Lives of Eleanor of Provence and Eleanor de Montfort*, Pen & Sword History, Barnsley, 2019

Baker, Darren, *With All For All: The Life of Simon de Montfort*, Amberley, Stroud, 2015

Barrow, Julia, *Briouze, Giles de (c. 1170–1215), bishop of Hereford* (article), *Oxford Dictionary of National Biography*, Oxford University Press, online edition, 26 May 1216

Bartlett, Robert, *England Under the Norman and Angevin Kings, 1075–1225*, Oxford University Press, Oxford, 2000

Bartlett, W.B., *Richard the Lionheart: The Crusader King of England*, Amberley, Stroud, 2018

Bateson, Mary, *Medieval England 1066–1350*, Lecturable, e-book

Bémont, Charles and Gabriel Monod, *Medieval Europe, 395–1270*, Lecturable, e-book, 2012

Blackburn, Robert, *Britain's Written Constitution* (article), bl.uk/magna-carta, 13 March 2015

Boyd, Douglas, *Eleanor, April Queen of Aquitaine*, Sutton Publishing, Stroud, 2004.

Brand, Paul, *Bigod, Hugh (b. in or before 1220, d. 1266)* (article), *Oxford Dictionary of National Biography*, Oxford University Press, online edition, 3 January 2008.

Brindle, Steven and Agnieszka Sadraei, *Conisbrough Castle, English Heritage Guidebook*, English Heritage, London, 2015

Brooks, Richard, *The Knight who Saved England, William Marshal and the French Invasion, 1217*, Osprey Publishing, Oxford, 2014

Burke, John and John Bernard Burke, *A Genealogical and Heraldic Dictionary of the Peerages of England, Ireland and Scotland*, Henry Colburn, London, 1846

Campbell, Bruce, *Britain 1300* (article), *History Today*, Volume 50 (6), June 2000

Cannon, John, editor, *The Oxford Companion to British History*, Oxford University Press, Oxford, 1997

Carol, *Eleanor of Leicester: A Broken Vow of Chastity* (article), historyofroyalwomen.com, 28 February 2017

Carpenter, David, *Revival and Survival: Reissuing Magna Carta* (article) bl.co.uk/magna-carta/articles, 13 March 2015

Castor, Helen, *She-Wolves: The Women who Ruled England before Elizabeth*, Faber and Faber, London, 2010

Chadwick, Elizabeth, *Clothing the Bones: Finding Mahelt Marshal* (article), livingthehistoryelizabethchadwick.blogspot.com, 7 September 2008

Chadwick, Elizabeth, *Roger Bigod Earl of Norfolk circa 1140–1221* (article), the-history-girls-blogspot.com, 24 November 2018

Chadwick, Elizabeth, *Roger Bigod II Earl of Norfolk* (article), livingthehistoryelizabethchadwick.blogspot.com, 12 June 2009

Church, Stephen, *King John: England, Magna Carta and the Making of a Tyrant*, Pan MacMillan, London, 2015

Cockerill, Sara, *Eleanor of Castile: The Shadow Queen*, Amberley, Stroud, 2014

Cole, Margaret Wren, *Llywelyn ab Iorwerth: The Making of a Welsh Prince*, Phd thesis, ethos.bl.uk, January 2012

Connolly, Sharon Bennett, *Heroines of the Medieval World*, Amberley, Stroud, 2017

Corvi, Steven J., *Plantagenet Queens and Consorts: Family, Duty, Power*, Amberley, Stroud, 2018

Crouch, David, *Breteuil, Robert de, fourth earl of Leicester* (article), *Oxford Dictionary of National Biography*, Oxford University Press, online edition, 24 September 2004.

Crouch, David, *Marshal, William [called the Marshal], fourth earl of Pembroke (c. 1146–1219)* (article), *Oxford Dictionary of National Biography*, Oxford University Press, online edition, 24 May 2007

Crouch, David, *William Marshal*, 3rd edition, Routledge, Abingdon, 2016

Danziger, Danny and John Gillingham, *1215: The Year of Magna Carta*, Hodder & Stoughton, London, 2004

Davis, H.W. Carless, *England under the Normans and Angevins 1066–1272*, Lecturable, ebook

Davis, William Stearns, *A History of France from the Earliest Times to the Treaty of Versailles*, The Riverside Press, Cambridge Massachusetts, 1919

Douglyn.com/BraoseWeb, accessed 10-17 March 2019

Duducu, Jem, *Forgotten History: Unbelievable Moments from the Past*, Amberley, Stroud, 2016

Duruy, Victor, *History of the Middle Ages*, Lecturable, e-book, 2012

Eales, Richard, *Ranulf III [Ranulf de Blundeville], sixth earl of Chester and first earl of Lincoln* (article), *Oxford Dictionary of National Biography*, Oxford University Press, online edition, 4 October 2008

Ela, Countess of Salisbury (article), medievalwomen.org

Epistolae, *Eleanor of England* (article), epistolae.ctl.columbia.edu/women

Epistolae, *Isabel of Angoulême* (article), epistolae.ctl.columbia.edu/women

Eva Marshal, Revolvy.com, accessed 13 March 2019

Farrer, William and Charles Travis Clay, editors, *Early Yorkshire Charters, Volume 8: The Honour of Warenne*, Cambridge University Press, Cambridge, 2013 edition, first published 1949

Faulkner, Kathryn, *Beauchamp, de, family* (article), *Oxford Dictionary of National Biography*, Oxford University Press, online edition, 23 September 2004

Flanagan, M.T., *Clare, Isabel de, suo jure countess of Pembroke (1171x6–1220)* (article), *Oxford Dictionary of National Biography*, Oxford University Press, online edition, 23 September 2010

Ford, David Nash, *Matilda de St Valery, Lady Bergavenny (c. 1153–1210)* (article), berkshirehistory.com, 2003

Fraser, Antonia, *The Warrior Queens: Boadicea's Chariot*, George Weidenfeld & Nicolson Ltd., London, 1993

Gardiner, Juliet and Neil Wenborn, editors, *History Today Companion to British History*, Collins & Brown, London, 1995

Gillingham, John, *John (1167–1216)* (article), *Oxford Dictionary of National Biography*, Oxford University Press, online edition, 23 September 2010

Gladwin, Irene, *The Sheriff: The Man and his Office*, Victor Gollancz, London, 1974

Golding, Brian, *Canville [Camville], Gerard de (d. 1214)* (article), *Oxford Dictionary of National Biography*, Oxford University Press, online edition, 28 September 2006

Goubert, Pierre *The Course of French History*, Routledge, London, 1991

Grant, Lindy, *Eleanor of Aquitaine* (article), *BBC History Magazine*, August 2016

Green, Mary Anne Everett, *Lives of the Princesses of England from the Norman Conquest*, Volume 1, Longman, London, 1857

Green, Mary Anne Everett, *Lives of the Princesses of England from the Norman Conquest*, Volume 2, Longman, London, 1857

Grey, Madeleine, *Four Weddings, Three Funerals and a Historic Detective Puzzle: A Cautionary Tale* (article), 2014, https://biography.wales/article/s12-JOAN-TYW-

Hallam, Elizabeth, editor, *Chronicles of the Age of Chivalry*, Tiger Books, Twickenham, 1995

Hallam, Elizabeth, *Eleanor, Countess of Pembroke and Leicester (1215?–1275)* (article), *Oxford Dictionary of National Biography*, Oxford University Press, online edition, 23 September 2004

Hallam, Elizabeth, editor, *The Plantagenet Chronicles*, Tiger Books, Twickenham, 1995

Hanley, Catherine, *The Battle that Saved England* (article), historiamag.com, 20 May 2017

Hanley, Catherine, *Nichola de la Haye* (article), catherinehanley.co.uk

Hanna-Black, Sara, themortimersblog.wordpress.com

Hilliam, David *Kings, Queens, Bones and Bastards: Who's Who in the English Monarchy from Egbert to Elizabeth II*, The History Press, Stroud, 2008 (first published 1998)

Hilton, Lisa, *Queens Consort: England's Medieval Queens*, Orion Books, London, 2008

Huizinga, J. *The Waning of the Middle Ages*, 4th edition, The Folio Society. London, 2000

Hume, David, *The History of England, Volume I*, public domain, ebook

Joan, Lady of Wales (c. 1191–1237) (article), englishmonarchs.co.uk, 2004

Johns, Susan M., *Alice* [married name *Alice de Lusignan*] *suo jure countess of Eu* (article), *Oxford Dictionary of National Biography*, Oxford University Press, online edition, 23 September 2004

Johns, Susan M., *Briouze, Loretta de, countess of Leicester (d. in or after 1266)* (article), *Oxford Dictionary of National Biography*, Oxford University Press, online edition, 28 September 2006

Johns, Susan M., *Haie, Nicola de la (d. 1230), landowner* (article), *Oxford Dictionary of National Biography*, Oxford University Press, online edition, 23 September 2004

Johns, Susan M., *Warenne, Isabel de, suo jure countess of Surrey (d. 1203)* (article), *Oxford Dictionary of National Biography*, Oxford University Press, online edition, 2004

Jones, Dan, *The Plantagenets: The Kings Who Made England*, Kindle edition, Harper Collins, London, 2013

Jones, Dan, *Realm Divided: A Year in the Life of Plantagenet England*, Head of Zeus, London, 2015

Jones, Dan, *What Was Magna Carta and Why Was it Significant?* (article), hitoryhit.com, 15 June 2018

Jones, Michael, *Eleanor [Eleanor of Brittany] suo jure duchess of Brittany* (article), *Oxford Dictionary of National Biography*, Oxford University Press, online edition, 3 January 2008

Jones, Terry, *Terry Jones' Medieval Lives*, BBC Books, London, 2005

Kemp, B.R., *Longespée, Nicholas* (article), *Oxford Dictionary of National Biography*, Oxford University Press, online edition, 27 May 2010

Koenigsberger, H.G., *Medieval Europe 400–1500*, Longman, New York, 1987

Kramer, Kyra Cornelius, *The Jezebel Effect: Why the Slut Shaming of Famous Women still Matters*, Ash Wood Press, Indiana, 2015

Lacroix, Paul, *Medieval Life: Manners, Customs and Dress During the Middle Ages*, Arcturus, London, 2011

Laffin, John, *Brassey's Battles: 3,500 Years of Conflict, Campaigns and Wars from A-Z*, Brassey's, London, 1995

Lawless, Erin, *Forgotten Royal Women: The King and I*, Pen & Sword Books, Barnsley, 2019

Lewis, Matthew, *Henry III: The Son of Magna Carta*, Amberley, Stroud, 2016

Leyser, Henrietta, *Medieval Women: A Social History of Women in England 450–1500*, Phoenix, e-book, 2013

Lloyd, Simon, *Longespée, Sir William* (article), *Oxford Dictionary of National Biography*, Oxford University Press, online edition, 27 May 2010

Maddicott, J.R., *Montfort, Simon de, eighth earl of Leicester (1208–1265)* (article), *Oxford Dictionary of National Biography*, Oxford University Press, online edition, 3 January 2008

Magna Carta, salisburycathedral.org.uk

Magna Carta Project, magnacartaresearch.org

Magna Carta Quotations, magnacarta800th.com

McConnell, Ally, *The Life of Ela, Countess of Salisbury* (article), Wiltshire and Swindon History Centre, wshc.eu, 15 September 2015

McGlynn, Sean, *Blood Cries Afar: The Magna Carta War and the Invasion of England 1215–1217,* The History Press, Stroud, 2015, ebook

Marlow, Joyce, *Kings & Queens of Britain*, 6th edition, Artus Publishing, London, 1979

Martindale, Jane, *Eleanor, suo jure duchess of Aquitaine (c.1122–1204)* (article), *Oxford Dictionary of National Biography*, Oxford University Press, online edition, May 2006

Matthew, Donald, *King Stephen*, Hambledon and London, London, 2002

Mcglynn, Sean, *King John and the French Invasion of England* (article), *BBC History Magazine,* Vol. 11, no. 6, June 2010

Messer, D.R. (2018), *Joan (Siwan) (died 1237), princess and diplomat* (article), *Dictionary of Welsh Biography*, https://biography.wales/article/s12-JOAN-TYW-1237, 19 Aug 2019

Morris, Marc, *A Great and Terrible King: Edward I and the Forging of Britain*, Windmill Books, London, 2009

Morris, Marc, *From Friendly Neighbours to Bitter Enemies* (article), *BBC History Magazine,* Vol. 9 no. 3, March 2008

Morris, Marc, *How Important was Magna Carta* (article), historyhit.com, 24 September 2018

Morris, Marc *King John: Treachery, Tyranny and the Road to Magna Carta*, Windmill Books, London, 2015

Mount, Toni, *A Year in the Life of Medieval England*, Amberley, Stroud, 2016.

Mundy, John H., *The High Middle Ages 1150–1309*, The Folio Society, London, 1998

Musgrove, David, *100 Places that Made Britain*, BBC Books, London, 2011

Nelson, Jessica A., *Isabella, Countess of Norfolk* (article), magnacarta800th.com

Nelson, Jessica, *Isabella [Isabella Bigod]* (article), (article), *Oxford Dictionary of National Biography*, Oxford University Press, online edition, 13 September 2018

Newcomb, Charlene, *John's Man in Lincoln: Gerard de Camville* (article), englishhistoryauthors.blog.uk, 4 October 2015

Nichols, John A., *Warenne, Isabel de [married name Isabel d'Aubigny] , countess of Arundel* (article), *Oxford Dictionary of National Biography*, Oxford University Press, online edition, 23 September 2004

Norton, Elizabeth, *She Wolves: The Notorious Queens of England*, The History Press, Stroud, 2008

Oliver, Neil, *The Story of the British Isles in 100 Places*, Penguin Random House, London, 2018

Ormrod, W.M., *English Historical Review* (article), December 2015

Patterson, Robert B., *Isabella, suo jure countess of Gloucester (c. 1160–1217)* (article), *Oxford Dictionary of National Biography*, Oxford University Press, online edition, 2004

Phillips, Charles, *The Illustrated Encyclopedia of Kings and Queens of Britain*, Hermes House, Leicestershire, 2011

Power, Eileen, *Medieval English Nunneries c. 1275–1535*, Cambridge University Press, London, 1922

Price, Rich, *King John's Letters*, Facebook Study Group, 20 June 2016 onwards

Ramirez, Janina, *Julian of Norwich: A Very Brief History*, London, SPCK Publishing, 2016

Rees, William, editor, Calendar of Ancient Petitions Relating to Wales (Thirteenth to Sixteenth Century), Cardiff, University of Wales Press, 1975. Ridgeway, H.W., *Munchensi, Warin de* (article), *Oxford Dictionary of National Biography*, Oxford University Press, online edition, 23 September 2004

Robertson, Geoffrey, *Magna Carta and Jury Trial*, (article), bl.uk/magna-carta, 13 March 2015

Ross, David, *Scotland: History of a Nation*, Lomond Books Ltd., Broxburn, 2014

Saul, Nigel, *Geoffrey de Mandeville* (article), magnacarta800th.com

Scott, W.W., *Ermengarde [Ermengarde de Beaumont] (1233)* (article), *Oxford Dictionary of National Biography*, Oxford University Press, online edition, 23 September 2004

Scott, W.W., *Margaret, countess of Kent* (article), *Oxford Dictionary of National Biography*, Oxford University Press, online edition, 23 September 2004

Scott, W.W., *William I [known as William the Lion] (c. 1142–1214)* (article), (article), *Oxford Dictionary of National Biography*, Oxford University Press, online edition, 23 September 2004

Seward, Desmond, *The Demon's Brood*, Constable, London, 2014

Southern, R.W., *The Making of the Middle Ages*, 4th edition, The Folio Society, London, 1998

Stacey, Robert C., *Bigod, Roger, fourth earl of Norfolk* (article), *Oxford Dictionary of National Biography*, Oxford University Press, online edition, 23 September 2004

Stacey, R.C., *Divorce, Medieval Welsh Style*, (article), *Speculum*, Volume 77, issue 4 October 2002, University of Chicago Press

Starkey, David, *Magna Carta: The True Story Behind the Charter*, Hodder, London, 2015

Strickland, Matthew, *Enforcers of Magna Carta (act, 1215–1216)* (article), Oxford Dictionary of National Biography, Oxford University Press, online edition, 22 September 2005

Strickland, Matthew, *Longespée [Lungespée], William, third earl of Salisbury* (article), *Oxford Dictionary of National Biography*, Oxford University Press, online edition, 27 May 2010

Stringer, Keith, *Alexander II (1198–1249)* (article), *Oxford Dictionary of National Biography*, Oxford University Press, online edition, 23 September 2004

Stringer, Keith, *Joan (1210–1237)*(article), *Oxford Dictionary of National Biography*, Oxford University Press, online edition, 23 September 2004

Swaton Parish Council, *The History of Swaton* (article), swaton.org.uk

The Historier, *The Treaty of Kingston: On this Day and on this Spot?* (article), anhistoriersmiscellany.com, 12 September 2017

Thompson, S.P., *Mary [Mary of Blois], suo jure countess of Boulogne (d. 1182), princess and abbess of Romsey* (article), *Oxford Dictionary of National Biography*, Oxford University Press, online edition, May 2014

Tickhill Castle Guide Leaflet, *Lords of the Honour of Tickhill*, author unknown, 2017

Tranter, Nigel, *The Story of Scotland*, e-book, 4th edition, Neil Wilson Publishing, 2011

Turner, Ralph V., *Aubigny, William d', [William de Albini], third earl of Arundel* (article), *Oxford Dictionary of National Biography*, Oxford University Press, online edition, 23 September 2004

Turner, Ralph V., *Briouze [Braose], William de (d. 1211)* (article), *Oxford Dictionary of National Biography*, Oxford University Press, online edition, 28 September 2006

Vincent, Nicholas, *Canville [Camville], Richard de (d. 1191)* (article), *Oxford Dictionary of National Biography*, Oxford University Press, online edition, 23 September 2004

Vincent, Nicholas, *Feature of the Month: May 2015 – A Glimpse of London, May 1216* (article), The Magna Carta Project, magnacarta.cmp.uea.ac.uk, May 2015

Vincent, Nicholas, *From the Tower: John Sends a Coded Message to His Queen* (article), The Magna Carta Project, magnacartaresearch.org, accessed 19 May 2019

Vincent, Nicholas, *Isabella [Isabella of Angoulême], suo jure countess of Angoulême (c. 1188–1246)* (article), *Oxford Dictionary of National Biography*, Oxford University Press, online edition, 5 January 2006

Vincent, Nicholas, *John Deals with Loretta de Braose and Isaac of Norwich* (article), The Magna Carta Project, magnacarta.cmp.uea.ac.uk

Vincent, Nicholas, *King John's Blood Lust* (article), *BBC History Magazine*, April 2019

Vincent, Nicholas, *King John's Evil Counsellors (act. 1208–1214)* (article), *Oxford Dictionary of National Biography*, Oxford University Press, online edition, 4 October 2008

Vincent, Nicholas, *Lacy, John de, third earl of Lincoln* (article), *Oxford Dictionary of National Biography*, Oxford University Press, online edition, 23 September 2010

Vincent, Nicholas, *Richard, first earl of Cornwall and king of Germany* (article), *Oxford Dictionary of National Biography*, Oxford University Press, online edition, 3 January 2008

Vincent, Nicholas, *Tournaments, Ladies and Bears* (article) and *The Magna Carta Project* (article), magnacartaresearch.org, accessed 27 November 2018

Vincent, Nicholas, *Warenne, William de, fifth earl of Surrey [Earl Warenne]* (article), *Oxford Dictionary of National Biography*, Oxford University Press, online edition, 23 September 2004

Walker, R.F., *Marshal, William, fifth earl of Pembroke (c. 1190–1231)* (article), *Oxford Dictionary of National Biography*, Oxford University Press, online edition, 22 September 2005

Ward, Jennifer C., *Lacy [née Quincy], Margaret de, countess of Lincoln* (article), *Oxford Dictionary of National Biography*, Oxford University Press, online edition, 3 January 2008

Waugh, S.L., The Lordship of England: Royal Wardships and Marriages in English Society and Politics, 1217–1327 (article) (1988)

Weir, Alison, *Britain's Royal Families: The Complete Genealogy*, 2nd edition, Pimlico, London, 1996

Weir, Alison, *Eleanor of Aquitaine: By the Wrath of God, Queen of England*, Jonathan Cape, London, 1999

West, F.J., *Burgh, Hubert de, earl of Kent (c. 1170–1243)* (article), *Oxford Dictionary of National Biography*, Oxford University Press, online edition, 3 January 2008

Whittle, Elisabeth, *Abergavenny Castle* (article), castlewales.com, 1992

Why Magna Carta Matters (article), historyextra.com, 23 January 2013

Wilkinson, Louise, *Isabella of Angoulême, wife of King John* (article), magnacarta800th.com

Wilkinson, Louise, *Isabel of Gloucester, wife of King John* (article), magnacarta 800th.com

Wilkinson, Louise, *Joan, daughter of King John* (article), magnacarta800th.com. 2016

Wilkinson, Louise, *Margaret, Princess of Scotland* (article), magnacarta800th.com

Wilkinson, Louise, *Women in Thirteenth-Century Lincolnshire*, Boydell, Suffolk, 2007

William Marshal, Earl of Pembroke (article), englishmonarchs.co.uk, 2004–2018

William de Warenne, 5th earl of Surrey (article), howlingpixel.com

Williamson, David, *Brewer's British Royalty*, Cassell, London, 1996

Wilson, Derek, *The Plantagenets*, Quercus, London, 2011

The Woes of King John Parts I and II (article), weaponsandwarfare.com, 7 June 2016

Wright, James, *A Palace for Our Kings: The History and Archaeology of a Mediaeval Royal Palace in the Heart of Sherwood Forest*, Triskele Publishing, London, 2016

Yonge, Charlotte M., *History of France*, D. Appleton and Company, New York, 1882

Index